PRAISE FOR FINDING KANSAS

The following comments are from professionals in the field of Autism and Asperger's Syndrome. Because they are employed by organizations and schools, they have requested that their names not be used so as not to imply endorsement of this book by their employers.

"Aaron Likens has developed a new vocabulary that will change how parents and therapists talk about Asperger's."

Special Education Teacher
St. Louis, MO

"I've been diagnosing children with autism and Asperger's for years. After reading just two chapters of Aaron's book, I now know what it feels like."

Licensed Clinical Social Worker
St. Louis, MO

"This book should be required reading for every masters level social work student in the country. Mr. Likens has described in real terms what we have theoretically been teaching for years."

PhD. Researcher
A major university

"I am going to retire soon. I wish I had had this book twenty years ago. I could have helped so many students, especially the boys, if I had understood what was going on in their heads."

Special Education Teacher
Baton Rouge, LA

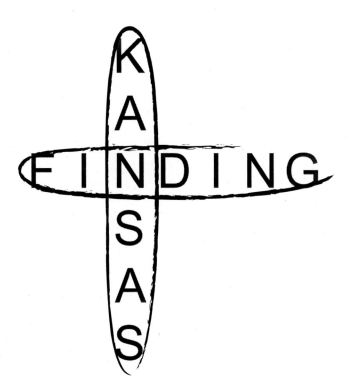

FINDING KANSAS

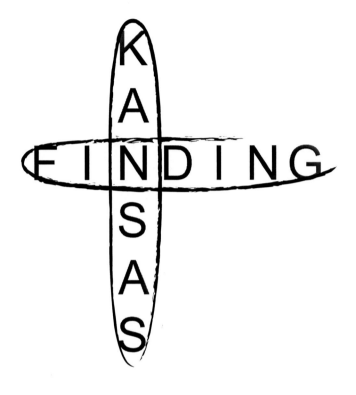

Decoding the Enigma
of Asperger's Syndrome

AARON LIKENS

TATE PUBLISHING & Enterprises

Published by Tate Publishing & Enterprises, LLC
127 E. Trade Center Terrace | Mustang, Oklahoma 73064 USA
1.888.361.9473 | www.tatepublishing.com

Tate Publishing is committed to excellence in the publishing industry. The company reflects the philosophy established by the founders, based on Psalm 68:11,
"The Lord gave the word and great was the company of those who published it."

Published in the United States of America

ISBN: 978-1-60604-560-2
1. Bibliography & Autobiography: Personal Memoir
2. Psychology: Mental Health: Aspberger's/Emotions

08.08.18

DEDICATION

To the real Emily.
After this I hope you will understand.

And to Bill Varner for having
faith in this book.

TABLE OF CONTENTS

de·cod·ing
To convert from a scrambled electronic signal into an interpretable one.
To extract the underlying meaning from: decode a complex literary text.

e·nig·ma
1. a puzzling or inexplicable occurrence or situation
2. a person of puzzling or contradictory character
3. a saying, question, picture, etc., containing a hidden meaning; riddle

www.dictionary.com

Asperger's Syndrome, like autism, is on the rise. Many claim it is due to vaccines, some say genetics, some say ultrasounds. Regardless of the cause, to understand the "official" description of Asperger's Syndrome (AS), it is important in understanding what Aaron Likens has written. This is not a book about what; it is an exploration of one young man's attempt to explain to himself and others the why of AS.

WHAT IS ASPERGER'S SYNDROME?

by Barbara L. Kirby
Founder of the OASIS Web site (www.aspergersyndrome.org)
(Online Asperger Syndrome Information and Support)
Co-author of The Oasis Guide to Asperger
Syndrome (Crown, 2001, Revised 2005)

Asperger Syndrome (AS), or (Asperger's Disorder), is a neurobiological disorder named for a Viennese physician Hans Asperger, who in 1944 published a paper that described a pattern of behaviors in several young boys who had normal intelligence and language development, but who also exhibited autistic-like behaviors and marked deficiencies in social and communication skills. In spite of the publication of his paper in the 1940s, it wasn't until 1994 that Asperger Syndrome was added to the DSM IV (Diagnostic and Statistical Manual of Mental Disorders, 4th edition) and only in the past few years has AS been recognized by professionals and parents.

Individuals with AS can exhibit a variety of characteristics, and the disorder can range from mild to severe. Persons with AS show marked deficiencies in social skills, have difficulties with transitions or changes, and prefer sameness. They often have obsessive routines and may be preoccupied with a particular subject of interest. They have a great deal of difficulty reading nonverbal cues (body language), and very often the individual with AS has difficulty determining proper body space. Often overly sensitive to sounds, tastes, smells, and sights, the person with AS may prefer soft clothing, certain foods, and be bothered by sounds or lights no one else seems to hear or see. It's important to remember that the person with AS perceives the world very differently. Therefore, many behaviors that seem odd or unusual are due to those neurological differences and not the result of intentional rudeness or bad behavior, and most certainly not the result of "improper parenting."

By definition, those with AS have a normal IQ, and many individuals (although not all) exhibit exceptional skill or talent in a specific area. Because of their high degree of functionality and their naiveté, those with AS are often viewed as eccentric or odd and can easily become victims of teasing and bullying. While language development seems, on the surface, normal, individuals with AS often have deficits in pragmatics and prosody. Vocabularies may be extraordinarily rich, and some children sound like "little professors." However, persons with AS can be extremely literal and have difficulty using language in a social context.

At this time there is a great deal of debate as to exactly where AS fits. It is presently described as an autism spectrum disorder, and Uta Frith, in her book Autism and Asperger's Syndrome, described AS individuals as "having a dash of Autism." Some professionals feel that AS is the same as High-Functioning Autism, while others feel that it is better described as a Nonverbal Learning Disability. AS shares many of the characteristics of PDD-NOS (Pervasive Developmental Disorder; Not otherwise specified), HFA, and NLD, and because it was virtually unknown until a few years ago, many individuals either received an incorrect diagnosis or remained undiagnosed. For example, it is not at all uncommon for a child who was initially diagnosed with ADD or ADHD be re-diagnosed with AS. In addition, some individuals who were originally diagnosed with HFA or PDD-NOS are now being given the AS diagnosis, and many individuals have a dual diagnosis of Asperger Syndrome and High-Functioning Autism.

1 What is Asperger's Syndrome?, Barbara L. Kirby, http://www.udel. edu/bkirby/asperger. Used with permission.

FOREWORD

I have been asked to write a brief description of my impression of the "clinical" value and importance of Aaron Likens' writings. I feel honored by this opportunity. At the same time I also doubt if I am capable of providing anywhere near a comprehensive interpretation or analysis of the value and meaning of Aaron's truly remarkable writings. However, there are a few observations I feel confident in making: These writings are of prodigious value to anyone interested in autistic-spectrum disorders, especially Asperger's Disorder, whether they be a mental health professional, researchers in the field, family members, or other persons with similar disorders. There is always a desire to secure some exacting definition of a particular disorder such as Asperger's, a tendency to see each person as part of a more or less homogeneous group. This categorical thinking has been yielding (especially in the conception of autistic disorders) to the notion of a continuum, which may be fore descriptive and individualistic. In this regard the term autistic-spectrum disorders has increasingly gained acceptance.

As a mental health professional who has specialized in the field of autistic-spectrum disorders for nearly twenty years, the only apt comparison I can make of Aaron's writings is the effect of Temple Grandin's first book, *Emergence*. Her personal account of the "experience" of autism was a revelation. It shattered many myths and previously accepted "facts" about autism. Her book permanently changed the previously limited understanding of autistic disorders.

I believe Aaron's writings have the same potential regarding Asperger's Disorder. He reveals depths of emotion, social comprehension, nuances of cognition and perception, and especially the potential for something close to "recovery." I believe its potential benefits are invaluable and capable of changing lives.

One of the changed lives has been my own. Aaron's writings and our conversations have granted me clinical insights, a new understanding, and subsequently more effective care for my other clients with autistic-spectrum disorders.

It is difficult to keep this introductory statement brief because of the broad range of subjects he addresses; the questions raised by his intensely personal observations and analyses have implications beyond this field and the expertise of this professional.

First, I think it is important to note that unlike most current books on the subject of Asperger's, this is not a "how to" (treat symptoms, etc.), but a "how did" book. It is Aaron's intensely personal journey, begun half unconsciously, its purpose emerging intuitively. The process has been self-healing, but the product, like many literary journeys—from Homer and Dante to James Joyce's re-visitation of Homer's hero in Ulysses—Aaron's writings speak to us all. When he came to realize its potential value to others, he unselfishly decided to share it.

Aaron presents his writings as a series of essays arranged in chronological order (in keeping with the typical preoccupation with sameness, order, and predictability that is a hallmark of these disorders). In many ways his descriptions and observations about himself reflect those made by Temple Grandin, as well as other observations and testimonials regarding the autistic experience. His personal experience and even the words used to describe these experiences are often strikingly similar (although Aaron has never read her work), but beyond sharing certain clinical symptoms (as one would expect), Aaron has written a very different document.

Aaron has subjected himself to a rigorous self-examination, using himself as the subject of this "study," a study of the nature and experience of Asperger's Disorder. He has bravely exposed us to his inner world. He queries himself relentlessly about the nature, meaning, and implications of his thoughts, feelings, and perceptions. In the course of this self-examination, he diligently applies logic, metaphor, analogy, and self-reflection to this "question" of his life, which most compels him.

In the course of this personal odyssey, however, he becomes much more than a clinical study of Asperger's, for his personal queries eventually pose the same strenuous questions about the human experience that have challenged philosophers since antiquity: What is the meaning of our lives and actions? How do we reconcile our experience with that of others? Where does the Truth lie? What is Love? Does freedom equal love?

Aaron does not ask these questions casually or as a kind of intellectual dalliance. (He is no dilettante.) He poses these earnestly, for he perceives this is the only place where his personal salvation may be found. This is one of the most fascinating and unique aspects of his writings to me.

Aaron examines everything with the tool of reason and logic. This is the fateful manifestation of autistic preoccupation with sameness, predictability, and cognitive inflexibility. Aaron is compelled to seek according to this method, applying "reason" to all matters and questions. This seemingly innate methodology makes for a unique, self-made form of "philosophical inquiry." When I say "self-made," I mean this literally, for Aaron reads very little and is completely unacquainted with the discipline or any of its most notable contributors.

The unfortunate aspect of this comprehensive philosophical mode of inquiry is, of course, the fact that our lives, our personal problems, and experiences can be only partly (even marginally) resolved by logic and reason. Aaron's cognitive inflexibility may be seen as a manifestation of the autistic tendencies as mentioned before and the pressing need to abolish ambiguity. In Aaron's case, owing largely to his extremely high intelligence, this preoccupation with order goes beyond arranging routines and establishing and imposing order on his environment. He imposes this philosophical mode of thinking as the sole means of understanding himself, the world, and others. The result is a kind of "tyranny of reason." In Aaron's words, he "asks questions on paper to come up with some reasoning for someone who lives in a world of contradictions and paradoxes that have no answers or resolutions … a world within a world; a prison, chained by one's mind." The expression "being on the horns of a philosophical dilemma" acquires a terrible disproportion here, a metaphorical "goring" of human potential and experience that is particularly bloody.

Aaron loves metaphor and hyperbole such as this. It is one of the elements that make his writing so enthralling. He has a marvelous sense of irony and a prose-style that is rich with emotional revelation, wit, and a wonderful absurdist sense of humor. An incipient depth of emotion is given greater weight and meaning more often by implication rather that explication. This is especially the case when he writes of the death of a friend (his cat) and his romantic experiences. But his writer's flair is also evident when he examines the value and torment of his prodigious memory, his work experiences, his fears, and his despair. He is often given to morbid recollection, doubt, and hopelessness, but there is also the zest and excitement of release, joy, and peace, and even moments of serene and blissful happiness.

Where does he find this illusive "happiness" we all seek? On eanswer he discovers is in playing games such as Monopoly. In asking himself why this is so, he finds compelling answers regarding his Asperger's mentality; the fact that games have clear rules that temper the "unpredictable," that "there's no better feeling that the unpredictability of a game set with predictable rules." He sees he is temporarily "free of my mind … of all the other mental anguish … the chains that make me overanalyze life, the critical mind … The real world and my world coincide, and happiness is found through the medium of the game." These observations and conclusions correspond with our current understanding of autistic-like mental processes.

But a more comprehensive, even profound fruit arises from Aaron's study of himself. It is an existential, even spiritual observation that "within rules comes knowledge of boundaries and limitation … [that] I am free because there are limits … " The notion that in order to find life-sustaining meaning and true freedom we must know our limitations, Aaron concludes that limitations set the boundaries in which we can truly know ourselves.

As I cautioned previously, I had difficulty keeping this concise. There are so many other aspects of Aaron's writing and of our therapeutic relationship left untouched. I hope I have this opportunity at some point.

I know that the general "rule" regarding getting a book published is that, well ... "That isn't going to happen." On the other hand, I find hope in one of Aaron's many pithy aphorisms, "The rule that saved my life was the rule that there is an exception to every rule."

Mark A. Cameron, Ph.D., M.A.
St. Louis, Missouri

PROLOGUE

"Aaron doesn't socialize real well with the other kids," the preschool teacher said. "But I think it is probably due to his high intelligence." Year after year that's what I heard, and year after year I believed it. In fact, it was rather a proud moment at every parent-teacher conference when the teacher would say, and I could tell it was coming, "I think it is probably due to his high intelligence."

Aaron was intelligent. He knew the alphabet by the time he was eighteen months. By the time he was three he could spell all the words on his Speak 'n Spell. During his fifth year he got his first Monopoly game and was the banker. Before his sixth birthday I stopped playing Monopoly because I always lost. Before he was seven he taught himself the multiplication table after he asked me what the "x" meant in one of his sister's math problems. Boy oh boy, was I ever a proud papa.

There was one big problem: Aaron didn't want to go to school, especially if there was the threat of severe weather. He also didn't want to go to school if the sun was shining; or if it was Monday, Tuesday, Wednesday, Thursday, or Friday. I think from the second grade on he missed more days in the school year than he attended. Yet, he was always one of the top students in the class. Oh, did I tell you it was probably due to his high intelligence?

As a Lutheran pastor, much of my time was spent "saving" the world. I didn't really notice the lack of friends in Aaron's life. In fact, looking back on it, I was his best friend.

When Aaron was born, he and his mother did not bond. She went through a bout of postpartum depression, and I, more or less, took care of Aaron. I was a pastor in a small town in western Nebraska with a small church and a lot of time on my hands.

I really didn't notice a problem at six months; when most children start taking solid food, his mouth wouldn't work to swallow. When he was two and really spoke no intelligible words, I figured it was because his older brother and sister did most of the talking for him.

I could go on and on about the "whens," but I won't. Suffice it to say there were so many things I didn't notice, or chose to deny, or took pride in—"I think it is probably due to his high intelligence." I didn't see any "real" problem, but then I never noticed dirty socks either.

At one point, because of his fear and unwillingness to go to school, I called the "mental health care provider" that served pastors of the Lutheran Church-Missouri Synod. They gave me the name of psychiatrist in Clayton, Missouri, a suburb of St. Louis. During the one-hour visit, the aged doctor and former head of the child psychiatric department at Washington University's School of Medicine smoked a half a pack of cigarettes and then told us that Aaron would probably grow up to be a serial killer. I wondered if this was "due to his high intelligence." Arrgh!

About six months later another noted child psychiatrist in the St. Louis area said he thought Aaron suffered from PPD-NOS, Pervasive Developmental Disorder-No Other Symptom. As Aaron, his mother, and I sat there, I asked, "My oldest son had ADD, and we took hope in the fact that great people like Thomas Edison reportedly were ADD. Is there anyone like that concerning this PPD thing?"

"Oh yes," the doctor quickly replied. "Ted Kaczynski, the Unabomber."

Well, now I'd been told my son would probably be a serial killer and he has the same traits as the Unabomber. Instills a lot of hope, don't you think?

In 1998 Aaron's mother and I separated, and in 2000 we were divorced. Much of my relationship with Aaron up to that point had been spent playing games, going to races, or racing go-karts. I remarried in 2002, and in July of 2003 Aaron moved in with me and his stepmother, Mary. She saw many things that I hadn't. She didn't know what the problem was, but she certainly knew there was a problem.

It wasn't until Aaron was twenty years old that I read an article in a Sunday news magazine that talked about savant traits in children with Autism. Aaron wasn't one of those math wizards, nor did he know the batting average of every baseball player in the history of the world. He did know a lot about auto racing, but the characteristics that stood out the most were his eye-to-hand coordination and his reflexes.

I did some research on the Internet and read about PDD-NOS, Autism, and Asperger's. I began to realize that I had bought into the lie of "It is probably due to his high intelligence." Mary was right. There was a problem. Aaron was intelligent, but he was also a very unique member of the Autism Spectrum Disorder.

I called the Judevine Center in St. Louis, a most noted organization that works with ASD children from diagnosis to treatment, and scheduled an evaluation. Prior to making that appointment I spent a great deal of time talking with Aaron about my conclusions. As I shared with him the characteristics of Asperger's as found in the DSM (Diagnostic and Statistical Manual of Mental Disorders) and what I had found on the Internet, he kept asking me, "But what does this mean?" I didn't have a complete answer, but I did tell him whatever we found out from a diagnosis, progress and change would be difficult.

It was November of 2003. Aaron and I had traveled to the Washington D.C. area to visit my sister for Thanksgiving. We usually left my sister's condo, got on Leesburg Pike (VA 7), and traversed across northern Maryland to Morgantown before heading north to Pittsburgh. Because of heavy snow in northern Maryland, we headed south on I-81, took I-64 to the west, and were headed into Charleston, West Virginia. I can clearly remember the light snow falling, the fog that hovered over the Kanawha River, and the snowplow in front of us.

"Aaron," I said, "I don't know what the future holds. I do know that I haven't been a very good father because I have ignored the suffering I have seen you go through. We're going to do this thing with Judevine, and no matter what it takes, how much it hurts, or how hard it is, we are going to do it."

As the day neared for the appointment, Aaron told me that he didn't want to talk much to whoever would be doing the assessment. I told him, "Why don't you write a short essay and call it 'I Wish' and describe how you wish your life was." He did. Unfortunately, the document was not saved, and the essay has disappeared from his file.

That was the beginning of what you are about to read. Since then, Aaron has continued to write. It has been the most therapeutic treatment he has ever received. The amazing thing is that he did it all himself. What he has gained is invaluable. What others will learn and realize about ASD will be priceless.

I believe that like the cryptographers who cracked the code of the Enigma machine used by the Germans, Aaron has begun the process of decoding the enigma of Asperger's Syndrome.

His father
Spring 2007

IN THE END

After writing for over a year now on my experiences and thoughts regarding Asperger's, I feel it is proper to write a final chapter. I write this in the same room I wrote "Scream" and "School" some nineteen months ago. This room is room number 312 in the Imperial Hotel in Kisumu, Kenya. This is a fitting place to write my final chapter because it was in this very room, on this very bed, that I first thought that my writings may actually be used for something. From that point on, I took my insights very seriously.

So with all that I have written, what have I learned? I have come to understand for one that I am, indeed, different. It's not that radically different, though, but just a different understanding of the world.

I have learned that I am very lucky to have such great parents who allowed me to be me. I have realized that I have had many experiences that "normal" people will never have. I believe that both of those things have allowed me to write such neat material.

To be continued...

IN THE END II

Just a note from Dad … (Sound of screeching brakes!)

Okay, so wait a minute. You might be asking yourself two questions: Why start with "In the End," and what was this twenty-two-year-old kid doing in a hotel room in Kisumu, Kenya? Good questions.

Aaron starts with the end in order to have a better understanding of the beginning. My stepson, Michael, will often videotape a St. Louis Cardinals game and is devastated if he finds out what the score is before he watches the tape.

I remember working at WPTA-TV in Ft. Wayne, Indiana, while I was going to Concordia Theological Seminary. The 1980 Olympics were on. ABC was not going to show the hockey game between the U.S. and the U.S.S.R. until after the newscast: it was February 22, 1980. The Miracle on Ice was about to be seen at 11:30 p.m., EST.

Around 10:30 p.m. each night, one of the two anchors would do a live "teaser" about what was going to be on the news. Fred DeBrine pulled up to the news desk in the "newsroom set" and said, "If you don't want to know who won the U.S./U.S.S.R. hockey game, turn off your television." He then proceeded to give the score an hour before the start of the game.

The phones in the newsroom went wild. The local newspaper

slaughtered Fred and the station for giving away the score. It was not a pinnacle moment for the station.

Why start with the end? So that you don't have to wait to find out whether my son survived the diagnosis, the realization of his disabilities, and the daunting future that faces him. In this situation I think it is really is good to know the score beforehand.

The love and respect I have for Aaron is outside my vocabulary. The pain I have felt for him as I have watched him struggle with the realities of Asperger's has been intense. At one point in time a person from the Judevine Center was coming to meet with Aaron's stepmother, Mary, and me once a week at our office to help us understand this disorder. One afternoon he said, "As intelligent as Aaron is, he would probably be happier if he was more autistic and didn't realize what he was missing in life."

Aaron is very aware of what he is missing. He grieves deeply about what he is missing. He cries about what he is missing. But he also realizes that this book will make a difference in the lives of many people. He also realizes that if you are reading this, he will get some royalty and, as he often says with a smile on his face, "I guess that will make it worth it."

Now, why was he in Kenya? We were on a filming trip for LCMS World Relief and Human Care, the mercy arm of the Lutheran Church-Missouri Synod. Shortly after Aaron moved in with my wife, Mary, and me, she was concerned about how much Aaron worried when I was out of town. Prior to his departure from living with his mother, Aaron traveled with me as my sound engineer for the concerts I performed. He was my copilot, confidant, and friend. There were times, however, that I had to fly somewhere to film an interview or to go to a meeting. This was when the worry would set in.

In the fall of 2004, I signed a contract to film a project in Lithuania. Mary was greatly concerned about how Aaron would deal with me being out of the country for two weeks. She suggested I take him with me. I talked with the client, and an agreement was struck that anytime I traveled overseas Aaron would go with me and shoot still pictures.

You will read about Palanga, Lithuania, and other places he's been.

This is why he wrote "In the End" in room 312 at the Imperial Hotel in Kisumu, Kenya. In this room, as he said, "This is a fitting place to write my final chapter because it was in this very room on this very bed that I first thought that my writings may actually be used for something. From that point on I took my insights very seriously."

The first time we were in Kenya, we were attacked by a mob of homeless boys. You'll read about that from Aaron. You are also going to read about other adventures and misadventures. In fact, you will learn more about Aaron from Aaron than I could ever tell you.

As Dr. Cameron said in the foreword:

> Aaron has subjected himself to a rigorous self-examination, using himself as the subject of this "study," a study of the nature and experience of Asperger's Disorder. He has bravely exposed us to his inner world. He queries himself relentlessly about the nature, meaning, and implications of his thoughts, feelings, and perceptions. In the course of this self-examination he diligently applies logic, metaphor, analogy, and self-reflection to these questions of his life that most compel him.

It is important to understand that Aaron doesn't necessarily present Asperger's Disorder as a set of symptoms. He digs far beneath the intellectual, academic, medical, and psychological definitions, and will give you the privilege of learning not "what" Asperger's is, but rather "how" it is to live with it.

If you took the time to thumb through this book and read the chapter titles, you would find some very interesting and intriguing titles. Titles such as: "Film Theory," "See," "I versus It," "The Conscious Coma," and "Faking Kansas." I won't try to explain them, but on your journey through Aaron's mind you will discover a world you did not know existed. It is the world of Finding Kansas.

Keep in mind that this book was not written in order to write a book. These writings expose the heart and emotions of a young man who has been willing to sacrifice his thoughts and feelings that most of us are afraid of. His journey of exploration is about to become yours.

Bon voyage.

FINDING KANSAS: THE SITUATIONAL HANDICAP

Just a note from Dad ... This piece is one of the most significant in this book. It is so significant that some professionals at one of America's top autism organizations have adopted Aaron's definitions of a Situational Handicap.

Some people who know me and know that I have Asperger's think that there's nothing wrong with me. These people, however, only see me in certain situations and have no idea how paralyzed I can be in some situations. This can be very aggravating, because I know something isn't perfect with me, but when I hear such remarks as, "Oh, you're fine," or "I can't see how you have that at all," it really bothers me.

To make a good example, let's say a person is paralyzed. However, for reasons unknown, this person is perfectly fine anytime they are in the state of Kansas. If you saw this person while in Kansas, you'd flat out tell them, "Hey, you're not paralyzed!" At the time this comment would be true, but to the person, they know that the second they leave the state they are paralyzed again.

Now this person, knowing the magic of Kansas, would probably sell his home in whatever state he's in and move to Kansas so he would not be paralyzed. This is exactly how I try to be in life in regards to finding my Kansas.

When in my comfort zone, I am like that man in Kansas; there is nothing wrong, and I appear to be a normal individual. My ultimate Kansas is anything to do with racing. I am now the race director of two different series, and while at my post, I am firm and confident. These two traits can't be used to describe me very often in a social setting.

After the first race weekend this year on a Monday, I went to a video game store to make a purchase. I walked into the store, making no eye contact with anyone, and was first asked the most horrifying question I know: "Sir, can I help you find something?" I instantly and passively said no, and a couple seconds later I said the title of the game I would like to purchase. The store clerk then, trying to make small talk, barraged me with several open-ended questions that I made closed-ended questions with simple yes or no answers. The clerk kept going, and he eventually said, "Umm, do you talk? I haven't gotten any words out of you!" As if I didn't already know it, this was a firm example (sorry for the cliché) that I wasn't in Kansas anymore.

This flip-flop difference for those around me could be very confusing. If my shadow could talk, it would certainly wonder how I can be the main guy at the race track but as passive as a sleeping kitten in a store setting.

As in the example, the guy would certainly want to live in the state that he can walk in. So too I want to do everything I can to not leave this magical state's limit. In simpler terms, you could call this a comfort zone, but that term isn't strong enough. A comfort zone seems to describe a place that is just slightly better than a normal zone. In my life, it's more like livable zone and life is horrible and all is worthless zone. There is no comfort zone, no middle ground, and it's either one or the other. Going into that game store, I wished so hard that the clerk would expedite the transaction because I didn't want to be put in that open-ended conversation that I'd know I'd make close ended, and the awkwardness that comes with that is simply unbearable for me.

Let's say you're the paralyzed fellow. How would you feel if you're walking along by the state border of Oklahoma and you venture into Oklahoma, and the instant you do you become paralyzed? One minute you are walking firmly and the next minute you are defenseless and helpless. One second you're self-sufficient and the next you have no ability to do anything. If this happened once, I'm sure you'd do everything you could to stay within Kansas.

Everyone has to do things they don't like. Most people have a tolerance, though, for these things. That example I used of the game store still hurts. Those open-ended questions with no meaning behind them have a significant meaning for me. I have to be crafty to survive each day, and the solution I see to avoid this is to just purchase everything via the Internet.

I used to work at a video game store and had no problem approaching customers. This is yet another example of this two-sided coin, or rather alter ego. The company line on talking to customers was to greet them and ask them the question from hell ("Can I help you find…") within five seconds of the time they enter the store. This I could not do. I could approach the customer once I knew what they were looking for. Once I knew that, I could make the game plan and I would have the bases covered. So I said I had no problem with them; I guess it's more like it was almost no problem, as long as I knew what they were focused on.

What everyone needs to know about this is the fact that there is this situational handicap. I can be fine and dandy driving in the car somewhere, but when we get to the destination and there are other people, I am not who I was. From being able to run like an Olympian, I become as helpless as a bedridden cripple. Imagine the distress that comes with this! One minute I am like a person who has won the gold medal, and in an instant I become nothing more than an extra in a movie that has no lines while lying in a bed. I am seen but not heard.

With all this said, I do everything I can to stay in my state of Kansas. Being outside is so unbearable to a point that sometimes the question of, "Is life worth this?" comes to mind. The hardest part of this all is when someone only knows me when I'm in my Kansas, and then they see me outside my livable state. It's like being completely naked and being powerless to do anything. Whatever person this is has seen me firm and confident and now they see the true me. Once they see both sides, I'm sure they ask themselves questions as to what on earth is going on with me.

I know I refuse to do many things with people because of all these facts. I hope they realize, though, that being outside my state, I feel like life isn't worth living. It's like having two choices—running like the wind or being stationary and blind. Like anyone's answer, I'd choose to run like the wind, but when I'm in Kansas, I don't just run, I fly.

A TEACHER
REMEMBERS

In the process of finding help for Aaron, it was recommended that I contact the State of Missouri Department of Mental Health. I had to provide evidence that Aaron had had difficulty in school. I contacted Mrs. Janice Nafzger, Aaron's fifth-grade teacher. We moved in December of 1993 to St. Louis from Indianapolis. It wasn't long before Aaron began developing migraine headaches. In March of 2004, Mrs. Nafzger wrote the following:

J.T., Assessment Team Secretary
State of Missouri Department of Mental Health
St. Louis Regional Center for Developmental Disabilities
St. Louis, MO 63103

Dear Ms.————:

I received a letter from Jim Likens a few days ago, asking that I write to you regarding his son, Aaron Likens. While it has been ten years since I have seen Aaron, I have very vivid memories of the months he was in my fifth-grade class at Word of Life Lutheran School in St. Louis, Missouri.

Aaron Likens enrolled at Word of Life School and was assigned to my classroom in December 1993. My class numbered twenty-two children when he arrived, with thirteen of them being boys who were competitive in academics as well as athletics. It was a typical, normal class of excitable fifth-graders. Upon receiving word that we were going to get a new student, my class was eager and excited to be getting a new boy!

I remember the day Aaron arrived. A quiet and seemingly shy little boy entered the classroom, appearing guarded and reserved. While the other children tried to involve Aaron and help him acclimate into the group, Aaron appeared aloof or disinterested or unfriendly. The other children did not know how to relate to him or understand him. After several days, the other children ceased actively trying to help Aaron adjust or become his friend. Aaron was very preoccupied with racecars at that time. He would react a little more positively when other children asked him questions about racing. (See the "Best Day" coming up next.) Unfortunately for Aaron, no other student shared his interest in racing.

When I first met Aaron, he was small in stature and seemed somewhat frail to me. He suffered from migraine headaches. As a result of the headaches, he frequently left school during the school day. As his teacher, I questioned if his sickness was of a physical nature, but when he said he had a headache, he literally could not remain in the classroom. Aaron was absent many days from school during the six months he was in my class.

Aaron exhibited a great fear of storms and thunderstorms. I particularly remember one stormy day. Dark clouds gathered and darkened our classroom rather quickly. Windows covered one entire wall, so the storm could not be ignored. Aaron panicked. We had to call his mom to come to take him home.

An interesting development occurred about a month after Aaron arrived in my class. Another boy, a very high-functioning Down syndrome child, enrolled in the Resource Room of our school and was assigned to my classroom for his homeroom. "Chris" had a bubbly personality and funny sense of humor, which enabled him to become the center of attention when he was in the classroom for non-academic subjects or other activities. I mention this fact because it appeared that as the days and weeks passed by Chris became the class "darling," and Aaron, in contrast, faded more and more into the background with his quiet personality and inability to establish interpersonal relationships.

Quite understandably, Aaron's inability to develop relationships or friendships with the other students inhibited his interest in school. It became like a vicious cycle. He generally appeared to be unhappy. He did not enjoy recess, art, or gym. Academically, Aaron performed quite well for a student who was so often absent from school.

Word of Life is a Lutheran Parochial School. I received my college training at Concordia Lutheran Teacher's College in River Forest, Illinois. I received training to minister to children in our church and school. In addition to being trained to teach the academic subjects, I was taught to share the love of Jesus Christ and to teach acceptance and love for others. While the other students were not mean to Aaron or did not bully him, I felt that the ignoring or indifference shown toward Aaron was even more hurtful than outward rejection.

The other children in my class sensed that Aaron had problems, but neither they nor I understood the nature of his disability. I am not trained in special education, and it does take time for a classroom teacher to really get to know students. Aaron was in our school only a short time before I was aware that there were serious problems. But there was no diagnosis, and I was aware that his parents were also searching for answers. We had no answers for why it was so difficult for Aaron to relate to peers or be able to make friends.

I hope that these comments from my experience ten years ago will be helpful to you in your work with Aaron. If I can be of further assistance to you, please feel free to contact me.

Sincerely yours,
Mrs. Janis E. Nafzger

Just a note from Dad... Mrs. Nafzger pointed out that Aaron "would react a little more positively when other children asked him questions about racing." Like most children with AS, Aaron had a special interest, an interest that put his life on the edge every time he participated in it.

In his first college course, English Comp 101, he had to write an essay entitled "The Best Day." From that day on, the quote below became the essence of his life.

"I've wanted to race since I was five years old. That's plan A for my life. There is no plan B."

THE BEST DAY

An essay by Aaron Likens
(Written for English Comp 101, Meremac Community College)

It was a cool, humid April morning. It was 5:00 in the morning, still two hours before I had to get up, but I just couldn't sleep and was counting down the minutes until I had to go. My dad was shocked to see me up when he awoke, but if you've waited for something all your life, you wouldn't be able to sleep either. When we left the house, the sunlight was just breaking through the clouds and burning the mist-like fog away. About a mile from home, we stopped at a donut shop and got some donuts. As we pulled away, I told my dad that I was too nervous to eat. He reminded me that there are starving children in Bolivia that would give their left kidney to eat just one donut. He said that jokingly, of course, but I took it to heart and slowly worked down my two glazed donuts.

So where were we going that had me so nervous I felt like one of those knots you can't get out of your shoelaces? We were headed to Widman Raceway for my first go-kart race. I was just twelve years old, but it felt like two hundred years waiting to get my chance to race. On the drive to the track, I began to ponder how I got to this opportunistic point in time where I'd get the chance to start what I had envisioned myself doing since I was just the age of two.

To say that my start in racing was lucky for me is an understatement.

You see, my dad had been a pastor in Indianapolis, and, of course, being a pastor, you are expected to work on Sunday. Also living in Indy, they have a little thing known as the Indianapolis 500, and being a little kid exposed to drivers and fast cars from my dad taking me to the practice runs, I got the itch to race at an early age. But we never went to the actual race though, because my dad was a pastor, and that made racing on Sundays very difficult since most racing of any sort takes place on Sunday. Well, he got a job in St. Louis in 1993, so we moved there, and the job he had did not require his services on Sunday. One hurdle down! The other, however, was the difficult one—money. Buying a go-kart and all the related equipment that is required was more than he was able to afford. I still had hope though. I prayed every night that somehow, someway, I'd get the chance, even if it were just once. There's a common saying that when one door shuts, another opens. That plays true with what happened: One night in 1994, some thieves who obviously had a misunderstanding of what "Thou shall not steal" meant decided they'd steal my dad's table saw from our garage. As it turns out, the insurance company gave him a check for his loss, but instead of buying another table saw, he figured that since the amount of the check was roughly the amount of everything needed to start racing, it must be a sign, so I got a go-kart.

It was a long road indeed, but now all my waiting was about to be put to rest. We pulled up to the track, and at the gate we had to sign in. As my dad was filling out all the insurance papers, I looked around the track. Widman Raceway was nestled down a hill off a road. The grass was neatly trimmed, and hay bails lined the turns. The ground was very muddy from all the rain the previous week, so walking around was like stepping on sponges because water and mud seeped from the ground on every step. I heard my dad tell me to come and sign papers, so I went over to the table and signed where the lady told me to sign. I began to read the paper I had just signed, and when I got to the part about how racing is dangerous and can lead to injury, death, or paralysis, I elected to stop reading and just signed on the dotted line. As I put the piece of paper on the table and started my way back to the van, the lady asked me, "So, today's your first race?"

"Yes, and I can't wait!" I replied enthusiastically

She answered back just as I was entering the van, "Well then, enjoy yourself, have fun, and don't worry how you do."

Enjoy myself? Enjoy myself? I wasn't here to just have fun and enjoy myself, I was here to win or at least finish in the top five.

We pulled into our pit spot and unloaded the van. Most people had trailers to put their karts in, but we had to stuff all of our equipment into the back of a Ford Aerostar van. By the time we got fully unloaded, there were just about ten minutes before my first practice session. We hurried down to the grid, and I got into my suit, helmet, and rib protector and anxiously waited until I received the signal to enter the track. When the signal was given for my division to enter, the pack of karts I was in stormed onto the track. Slight problem though, since it was so cold the tires' cohesion weren't as good as if it were a hot day, so the first turn I entered I spun like a revolving top. Didn't hit anyone or anything, but I felt very stupid. The rest of the session I was beating myself up emotionally even though through the rest of it I passed most of the karts I would later be racing.

After one more practice session, it was time for the drivers' meeting. The race director talked for a while, and then the flagman, an old man who had to be at least in his seventies, looking as if he hadn't eaten any food for years, told everyone how he wanted the field aligned as they came to the start. After the meeting, the race director wanted to meet with all the rookie drivers to go through racing procedures. He explained the flags and how the race day would work. There'd be two heat races and then a feature race. He then told us, for our first three race weekends, we'd have to start in the back of the pack for safety reasons. He then said, "And remember, it's your first race, don't be concerned with how you do, just have fun." Everyone kept saying that, as if we had no chance of finishing in the top five positions. It was driving me up a wall. I knew I was good, at least I always won in the video games I played, but why did everyone count all of us out?

Twenty minutes passed after the driver's meeting, and then it was time for my race to commence. We started our motors and waited. As I waited eagerly for the race that preceded us to finish, my mind began racing at a ferocious pace. I thought about the insurance papers I had read and how serious injury or even death can occur. I thought about what my mom said as I left my house, "Now, Aaron, whatever you do, just don't get hurt. You hear me, don't get hurt." And as I pondered that, I finally realized that this was a dangerous activity. I mean, hurling your body in a moving projectile at speeds in excess of forty miles per hour without a seatbelt or roll cage two inches off the ground isn't the safest sport a twelve-year-old could be competing in. My mind continued to race around like a dog chasing its tail until I got the signal to roll. As soon as I started to roll and pick up speed, every thought about how dangerous this was and what my mom told me vanished quicker than lasagna fed to Garfield. We did one warm-up lap, and then it was time to take the green. I was starting fifteen out of seventeen, and as we rolled off the final corner, the green flag was displayed, and we were off. That start was one of the most nerve-racking moments in my life, because there was a kart behind me, a kart beside me, and thirteen karts in front of me. As we entered turns one and two, a couple of karts in front of me tangled and spun. Oh no, I said to myself, I'm going to get hurt right away. What's my mom going to think? I pulled off a great move and avoided the two pirouetting karts and in the process advanced to eighth place.

The late Allen Barckledge (a TV-station helicopter pilot in the St. Louis market who was killed in a helicopter accident) was the club announcer at the time, and he was calling the race I was in. By lap four out of ten, I had moved up to second and was challenging for the lead. I went for the lead going into turn one; Allen was enthusiastic to say the least. "And that's Aaron Likens challenging the leader, Justin Rodriguez, going into turn one. Side by side they go, and oh! They've touched, and Aaron's going to spin, whoa, he saved it. How did he save that? I can't believe this is only Aaron's first race." I didn't quite pull the pass off, but I had another chance on the final lap. Allen commented, "Coming out of the final turn, Aaron to the inside for the lead, nope, not going to get the win, but a valiant effort for just his first race."

As I pulled off the track and onto the scales, everyone was giving me the thumbs-up sign and clapping. The feeling at that point in time was simply indescribable. Think of pure happiness and multiply that by ten. The look of disbelief on my dad's face was priceless. I knew he thought I'd do decently, but I don't exactly think he was expecting me touching side pods with the leader of the race. As we lifted the kart onto the scale and weighed, I asked my dad, "How'd

I do?" He didn't reply, which for me was the best response. He was in a total state of shock.

The following race wasn't as eventful, and I didn't do as well, finishing fifth. Still impressive being my first race, but at the same time disappointing since I started off with a second; I was hoping to pull off a win. Finishing where I finished both races would've entitled me to a third starting spot, but since it was my first race, I'd be back in fifteenth again.

It was getting late in the day. The sun was now in the western part of the sky, and clouds had begun to hesitantly drift into the area. The aroma of kart exhaust was very apparent in the air. With just about ten minutes to go until my race, I asked my dad, "How do you think I'll do in this final race?"

"You'll do just fine," he replied.

"Are you sure?"

"Absolutely," he said calmly.

It turned out I did do well, finished fourth in the feature for an excellent day overall. As we were heading home, I asked my dad, "So, Dad, how'd I do today?"

"Well," he responded, "let's just say you've got it. Someday, you're going to win the Indianapolis 500."

Wow, I thought, maybe I actually do have it. And at that point in time, I decided that racing was going to be my career choice, and if I got as far as I had gotten, nothing was or is going to stop me from my dream.

THERE IS NO PLAN B

Just a note from Dad.

Ever heard or read that verse from the Bible that says, "All things work together for good for those who love God and care called according to his purpose"? My grandmother used to tell me that all the time about my alcoholic, mentally ill father. At the time I hated her for it. At the age of sixty I look at my life, especially as a pastor in the Lutheran Church-Missouri Synod, and what I learned as a child really made a difference in my ministry.

That day I told Aaron, "Let's just say you've got it. Someday, you're going to win the Indianapolis 500," was, as I look back, one of the saddest days of my life.

You see, and you will learn from Aaron, when something happens the first time, it always has to be like that. If your dad says you're going to win the Indy 500, it's not a question of "if"; it's a question of, "Are we there yet?"

I implanted in Aaron's mind the reality that it would happen. It hasn't. It has created great pain and sorrow for both of us.

I sent to him to racing schools in Las Vegas and Tampa. He was one of the fastest students they'd ever had. We raced go-karts for six years and then abandoned them for a ride in the big time. We had a deal with an ARCA team, a race series just under the ranks of NASCAR, and it went sour when we found out the team had an illegal car. I talked to sprint car owners, and if Aaron had had track time, he would have had a ride. He didn't have track time. He had a chance to race in the training series for the Champ Car Series, and I didn't have sixty thousand dollars. He had everything needed for Plan A except for one thing: a dad with a million bucks.

But if we had landed that ARCA ride, or sprint ride, or if I had had sixty thousand dollars, this book would not exist. You see, how Aaron dealt with his disappointments was to write. He had plenty of disappointments. Many nights I sat up with him while he cried. Many days I hated myself for not being able to deliver on that statement that took on the power of a promise: "Let's just say you've got it. Someday, you're going to win the Indianapolis 500."

Things really do work out. Most of the time, however, it's not like we think they should. But then, since when did God start asking his creation how to do things?

The disappointment of not getting a big-time ride was a daily reality for Aaron. There was one bright spot though: Emily (not her real name). It was Emily who started Aaron on this journey of writing.

This is where Aaron began.

EMILY

This will be somewhat confusing. I'll state my feelings one way and then probably contradict myself a few lines later. The best way for me to write on this topic is in chronological order.

It was going to be my final year in junior bowling leagues because I wanted to move up to the adult leagues as soon as I hit eighteen, but, at the same time, I was pondering retirement from the sport because it just wasn't that much fun. I bowled twice a week (Wednesday and Saturday), and I also worked at the same bowling alley twice a week. I knew I'd be on the Wednesday league, because I started work immediately after the 3:30 league, but Saturday leagues were in the morning, and I didn't have a team going into week one, so I was pondering just pre-bowling every week. I decided to show up for week one just to see which team I'd be on. As I entered from the west entrance, I saw that on lane one were the initials AL and also ES. I knew of Emily because I had bowled against her the previous year, but I didn't know her age, and I figured she had a boyfriend because she bowled with some weird guy, but where was the weird guy this season?

As I sat down, I also noticed that there were no other initials on the scoring screen, which meant that it was just going to be Emily and me. This was good and bad. Bad in the sense that on week two for us to win, we would have to have had a combined score of 650 to win the game (which is impossible; a maximum score for two people in one game is 600), but good in the sense that I do much better one-on-one than I do with a third party involved. But again, I didn't know her age, didn't know her voice, so I figured I'd give it one week and then pre-bowl out.

Emily arrived one minute after the start of practice (remember that statement), and because I couldn't remember exactly what she looked like, I didn't recognize her at first. I did, however, remember that she threw a strange ball, and I was quite proud of my memory because no one throws a weirder ball than she does. Okay, enough about bowling physics.

Customary to my standards, I didn't acknowledge her existence for the entire practice session. As practice finished up, she finally said, "Hi, I'm Emily," and I replied with a nervous, "Hi, I'm Aaron," and also, for no apparent reason, I went to shake her hand. I have no idea why I did that, and I felt quite odd afterwards.

During the first three games of knowing each other, we found many topics to talk about. We talked about her dog, Mickey, and I talked about Missy (my dog) and how strange Siam (my cat) is. We continued, and I talked about racing; she talked about school, and there wasn't a silent moment. With so much talk and the fact that I bowled decently, I decided to show up for week two.

Week two was as talkative as the first, and it was that week that Emily mentioned she was hoping to be put on my team. Later she said she "had her eye on me," whatever that means. Week three I would be gone to a race in Rock Island, Illinois, which went horribly, but it gave me a lot to talk about the next week. That week saw the day I nervously asked for her e-mail address. It took me two-and-a-half games to finally ask, but I was shocked when she said, "Sure." I always think to the negative on any given situation, so I was expecting her to say, "No, you weird, weird person." But that wasn't the case, and we e-mailed each other in the middle of the week.

It was about mid-October when we scheduled our first "unofficial" date. Unofficial, because it would be illegal in her mom's eye to date me because I was only seventeen and she was nineteen, and that most certainly would lead to some sort of jail time. Whatever.

Anyways, we were scheduled to go cosmic bowling on a Friday night. I, in typical fashion, showed up an hour early and was waiting for her. Nine thirty came and passed and there was no Emily. Then

9:45 (oh, it starts at 9:30) came and went. Finally, I was getting a bit mad, but then she called the alley and the guy behind the desk gave me the phone. She told me that her mom wouldn't let her go out because there was a ten percent chance of freezing rain and/or sleet, which never happened—in fact, it didn't even rain a tenth of an inch for that matter. But I said fine, and I bowled by myself and had a 300 that night, so I didn't care. If only I knew what was to come in the coming years.

The next week the weather was fine (you'd expect that statement to come on if a sporting event was delayed), and she showed up five minutes after bowling started. I asked her why she couldn't veto her mom's idea that ten percent of freezing rain should stop her life. She didn't have an answer, but on that night I learned that her mom's name was Carolyn and that she was a nurse. This is important because that was Linda's mother's name and occupation, and even more coincidently, they both worked the night shift. (You'll learn more about Linda later.) So maybe in my mind somewhere there was a connection made, and maybe I tried to make Emily Linda. I don't know if that's true or not, but I think Emily might have looked like Linda, or at least maybe I saw Linda in Emily, or maybe not. Needless to say, my mind still ached for Linda (okay, it still does as I write this), even when I was with Emily.

Anyways, back to that night of bowling. We had fun, and our games were always close and competitive, so I was having a good time, and I even commentated like a psycho British announcer, which I guess she found amusing. As she drove me home I asked if she would like to come in and play the NES (Nintendo) game "The Three Stooges." I was shocked when she owned one. It's quite a rare game. She said yes, but first I made her nervous by saying she had to pass the "cat test." What's the cat test? Simply put, if both cats hissed she would have to leave. She actually got nervous, but as soon as she stepped into the house on Nottingham, both cats immediately started to want attention from her. We then proceeded to the sunroom and played both "The Three Stooges" and the video game version of "Family Feud." We played for quite a while and had a great time. Then she left and called me when she got back home. By this time we were talking on a regular basis on the phone, and I was quick to memorize both her home and cell phone numbers. The numbers became as much a part of her, in my mind, as her actual being. I have since realized that this is because when I'm away from someone, I don't remember their physical appearance, so their phone number, in essence, becomes them in my mind. I still have so much pain that I don't get to dial 965–82XX everyday.

So, it's now late October of 2000, and my mind always needing to know the official stance of any position needs to know if Emily and I are actually "dating." It took over two hours on the phone for me to actually ask the question, and then she was so quick on playing the age card. I figured that came from her mother, but would the police immediately have been to her house if she said yes? She figured it was so. Now mind you, we never touched hands or anything (except if someone got a strike or spare while bowling), but that didn't matter.

I was devastated. I needed that official status to feel secure. To make matters worse, while working at a video duplicator, I was constantly reminded of her via Saint Louis Bread Company's (her employer) ad campaign on the radio. But for me, just a week later I was headed to Vegas for my first experience at the Derek Daly Racing Academy.

I was stellar out there in Vegas, and there was that memorable presidential election that lasted longer than the NBA playoffs. Emily was quite the Al Gore supporter, and I knew when CBS awarded Florida to Gore that I wouldn't hear the end of it when I got home. Well, then Florida went to Bush and then back to Gore. During all this, my dad was asleep. I don't know how he knew, but he knew that this election wasn't going to be over on that night. Well, as you well know, it wasn't, and when I got back, Emily was very angry at the election results. This is quite the important topic coming up. When I asked why she wanted Gore, she didn't have an answer. Not one to give up, I kept asking, and she eventually came up with he was good for Unions. In other words, she wasn't thinking for herself. It was all what her mom wanted her to think.

Thanksgiving came and went, and she and I still were going cosmic bowling and talking on the phone even without having "official status." Then Christmas came, and I got back from Indianapolis late Christmas Eve and I called her and again, I asked, "What's the official status?"

Maybe I am too caught up in the whole needing-to-know-what's-going-on thing, but I just wanted, no, needed to know. Again, the age card was played, and there was no penetrating her mode of thought on the issue. Um, that sort of sounds likes me.

Then it was the first week of January, and, at the time, I was bowling in a high school travel league (even though I wasn't in high school). That first week of January 2001 was held at Tropicana Lanes. I bowled decently, and then Emily took me to Olive Garden. It was there that finally, yes, finally, "official status" was obtained. It was almost to the point that it was a game, but if she couldn't give the green light to an official relationship, then I was going to walk. I still remember the table where we sat. Today I try not to look at that table, because that was the place where the start of the finishing touches of this quagmire of life began.

The day before my eighteenth birthday, I officially met her parents. They took me to Red Lobster on Watson Road. I was quite nervous "meeting the parents," but they quickly liked me. That was what Emily said at least.

A couple Sundays later came the Daytona 500, but I also had to bowl in the travel league at Western Bowl. Emily came with me to the alley, and then we were to watch the rest of the race at my house. It was lap 150 when we finally got back to the house (I didn't bowl well because I was too busy trying to watch the race on the TV that was in the bar at the alley). Twenty laps later, the "Daytona Big One" happened while Fox was away at commercial. They (Fox) cut into their commercials, and the camera shot was that of a smoldering mass that was twenty-six racecars. It was quite apparent that Tony Stewart had flipped by the damage. My dad was working somewhere that day, so I immediately called him to tell him what had happened. As I was on the phone with him, the camera switched to an in-car shot of Stewart, who was not moving. This kept me on the phone longer, and as the replays showed, I relayed the images into words so my dad knew what had happened. I then hung up, and then ten minutes later, as the red flag was rescinded and the yellow came back out, I called again and told him that Stewart was conscious and alert. My dad then gave me the scariest prediction ever to come true on that call. He said that, "Earnhardt is going to crash in turn four of the final lap." I said, "Okay, whatever," and then went on watching the final laps.

Well, some laps later the white flag (signifying one lap to go) came out, and as the field came through three and four, I saw out of the corner of the camera a black car go to the apron and Mike Joy literally screamed, "Oh, big crash!" I had not seen the actual wall impact at that time, but I knew the angle had to be severe. At the same time my mom and Emily were talking about some irrelevant topic, but I knew that this crash was bad. I quickly called my dad and told him what had happened, and at the same time Ken Schrader approached the destroyed famous number "3" car and feverishly waved for medical personal. I said right then that this was bad. My mom and Emily didn't care about my feeling that this was bad, and Emily had a weird look on her face.

About an hour later came the official word that, indeed, Dale Earnhardt had died. I was never a fan of his, but death, regardless of whom it is, always affects me. I maintained my composure for probably thirty minutes, then I lost it. Emily was there for me, and she just held me as I cried away.

The last sentence of the paragraph above would sound like it would be quite the bonding experience, but sadly that was ruined ten minutes after she left. When she got home, she called me and yelled and asked why I was on the phone with my dad so much. She couldn't understand that this was the first Daytona 500 that my dad and I had not watched together since I had started racing. Also, the race had never experienced such accidents. And maybe she couldn't understand that I actually wanted to talk to my dad. You see, her dad's somewhat . . . slow. His wife controls all aspects of the family. And I mean all aspects. We were eating at Old Country Buffet one Sunday, and she literally told him, "You can't eat that." So maybe that's why Emily didn't understand my need to talk to my dad. But in this paragraph is another important topic—if she was so mad that I was on the phone, why did she just not say something then and there? I asked her that, and I was getting used to the fact that I wouldn't get an answer.

The next three months were quite routine. We went cosmic bowling on Friday and bowled in leagues, and she'd come over on Sundays. But during this time I started learning more about her and how she was supposedly "stalked" in high school, and how her mom had been thrown out of three different jobs because people threatened her life, and by each week the Sutherland family became odder and odder.

Here's an exact quote from my journal from May 23, 2001, "I don't know if I really like Emily. She is so odd. But I can't say goodbye for fear that I'll have a repeat incident of Linda. Oh, I am so trapped, what can I do?"

What could I do? I was trapped. Even in good times, I don't think I really cared for her. Even during the car ride to New Orleans for a youth gathering, I actually held her hand and looked into her eyes, but I was still filled with emptiness. Was I missing Linda? Did I just not like the girl? I don't know the answer to those questions, but I did know I didn't want to lose Emily. A true trap is what it was. I didn't really care for her, but I so dearly didn't want to lose her company.

Our time in the Big Easy was so memorable. We played, almost nonstop, the Play Station game "Pro Pinball: Big Race USA"—we practically played the game to death. We had all-access wristbands (we were there for a Lutheran youth convention), so we both had the feeling that we were better than the kids who were herded around like sheep, thirty thousand kids. And a moment I'll never forget is when we were playing the pinball game there in the hotel room and there were fireworks over the Mississippi River. Quite a scene it was indeed. If I were writing a movie, a scene like that would definitely be in it, because I assume that it would be quite romantic. Granted, I didn't feel anything like that, but I assume it would be.

Two days after we got back I had a crazy notion to go to the NASCAR Brickyard 400 in Indianapolis. At first Emily thought this was insane and that her mom would never allow it. She did allow it though, and we went on our one and only alone road trip. We stayed at my sister's and had a great time overall. We swam, went downtown, and I showed her where I lived. We didn't have the best of seats for the race, but a good time was had. That was the only experience during which I think I actually liked Emily. Maybe it was because she was free from her mother's sharp talons. I don't know precisely what it was, but, in essence, she was free. Sadly, that freedom didn't live on.

The beginning of the long end began early April 2002. I had a race in Quincy, Illinois, and Emily said she would drive up. She would have been twenty-one at this time. The hotel where I was staying was sold out, but the hotel across the way had vacancies. But Emily said there was no way she could drive the ninety miles there, and that she might get lost (even though she could simply follow the van I was traveling in and she had a cell phone), or that some weirdo would kidnap her from her hotel room. Irrational fears (okay, you, the reader, may not think anything of me for discounting someone else's irrational fears, so I think microwaves are dangerous, so what? It's not irrational!), I know, but what made it worse was the fact that she called me at 2:00 a.m. on the morning of the day we were supposed to leave.

What hurt the most was the fact that I know racing is dangerous, and I want those who say they love me to be there when such a dangerous hobby/career is being pursued. Quincy has one of the fastest and most dangerous tracks in the country. I, in fact, broke someone's arm at that track. (It wasn't my fault. Honest.) I knew that something bad could happen because of the fast speeds at that track. Okay, so I think something bad could happen at any moment, but that's beside the point. The point is that, in the eleventh hour, I was told she wouldn't be there. Sunday was actually a washout, but it still hurt that she wasn't there. When I got back, she told me if she had to do it over again she would've gone, because she then understood how much her being there meant to me.

Well, guess what? She would get her chance to do it all over again. One month later a race was scheduled for Springfield, Illinois, and this place is even easier to find. Hop on I-55 and go north. She said she would go, and we would even be able to stay at the same hotel. But guess what happened? If you said in the eleventh hour in the middle of the night she called me and told me that she might get lost and such, you win the prize. So she had the chance to do it all over again, and in the end I was burned again. This time it hurt twice as much because she promised that if she had to do it over again, the result would be different. The chance was there, but history repeated itself. That was the first of many times I broke up with her. I think I did so just to get some emotional reaction out of her. You see, she was much like a boulder—rather plain, cold, and emotionless. I never knew how she felt about me, so if she tried to make things right after I broke up with her, maybe I would know she would miss me. Well, she was just like, "Okay," and went on talking about school. I got back with her officially the next day, and things went back to normal, or rather what was the norm. I don't think normal could ever be applied to my relationship with her.

A month later I went to meet a race team that was racing at Road America in Elkhart Lake, Wisconsin. After that I began to sense that Emily resented me for going. At least I took it as resentment. Maybe it was the fact that I could go somewhere on my own many miles away. I learned while I was there, in a phone conversation with her, that she had never been any farther east than my house in St. Louis, and never farther west than the I-270 Beltway, with the exception of driving on I-44 to go to Six Flags. I too would be somewhat envious if I was in some sort of geographical prison and someone I knew could, out of nowhere, drive four hundred miles to a town and state they never have been in and meet people they only talked to the day they left. Again, I too would be envious because her geographical prison and fear of new places is much like my internal prison. I was envious of her, how she casually talked to people about nothing at all. I can't "small talk." All my conversations have a point. I either make a humorous, sarcastic comment or give an opinion that you would probably remember if we had a conversation. But for Emily, she could just small talk all day long. And I wished so badly that I too could small talk.

Two weeks after Wisconsin, I went back to the Derek Daly School to take their advanced course. I was so quick that the instructor actually went out in a car to better his time to make it tougher for me to be faster than him. Emily could've cared less. When I told her, she told me that she was reading some book that her job was making her read.

Here's something I should've mentioned above. In April of 2002, she graduated from college. Her parents thought she could go into clinical psychology with just a bachelor's degree in psychology. She then found out that that's not the way the world works. Then in the following weeks she was denied entry into grad school. This, I think, was the start of her proverbial black hole. You have to understand that school was everything to her. If school was a person, she would marry it, no questions asked. So with being denied grad school and me traveling all over and having a ton of potential, I believe there was some resentment.

A month after Vegas, I was headed up to Benton Harbor, Michigan, to have a test in a Formula Mazda. I was so nervous headed into the test that it rivaled my first race. This was the first time I'd be in a legitimate racecar. In Vegas, they are racecars, but somewhat detuned.

But the Formula Mazda would be a race prepared on a real track with other drivers on the track. This would be something completely new for me. The morning of the test, the team owner had me drive around an access road to get the sequential shifting down, and shifting for me is much like having teeth pulled. It's tedious and not much fun at all. Thankfully, I had no problem shifting, but the sense of acceleration was something I had never felt before. Like many people with Asperger's, I'm very sensitive to the slightest changes in my physical environment. I'm telling you all this because, trust me, I'm building to something.

The sensation of deceleration when I hit the brakes was so great that breathing seemed impossible. The shoulder belts felt like they were crushing my chest. There was some of that in Vegas, but, for the first time in my life, when I put the accelerator to the floor, I sadly said, "My God!" I felt bad afterwards for saying that, but its sensations were so uncomfortable that I thought my racing career and dreams were going to die that day. Think about that for a second. You have lived your life for one thing and one thing only—racing. And now this force is making you ponder if you are capable of actually doing it. It would be like a little league baseball player being league MVP, and as soon as he sees a major league pitcher throw a ninety-seven-mile-per-hour fastball across the plate, he begins to wonder if he can hit the ball, much less not be afraid of the ball.

Well, I had my first on-track session, and the fear was quickly replaced by trying to get the double apex turn of five and six down perfect. I did about ten laps and then was brought in so the Porsche Club could use the track. In the next session, I did the unthinkable. With less than twenty-five minutes of on-track time, I was just about a second off the official track record and five seconds faster than the previous weekend's pole time. Think about the exhilaration that I should have felt. I mean, fifty minutes prior, my world was crumbling apart and now I'm running faster than anyone had been there in quite a while, and I was so fast that Mr. Team Principal spun out trying to keep up with me. At the end of the day he told me my talent was such that I was F1 material. Granted, few Americans have made it to F1, but to be told that my raw talent was of F1 caliber should've been something. There was no feeling though. I was just like, "Okay, so what?

That's just how I am." There was no feeling of glee from my shocking performance. And even less after I made a phone call.

"Hey, Emily, how are you?" I asked.

"Umm, fine and yourself?" she replied inquisitively.

"Well, I was just about a second off the official track record and I reached one hundred and—"

Just then she cut me off and then said, "Look, Aaron, I'm on break and I'm sipping a soda, do you think you could call me back?"

Call her back? Sipping a soda? I just did what probably hasn't been done since and she's sipping a soda? What's wrong with that picture? Is it just me, or if your significant other did something spectacular wouldn't you want to hear it? To make an analogy, it would be like winning $200,000 on a game show and having the other person say, "Oh, that's great, could you call be back? 'Seinfeld's' on."

So she could care less about my superior skill at driving a car. From her point of view maybe she thought, Well, look at him, he's good at something. I have a college degree and why is he getting to do these things and why is he able to travel? That might be a stretch of the imagination, but it's probably somewhere in the spectrum of what she was thinking.

To move ahead in time to 2003—now it's early June, and my mom goes insane for a day calling me a "retarded invalid" to my brother. There were other off-the-cuff comments that I don't care to repeat. My home life was shattered. These comments came after I had the joy of flagging on that Sunday. I was inches from putting a knife in my throat. My primary caretaker calls me an invalid, because at the time I was unable to work (I'll write one on the work topic, don't worry), I wasn't going to school, and I wanted to race. In the end, the knife was put down and I knew I had to get out.

So get out is what I did. I went to stay with my aunt in D.C. for two weeks, and when I got back I was living at my dad's. In the process, my sleeping hours adapted to my aunt's, and Emily, for no apparent reason, disapproved. "You mean you go to bed at eight and get up at six? Why the hell would you do that?" That statement came out of nowhere. Why would my sleeping hours affect her? I wish that was the primary point of concern when I got back.

When I returned, my sixteen-year-old Missy the Maltese was on her way out. She was probably ninety percent blind, and she just slept by the toilet at my mom's house while I was gone. When she made the move to my dad's, she just couldn't make the move, so the next morning I calmly and coolly told my dad that it was her time. Not a tear was shed until my dad cried; then I felt his pain. The loss of her still is inaccessible in my mind. Maybe it's because it would be too overwhelming, but in the least, it affected me horribly. I couldn't feel the pain, but the internal pain we can't feel changed me. Add on top of that, my living environment had changed—my mom keeps calling me and I don't want to listen—and add on top of all that Emily didn't understand a darn thing, and things were bound to get messy.

Four months after moving, I got the chance of a lifetime to move to Vegas and be a guest instructor at the Derek Daly Racing School. There was the place where a high percentage of my happy memories took place. Now at the same time I started taking Lexapro. Little did I know how badly that medicine would affect me, but the side effects were masked by the freedom I had in Vegas. But before I even left St. Louis, disaster struck.

Emily already was somewhat snooty about me getting the chance to go to Vegas. You could say that maybe she was going to miss me, but, sadly, that wasn't the case. She wasn't snooty until I told her how much I was going to get paid per day. You see, she's Miss College Degree, and she should have better pay than Mr. GED (even though I had the second highest score in the state up to that time. No big accomplishment if you saw some of the questions on that test). There was definitely a high level of resentment the weeks prior to my departure.

The week I was to leave had arrived, and we agreed to spend the entire Sunday together. We would start out by watching NASCAR from Talladega and F1 from Indy. Then we would eat at our restaurant that we frequented the most, Fortel's Pizza Den. It was going to be the best going-away day. Key phrase there is "was going to be." About halfway into Talladega, she said she was going to have to go home early to help clean out her mom's closet. Now I know you might say that's an excuse to do something else, but as I mentioned, her mom had quite the claws, so this sadly was the truth. So she left early, ruining the remainder of the day. It was going to get worse. With twenty laps to go in the race, I knew a big wreck was bound to occur. So I tried to call her to ask if she would at least turn it on just to listen to the race. Well, I never got in contact with her. Her home phone just went to voice mail, and her cell phone just rang. I tried calling every half hour. The big wreck happened, but I still hadn't heard from her. Now I was getting worried. Did she have a car wreck on the way home? Was she a greasy spot on the road? There were a ton of questions with no answers in sight. Five hours later she calls me and asks sternly, "Why in the world did you call my cell phone twenty-one times?" I then stated that I wanted her to watch the finish of the race and then I feared for her safety. This would seem to be a boyfriend concerned for his girlfriend's well-being. She didn't see it that way and fired back, "Aaron, you need to quit being so darn possessive!"

Whoa! Me? Possessive? That would be one word that never would describe my relationship with her, but I couldn't understand why she would say such a thing. In fact, I still don't know where it came from. Maybe it was deference from her mother's control of her to me. Whatever the case, I was planning on leaving for Vegas in two days.

Two days and I would be away from it all. Or so I thought. My new cell phone was delayed in the mail, so I had decided to spend the day with Emily before I left. One problem stood in the way though—her job. On Wednesday, she was working the twelve-to-five shift—an expendable shift, because there are multiple shift supervisors there, so they could live without her—but she just couldn't say no to her job. That hurt so badly because, as I've said before, I was headed to a dangerous job, and even the drive out there alone could be hazardous. But nope, the "job" held precedence over her boyfriend of over three years.

That evening she called me and said that if she had to do it all over again, she would have done it differently. Sound familiar? Well, guess what? The cell phone was delayed even more so. So on Friday she would have her chance to do it all over again. She was working the same shift and had the chance to right the wrong. She had the chance, but history once again repeated itself. She couldn't say no to her job. I don't want to sound so controlling that I expected her to drop everything to see me at the drop of a hat, but this was a special circumstance. Also, if she had a job where her presence on the job was a matter of life or death or if she was in absolute control (like being the head manager), I in no way would expect her to take off. But she never took off, so one day would not go on her "permanent record," as she put it.

That was the dagger that opened the wound that could not be healed, at least in the mental state I was in. While my time in Vegas was such a joy, at the same time I had the albatross of Emily in my mind. Every time I talked to her I just wanted to know why she couldn't see me before I left. All I wanted was something—whether it was because she just couldn't say goodbye or that she didn't really like me. Whatever it was, I wanted to know something. Anything. This was the enigma with Emily because, as in many cases, there was nothing. Maybe she got jammed in the same fashion that I get in, or maybe she couldn't deal with any emotions. Whatever the case, during my entire time in Vegas, I never once got any hint or any reasoning why Emily lied to me. She did say, however, "Well, I said that (do it different) because I didn't think I was going to get the chance and saying that would make you feel better. I could never say no to my job. They might talk about me while I was gone." Whatever.

When I got back, the Lexapro's side effects were starting to increase. Granted, they were so gradual I didn't notice them, but they made me something else. And on that fateful Christmas of 2003, I broke up with her for what would be the final time. That's the second worst thing I have ever done to somebody. To do it on Christmas is almost inexcusable. Regardless of any circumstance, Christmas should not be break-up day. But I once again had other elements affecting my judgment. So for the last time, I was "official" with Emily.

This so far has been pretty much a "bash Emily" affair, but I instantly missed her the day after, and I tried to get back to being official with her the next day. No such luck this time. History repeated itself, but this time it was me that repeated it. With Linda, I found out that not having her was worse than knowing her, and now with Emily, not being with her was worse than putting up with her constant lateness (I know I said remember that line, so, in a nutshell, she was always five minutes late) and small talk. I wanted her back. Badly.

I spent the first third of 2004 trying to get back with her, and I think she was extracting her revenge by saying, "I don't know. I just need time." That's probably a true statement, but the way she did it was like knowing an enemy's weakness and exploiting it for your personal gain. I was diagnosed with Asperger's two weeks after I broke up with her. And once she knew that's what I had, she seemed to use its symptoms to hurt me.

She knew I wasn't too thrilled to have the label of being a person with Asperger's. One night during bowling (we bowled on Monday nights on the same team and she bowled before my league on Wednesday nights), she was hinting that she would want to be "official" again. But just as the stock market can change in a heartbeat, so too did her mind. She handed me the coldest quote I think I could be handed. She sharply said, "Aaron, you have Asperger's, and I don't think anyone would want to know someone with that!" One word summarizes that: devastating.

Late one June afternoon, I attempted to call her cell phone to see how she was and got her voicemail. I hung up because I hate to leave messages. Besides, the caller ID is good enough. Well, to my surprise, her number called me right back. I answered, sounded elated, and it was some guy who sounded like he was half drunk and from the Bronx. I thought maybe Emily had changed her number, but then he mentioned that if I didn't stop calling his girlfriend, he would find me and cut off my hands then kill me. Needless to say, with my bleak outlook, I was sure mortal combat was about to ensue. I had a steak knife out, and I was ready to defend. I was shaking harder and more feverishly than the San Andreas Fault during a major earthquake. During the voice message that had those lines, I could hear Emily's friend Susan laughing. I knew it was some kind of hoax, but I couldn't let my guard down in case Mr. Bronx mafia man came over to de-hand me.

My dad called her cell phone then and Susan answered; my dad made it quite clear that it (death threats) was never going to happen again. If anything like that was pulled on me, he said people would pay dearly. The next day we actually got into contact with Emily, and she denied any knowledge of the incident and apologized for any stress caused by it. Her excuse was that she was at a party and she had her phone out on a table. The fallacies in that are that she didn't go to parties (as long as I knew her at least) and the biggest one was the fact that she never let her phone out of her hand or purse. Ever. I wouldn't hear from again her until December 31.

On my car ride back from Indy on New Year's Eve, I simply sent her a text message asking if she forgave me. She called and asked what that meant. This was the first time in nearly six months I had heard her voice, and I needed to hear it so bad. I explained that I just wanted to know if she forgave me for the previous year's Christmas, and she said yes. Then we talked like we weren't apart all those months. Thirty to forty minutes later she said she had to eat and that she would call me right back. Well, that was about forty days ago, and she still hasn't called back.

So now to the emotional side of me that I don't understand. As this piece of writing states, Emily was pretty inept when it came to a relationship and emotions. So why do I hurt so bad not having her? Is it simply because I have no one else? Or is it that she put up with me and accepted my views even when they were different from her own? Also, as I said earlier, I held her hand. I could hold her hand with no problem, but skin-to-skin contact with anyone else makes me feel uneasy. It's not that I'm concerned with germs or anything; it's just that skin feels weird. But with her, I could hold her arm or hand with no anxiety. So with her being the first girl that I felt comfortable with like that, I can see why there would be emptiness.

But with all the problems and meltdowns we had, why do I yearn to hear her voice? I know she never once let me know how she felt straightforward, but I miss her and there's nothing I can do to reverse it. There is no reset button. There is no Ctrl + Z. There is no coach's challenge to reverse the play. I have to live with the vacuum of Emily for the rest of my life. Even though I didn't care for her, I miss her. And there is no logic behind it. You could say it was all about a safety net and routine, but no routine is sound enough for me to live by it and be miserable.

When I talked with her in June, she said, "Aaron, I've done things you wouldn't be proud of." I have no clue what that meant, because she said she had no boyfriends. Maybe she started drinking. I say that because I am quite adamant on my no drinking or smoking policies. Or maybe she even started taking drugs. Do you see the dilemma here? There are a lot of questions with no answers. And as stated somewhere near the beginning of this piece, I said I need to know every official thing. I need to know more than that. I need to know what people are thinking, what's going to happen next, and stuff of that sort. As much as I need to know, I'm surprised I don't go as far as needing to know everyone's body temperature. The thing that hurts, and this also applies to Linda, is will I ever hear from them again? Will I see them ever again? Will I hear their voices? Or do I have to wait 'til the post-life show in heaven? So many questions, because for me all they are now are blurs in my memory and all I have to remember them physically is by their numbers.

Phone numbers.

LINDA

Just a note from Dad: Although Aaron wrote about Emily first, there was another girl. The chance encounter was like two ships running into each other in the night. It took a long time to recover from the collision.

There is no name that has more power over me than the name that is written above. And, sadly for me, it's quite a common name. So for this piece, as in "Emily," I will write in chronological order. This will probably be the toughest thing I ever write.

It was late June of 1999. My dad and I were headed up to Minneapolis to work at a convention. The trip got off to a great start when my dad had to stop and bought fifteen pounds of Life Savers, but at the same time I got a retail box of JuJubees that contained thirty-two individual boxes. The car ride up there was most uneventful, as it was Sunday and there weren't that many cars out and about. I was upset that I would miss the NASCAR race from Sears Point. In that race Steve Park and Ken Schrader both flipped in turn two. Irrelevant stat, but I remember everything about this time period, especially races.

The night we got to Minneapolis, we met with a pastor my dad knew. If I haven't mentioned it, my dad is a singer, songwriter, actor, and film producer. He had written and directed a Christmas special that was shown on nearly 150 NBC stations, and this pastor had been one of the stars of the show

The first day that the convention exhibit hall was open was July

2. My dad was going to put on a mini concert at the booth he shared with his video distributor, and to promote it I came up with the idea of becoming a human billboard. After about an hour of walking around I decided to take a rest at the booth. The Minneapolis Convention Center is big. Most of the people at this time were headed to the main hall for elections or devotions or something of the sort, so this would be a good time to take a rest.

As I was sitting there, I noticed this person standing near another exhibit. I thought I recognized her from my church as the vicar's wife. As I've said in other writings, I don't remember people, so in the end I was mistaken. But as she rounded the corner, she headed for me. I believe she first asked, "What in the name of Sam Hill are you wearing?" And I replied that I had to help my dad raise awareness of his concert, so I was willing to go to the bottom of the barrel to help out the cause. At this time I still thought this person was someone I went to church with, so I at least replied to stuff she asked me. Five minutes passed and I realized I didn't know this girl. How did I figure that out? Well, I finally looked at the nametag, and the hometown was Baltimore. So to whom was I talking? I would never have the nerve to talk to any girl because I felt that doing so was somehow illegal. I instantly started giving one-word answers.

She would have none of that though, and she was quite persistent in getting me to talk. Then she asked the question that would change my life forever: "Would you like to play "Uno"?" As you'll read in "Game Theory," you'll understand the importance of that question. Also, if you have a keen sense of knowing what is going to happen next, you know I said yes, because if I had said no, I would have not talked to her, and I would simply be writing about someone who just talked to me for five minutes, and if that was the case something truly would be wrong with me. But yes, I said yes firmly to that game of "Uno."

And boy, did we play "Uno." We must have played for two hours, and all the while we were talking about various topics. She had the same ire of Saddam Insane…ahem…I mean Hussein. She also believed that Clinton was just white trash and was a horrible moral influence on America. About this time she asked my age and I said sixteen, and then in typical Aaron fashion I did not return the question to sender, but she volunteered that her age too was sixteen. So it took a while, but I became the chatterbox as we shared stories of being a pastor's kid (her dad was a pastor), and then, for the first time in my life that I can recall, I actually started asking the first question in a chain of conversation, and, more importantly, I cared about her answer. I say this because before this day I never thought a girl would ever want to talk to me for any reason whatsoever, and I never cared about what someone else outside my family had to say about anything. So for the first time that rule I lived by was shattered.

Three hours had passed; then she remembered she had to meet her mom somewhere in the hall. She left really fast but said she'd return at some point in time. No time was given, so I went from experiencing something I never thought possible to losing it in less than five seconds. But wait, she left her backpack, so that meant she would have to come back at some point in time. My dad had been somewhere, and when he got back he wanted me to go back "campaigning" to get people to come to the concert. I made some sort of excuse, because there was no way I was going to lose sight of that backpack. That backpack was more than a backpack; it represented my lifeline to this person called Linda who took the time of day to talk to me. But where was she?

A snail-crawling hour and a half had passed. The time moved much like traffic seems to move when you are late for work. Standstill. Then through the crowd . . . was that her? Nope.

Two hours now, and as I had my back turned I heard a familiar voice that said, "Ready for a rematch?" It was her, and she was ready for some more "Uno." And I was quite ready to talk to her again while playing the game. After we played about a dozen hands, we decided to tour the convention exhibitor's hall. We walked and talked for another two hours and then got an ice cream cone at the concession stand that was open. We were two bored kids at an old women's convention who'd happened to cross paths.

Just being in Minneapolis took much work. I was supposed to have gone on some servant trip to upstate New York that I wasn't too excited about. So I was trying to find any reason whatsoever not to go to New York, and then I remembered my dad was going to the Lutheran Women's Missionary League convention in Minneapolis, so I asked if he needed help up there. At first he didn't consider it, but I was persistent and got my way. Looking back though, would I have the anguish to come if I had gone to New York?

It was 5:00 p.m., and the convention was closing for the day, so I asked Linda if I would see her the next day and she said certainly. Of course, with my negative outlook, I wondered if that was a true statement, and at dinner at the Holiday Inn Downtown I could think of nothing except Linda, who shattered all my thinking of the world and of myself. My dad was talking about who I thought was going to win the Pepsi 400 the next night, and I said I didn't know because it was a restrictor plate race, but I couldn't in any realm of possibility have given an answer because my mind was too busy contemplating the possibilities on whether or not Linda would be at the booth the next day. Finally, after three hours of trying to remember every conversation and every movement, I came to the optimistic conclusion that, indeed, I would see Linda the next day.

That evening my dad and I were watching the ESPN X Games, and on the night of the day I met Linda, Tony Hawk pulled off skateboarding's first 900. That, to this day, will instantly remind me of her. All I have to hear is either the number 900 or see an advertisement for any of Tony Hawk's video games and instantly I'm taken back.

July 3, the day that would change my life and the race that haunts me to this day, came with a stellar sunrise. We got to the convention center early, and instantly I was waiting for the reappearance of Linda. It was about 10:00 a.m. and there she was. My rare sense of optimism had been fulfilled. We started off just where we left off: talking about the downfall of Western civilization, the knucklehead who sat in the Oval Office, and so many other topics. Instead of trying to play "Uno" while old women were touring the booth, we headed to the hall and went upstairs. We continued to play "Uno," and we were joined by a pastor's kid who was from Michigan. Then his grandpa started playing. That lasted for about an hour until they went off to eat. That reminded Linda that she was to be in the hall to meet her mother so they too could go eat. She did the unthinkable; she invited me to go to lunch with them.

I quickly went into the exhibit hall to track down my dad, and he gave me the money and I was set to eat. I met her mother, who seemed to already know a lot about me from talking with her daughter, and she seemed to like me right off the bat.

As we walked aimlessly to a restaurant, the clouds in the skies were moving at a fast pace. A storm was moving in. In the end it missed downtown Minneapolis, but it certainly made me nervous, because I'm somewhat of a weather geek and the way the clouds were moving meant trouble. I wasn't the only one to notice this, as Carolyn, Linda's mother, knew this as well. Before moving to Baltimore they had lived in the heart of "tornado alley" in the state of Kansas. While looking for a place to eat, Linda's mother and I were talking about the weather. She knew about as much as me (and that's a lot) about the weather. The restaurant, however, wasn't a place where I would normally eat. But not to look weird I said okay. The place was on a street corner, and it was some sort of salad/soup joint.

Nothing on the menu looked appealing. Then I saw a soup that had tomatoes in it, so I figured I'd have a go with it. Well, I now know never to have gazpacho soup again! It was horrible! Cold soup? Who thought of this madness? I did enjoy the drink that I think was called Nantucket's Own. And on the cap it read "Jim Murphy will never be on a cap of Nantucket's Own." Quite humorous indeed.

Lunch ended, and we walked back to the convention center. It was on this walk that Linda attempted, I think, to try and hold my hand. First off, I try to avoid contact with people, and secondly, unless she virtually grabbed my hand, I would have no clue what someone's intentions were. Well, I do know she tried, because later she would tell me so.

Anyways, moving on, it was now about 2:00 p.m., and time was ticking. What time, you ask? Remember the race that haunts me that I mentioned? That's what was ticking. In order to make it back to the hotel, we would have to leave the convention center between 5:00 to 5:30 p.m. I made no efforts to cover up why I had to leave to Linda. I must have sounded quite stupid, because my dad and I were leaving back to St. Louis the next day, and for me Independence Day had a different meaning now. For in the end, America's Independence Day saw my independence leave me forever (at least up to the date that I write this). Okay, I jumped ahead a little bit... It was 2:00 p.m. and we went for the first time to the main hall to watch a black guy sing the anthem, or rather theme of the convention. It was some strange song that had no rhythm, and it kept stating, "Let freedom ring." How ironic, I guess. The theme was along the lines of let freedom ring, and for the first time in my life I was free: free from the negative self-talk that followed me around everywhere and free from the thought that under no circumstances could I be liked by someone else. Yes, for me this was Independence Day.

While in the main hall I finally made sure that communication would not be lost after the convention. I asked her if she had an e-mail address. She did, and I also got her phone number and Yahoo Messenger tag. I kept that sheet of paper for the longest time. More on that issue later.

The time to leave had arrived, and my dad had already loaded the van and was headed around to the front of the convention center. This was it. After all the games of "Uno," and after all the exploring and talking and emotion sharing, this was it—the hardest goodbye I have ever known. In retrospect, this goodbye was much harder than that of Missy (my dog who lived until 2003). Leaving this person named Linda, who I had just spent twelve hours with, was the hardest thing I ever had to do.

Two hours prior to this we had sat outside and just talked, both knowing what lay ahead. She later told me that she tried to hint that I should kiss her while we sat outside, but I was totally oblivious to that. I was too busy staring at the weird top of the AT&T building to notice anything that she was doing.

Back to the painful goodbye: For the first time I held someone else's hand, and with one painful hug she walked by me and then I watched as she slowly disappeared into the mass of people. For some strange reason I knew this would be the last time I would ever see this girl who changed my life. As I was walking out of the convention center, I saw my friend's mom from Indianapolis, and she stopped to talk; by this time buckets of tears were just waiting to erupt, so I said I was in a hurry and quickly proceeded to the van.

The Pepsi 400 at Daytona is normally one of the best races of the year. It is in my book because I cut my time short with the most wonderful person I ever met to watch it. And fittingly, to show me where my priorities should have been, the race just sucked. There were maybe two on-track lead changes. Pure boredom.

To make matters worse, all the while I was thinking that I may never see Linda again. I tried to convince my dad to stay for the last day of the convention, but he said it would be practically impossible to find one person amongst so many unless you had made arrangements to meet somewhere. Plus, he needed to get back to St. Louis to do something for some reason.

But wait, I had her e-mail address and phone number. I could e-mail her as soon as I go home, right? Wrong! Her grandma or aunt lived fifteen miles outside Minneapolis, and she wouldn't be home in Baltimore for another two weeks...two long weeks. I had given her my e-mail address and Yahoo Messenger screen-name and one night, out of the blue, Miss ***_***_2000 appeared on my screen with the message, "Hi, remember me?" Remember her? I had waited all 280+ hours for this moment. I once again was in communication with Linda. We talked for so many hours that night. Or rather we didn't talk, we "chatted."

As we were wrapping up our chat, she mentioned she was going to Panama with this Christian group for a mission trip. I knew nothing about this group, but I thought it was neat that she was willing to go to the slums of Panama to spread the gospel. Little did I know what this trip was going to bring.

Her trip coincided with a trip to Indianapolis that we had planned. I don't remember why we went, but while we were there it just so happened that the Brickyard 400 was that weekend, so we attended. She was gone for ten days and I was in Indy for five, so that still left five days of no contact. That bothered me. Would she be safe in Panama? Would she still talk to me when she got back? I'm so optimistic!

Just as had happened one and a half months before a random name appeared on my computer screen, and again was the message, "Hello, remember me?" It was Linda, but where was ***_***_2000? Now it was warriorgirl2000. I literally got misty eyed, because I became so attached to her first screen-name that it was almost like losing her again. If only I had realized that it was the beginning of the end of losing her.

What did that last sentence of the upper paragraph mean? She had changed her screen-name to further reflect her dedication to Jesus. She also, out of the blue, laid down the framework of rules that were to be followed if we were ever to meet again. Among them was no dating unless someone else was present. For example, a movie with just the two of us was simply out of the question. There were other off-the-wall things I can't recall, but they were quite odd.

It was now early October, and again a random name appeared on my computer screen; this time it was on_fire_with_god. Linda had changed it again because warriorgirl2000 didn't fully tell the world how dedicated to God she was. I knew at this point in time something odd was happening. At the time I did not know what a Charismatic Christian was, but if I had I would've played my cards differently, but then again, I couldn't accept someone else's view if I tried. I'm right, they're wrong, end of story. (Sorry, I got sidetracked.)

October 31, 1999 will mark the day that the beginning of the true black hole formed. I've mentioned this black hole before, and on this day the black dwarf star finally collapsed on itself, and it became this black hole from which I cannot escape. Watching the Littleton school massacre live and seeing dead, bloodied bodies on the ground created the black dwarf star. Two weeks later we left Oklahoma City the day before the F5 tornado hit, and then the following week I was to attend an Indy Racing League event in Charlotte, North Carolina, but I had a race of my own in Quincy, Illinois.

That was good for me because there was an accident and a tire went up and over the fence, killing three people and injuring many more. My dad had sold a sponsorship deal with a St. Louis company and the Jonathan Byrd race team. There was a high percentage that I would have been in that section where the tire landed because the tickets in that section belonged to the sponsor. Two years before, that's exactly where I was sitting during another IRL event. To make matters worse, at my counselor's office the week after the accident, I was reading Sports Illustrated and in their motor racing section they showed the bloody aftermath that the errant tire created. In the picture were two bodies covered up, obviously dismembered, with a river of blood running down the stairs. Indeed, the black dwarf had been created.

So now, on October 31, 1999, the star started to collapse. It wasn't something Linda said, but rather a race on television. It was the Marlboro 500 from the California Speedway. There was a minor accident on lap four that saw Richie Hearn lose it off turn two, and as he slowly crossed the infield grass he clipped some curbing that they had for the infield road course and his car nearly flipped. When I say nearly, the back end of his car came up maybe fifteen degrees, but it still was a hazard. After seeing that I immediately ran to the computer to write the head writer of motor sports for the Indianapolis Star-News about why they had such a dangerous curb where drivers could easily hit (he did a Q-and-A column).

There was nothing that could prepare me for what happened next. Here's how the ABC announcer's called it: "We're back to green and, Paul, you've got to remember with the new Hanford device the draft will be enormous…" The camera changed to a shot of a blue and white car spinning sideways, and Paul Page then took the mike, "Oh no…Oh my God, a horrible crash!" It was a horrible crash. Greg Moore's car hit that curbing that I was in the process of writing about, and it launched his car into a roll. His car viciously hit the inside wall and then proceeded in a horrible series of barrel rolls. The "tub" was destroyed on the first landing, and on the second landing during the rolls, Greg's head literally hit the ground and was crushed, and he was killed outright.

Why is this important? I've seen many drivers die in many races, but what was it about this one? For one, it could have been prevented, but that's not why. What chilled me was that I couldn't see it coming. As the quote said, Parker Johnstone was talking about the Hanford device, and the camera shot was on the two leaders, and then like a flash of lightning the shot changed to Greg's car and it was one-tenth of a second before his car was airborne. So it wasn't the death that hurt; it was the suddenness of it all.

One week later my mom and I ate at Olive Garden, and true to form I got the same thing I always get, a soup I'm not even going to try to spell and a Cherry Coke. And on this particular night I had my fair share of caffeine. So that night I was wired, and then I saw the movie that collapsed the black hole. *A Beautiful Life* had to have been the most depressing film I ever watched, but it made me realize something. We could die on any day at any second. So I e-mailed Linda that night saying how much I truly liked her and that I hoped, in the least, I would know her the rest of my life.

A cold, almost hostile response is what I got. It was something along the lines that such thoughts were ungodly. Whatever that means I still don't know. Three weeks prior she had sent me five pictures of her, so I at least had those. (Author's Note: Previous sentence should've been put in earlier, as I got five pictures of her in a letter that had a card that she stated that she was so thankful to God that she met me, and that she hoped I would be in her life forever.) Why now was it a crime for me to want to know her?

November 1999, and my dad and I were headed to Oklahoma City for Thanksgiving. And as much of a premonition that my dad had about the 2001 Daytona 500, I predicted that this would be a bumpy trip due to storms. My dad had a meeting in Branson, Missouri, and as we walked out of the theater, I warned him, "I smell big storms." Boy, was I right.

Three hours later, somewhere in northeastern Oklahoma, where the McDonald's stretches over the top of I-44, we hit it. According to the radio reports, tornadoes were everywhere. Oh, I haven't mentioned it, but at the time storms terrified me. I knew I was going to die before we reached Oklahoma City, and I knew this was going to be bad. We traveled to the next exit past the McDonald's and then turned. The first thing I did was call Linda.

It was 8:30 p.m. CST, which made it 9:30 p.m. in Baltimore. The phone rang and her dad picked up. From what I knew of him, he was a strict, overly legalistic pastor who'd probably never had a day of fun in his life. As soon as I asked if Linda was there, he responded harshly, "Do you know what time it is?" What time is it? I'm about to die, and he's concerned about time! Now, granted, he didn't know the circumstances, but I pleaded with him to talk to Linda. It wasn't until I mentioned that this might be the last phone call I ever make that I finally got to talk to Linda, "But only for five minutes!"

If you have ever been in a situation where you have no power and you know you are going to die, then you would understand how I felt. I needed to hear her voice before I died. (Sorry for the drama, but it sure seemed like it was going to happen.) She started out by telling me that it was "quite inappropriate" that I called her.

I replied with, "Umm, Linda, I might die here tonight."

"Why would you call me?" she countered.

"Because you know more about me than anyone else, and above all you're my best friend and I trust you," is what I said. That was enough, and she dropped the whole inappropriate thing... for now at least.

She prayed with me and asked God to keep me safe, and that obviously worked, and then five minutes was up and she had to go. By this time the super-cell storm had passed, so we decided to forge on to Oklahoma City. Somewhere between the McDonald's and Tulsa we ran into another storm. This time we were out in the open and there was no shelter. We parked under an overpass. Under that overpass, for the first time in my life, I felt true mortal fear. They say people snap when the stress gets too high. Well, I was at about 150,000 feet with no parachute or oxygen.

If you've ever flown in an airplane, you know the feeling of what it's like right before the plane takes off. Well, that's what my dad's van felt like. I knew instinctively by the way the rain shifted that there was a tornado in close proximity, but because it was pitch-black dark there was no way to tell where it was. A radio station in Tulsa had said there was one moving up I-44, and where were we? On I-44!

The sound of the wind sounded just like traveling in a high-speed racecar. It was roaring. There were lightning flashes every half second, and in the end it was the worst experience I have ever been through. I can tell you that being in a racing crash and seeing twenty karts heading right for me at a high rate of speed while I sat stopped, helpless in the middle of the track, was nothing compared to this. When I came to the conclusion that this was probably it, I reached into the glove compartment and took out my nametag from Minneapolis. It was the only connection I had with the one person outside my family that I would miss if I died. I held on to that so tightly that if we had been blown into the air, that nametag would have stayed in my frozen hand.

The storm passed, and we finally arrived at my great aunt's house (I think that's who she is, but ironically her name is... Linda). I immediately got my dad's laptop out and connected to the Internet to e-mail Linda and tell her that, by the grace of God, I was still alive. But guess what? She had already e-mailed me stating how wrong it was for me to call her at "that time of night." Okay, this is coming from the person who just two months prior told me that regardless of the time I could call her. Now I know people move on, but this had nothing to do with that.

I sent her somewhat of a stern e-mail, stating that I was happy to see she cared about my well-being, and then I debated the whole ungodly sense of calling past that taboo time of 9:00 p.m. In the end she conceded that she was wrong and she was just saying what her dad had told her. Sound familiar? If you read "Emily," you know that I cannot tolerate people who don't think for themselves. I know I think for myself, at least that's what people tell me (ha, ha, lame joke).

So the middle stanza of the end has been set. She didn't care about my near-death experience, and she can't think for herself, but at the same time her religious ways were getting wackier. I'm not going to say that I'm perfect when it comes to doctrine, but I've been told I have a good sense of it for someone who hasn't studied it at all. With my eye always on perfection, I always picked up the fallacies of a new belief system. She was ending e-mails with tag lines such as "doing God's work" and "wrapped up in God's blessings." Those are only two, and there's a third one that trumps them all, but as of this moment I can't remember it, but it was bad. It was getting to the extreme end of the wacky spectrum.

Now before I move on to the end of the game, I should mention that Linda and I were pretty much equals when it came to our ways of thinking. Our intelligence levels and the way we think were a lot alike. It was almost like the saying "Everyone has a twin somewhere"; in this case, my twin was Linda, except she was headed down a dangerous religious road.

Moving on a month to Christmas of 1999:

This was my most memorable Christmas on record. I had money from working at the bowling alley, so for the first time I used my money to buy people gifts. In fact, I bought my sister the ultimate gag gift. I bought her a gas pump nozzle. The eruption of laughter was well worth the thirty dollars I spent on it. What made it so great was I got every video and board game I wanted. What made it even more special was that I had my own room at my brother's and it was so cold. I love a cold bedroom as long as I have sufficient blankets. We were there for a week, and I did have e-mail.

Yes, I did have e-mail, and I was expecting a thank-you letter from

Linda for the forty dollars I sent her for her Romania mission trip that was coming up, but none came. She did send me an e-mail on the twenty-ninth stating that school was depressing her and other stuff I don't remember. I haven't really figured it out, but I sent the first of two goodbye e-mails on December 30, 1999. It was sort of a wake-up call, a honk of the old horn that I still existed.

It must have worked. On that memorable New Year's Eves, we talked on the phone for probably three hours working things out, and she mentioned that her mentor had died, but on the plus side she got a starring role in some school play production.

So things were worked out for a while. The religion was not. She was getting more charismatic by the day. I couldn't see it coming at the time, but the final episode of our relationship was beginning on the Friday before that year's Daytona 500.

It was the first NASCAR truck race at Daytona, and a little over halfway through the race another sudden crash of biblical proportions happened. Geoff Bodine was on the outside when the truck in front of him got together with another truck. Geoff had nowhere to go, nor did he have any time to react. As he impacted into the side of the track in front of him, he was launched skyward. He was headed straight for the catch fencing above the protective concrete wall. The truck exploded into a fireball, and the lower catch fencing cables sliced through the front rows of the grandstands. Then the truck tumbled like a toy car. While it was in the air another truck hit him, launching him once more toward heaven. In the end, Geoff suffered mild injuries and was back racing just seven months later, but the damage was final for me.

What damage, you ask? Just like Greg Moore and all the other sudden, unexpected incidents, I once more arrived at the death-at-any-moment mindset. Now, mind you, I am perfectly comfortable with my own death, but it's the death of those around me that I fear. And besides that, Linda's religion was getting to be too much for me, and it was sort of like the dot com stock bubble burst.

Linda, with this wacko group, was getting to the mindset that, "If I'm good, good things will happen and bad things will go away." That mindset is setting one's self up for a major checkmate, because when something bad happens, you will think one of two things: one is that you weren't good enough, and the second is the worst one—you come to the conclusion that there is no God.

So on February 13, 2000, I sent the ultimatum to her. Granted, I was pressured by my mom to do this, so maybe I wasn't thinking one hundred percent for myself, because I listened to her on this occasion. I simply sent Linda an e-mail stating what I believed were her distorted religious beliefs and told her that I thought she went that way due to her overly law-oriented father. That would be the last communication with her that I was sure she had read.

I did get a response. It wasn't a defense of her beliefs; it was very matter-of-fact. She said she didn't want to be a stumbling block to my faith. I had already sent her an e-mail saying I may have overreacted and that I would want to continue talking to her, but her last line summed it up: "Have a good life, and please never try and contact me again." So trying to help her in my own way backfired. I was sure that she would see that since I was willing to risk our friendship on this, she might see it my way, but my prediction was so horribly wrong.

The person who changed my life was now gone. The one who showed me that happiness could be found outside of a racecar was gone. I didn't obey her in regard to not contacting her. And ironically enough, one month after I sent that final e-mail, my dad had a trip and we drove through Baltimore. Linda and I had looked up on Mapquest to see how far apart we lived, and I knew she was just through the trees on the left side of I-95. Had I not sent that e-mail, I would've seen the face that I could not remember except for the outdated pictures.

Three months after the end, I sent her pictures back with a letter saying that I hoped she would forgive me and that I could not bear to see her, except for one picture that I would keep forever.

The reason I say forgiveness is that I came to the conclusion that no matter how wrong I thought she was, one must not go through the measures I took to try and make her see the light because obviously she didn't.

The one-year anniversary of our meeting was hard, but luckily for me I was in Alaska on a servant trip with my church. The flight back from Anchorage was on the same day that I said goodbye to Linda. It was the most lonely plane flight I had ever been on. Everyone I knew was sitting away from me due to some weird ticket glitch, so I had nine hours of self-reflection on the past year. Why did my trying to help backfire? Would I ever see or hear from her again? How did she do in that play she was gong to be in? Then it hit me. I actually cared how she did in that play. I had never cared about anyone else before, and now how I longed to know how she did.

I sent her a letter when I got back that was not answered, but I did have her Web site to hang on to. It was just poems that she wrote, but at least it was something. It had not been updated in some time though; in 2000 or 2001 it was shut down due to inactivity. That connection to Linda had been lost.

I may have seen her at the youth convention in 2001. There was this one person who rang a bell in my memory, and this person never made eye contact, nor did this mystery person say hello while I was passing out flyers. She talked to the next person handing out flyers, who just happened to be Emily. But I don't think I'll ever know if that was truly Linda or not.

To date I have had no communication with her whatsoever. The last time I tried to send a letter was when I was at my aunt's in 2003. I wanted to make sure I knew it was her receiving it, so I sent it priority mail with signature confirmation. I did get my wish of knowing if she received it, but I found that out by the "return to sender" she wrote on the package. In all my letters, all I wanted was some sort of forgiveness. I punish myself every day emotionally because I have no one to blame for losing contact with the most important person in my life except me. I knew it was her that wrote "return to sender" because I compared the handwriting from the paper she gave me in Minneapolis to that on the package and they matched.

I haven't asked any questions in a while, so what would make this better for me? If you, the reader, have an answer for that, please share it with me, because I've looked for that answer for nearly five years now. Half a decade and the wound just keeps getting deeper and deeper. For me there was and is no closure.

To make matters worse, in May of 2004, I had the opportunity to instruct at a stock car racing school in Pocono, Pennsylvania. I stayed at my aunt's in D.C. the night before I would head to upstate Pennsylvania. On my trek from D.C. to Pocono, Baltimore is a must travel-through city.

I was driving rather fast, but at the same time I was looking for the Baltimore-Washington International Airport because I have this fascination with airports and I wanted to see it from the road. While looking for BWI, I got stuck in the I-695 lane, an expressway to the Baltimore Beltway. This was on a Sunday, so traffic was very light, but the only exit from the road I was on was to head south on the beltway. Ironically for me, the first exit where I would be able to turn around was Linda's. Now what I'm going to say next is downright scary. Behind me, as I was waiting for the light to turn green, I saw Linda's dad. No kidding. I saw a picture of him in one of Linda's pictures, and he was driving the same car Linda said he drove and he had his pastor's collar on. God does truly have a sense of humor, doesn't he?

Later in 2004 I realized that I hadn't seen her picture or the slip of paper she gave me in Minneapolis in a while. I looked feverishly for it, but to no avail. It was nowhere to be found. And where's her picture? It was with that slip of paper and now it's gone too. My last remaining connection to the person that changed my life had been lost.

So again, what will make this better? I can't think of anything. All I want to know is if she forgives me. Now that I know I have Asperger's, it angers me even more because that might have been a contributing factor as to why I was so black and white on her religious beliefs.

But maybe someday, just like before, I'll get a random message from someone out of the blue, asking, "Hi, do you remember me?"

GAME THEORY

Just a note from Dad … When Aaron was five years old, I bought him his first Nintendo. It soon became all he did. While I had some concern about his obsession, I was too busy as a pastor to think much about it, and it kept him busy. What I soon found was that he was so good at playing the games, I enjoyed lying on his bed and watching him play.

He has perfected his abilities to the point that in the past five years, every racing game that has come out for the X-Box and the X-Box 360 Aaron has been number one in the world.

Is it bad or is it good? "Game Theory" might offer an explanation.

I've noticed that I am a different person when I play a game. Why is that? I have many theories that I'll try and talk through to see just what it is about a game that is so freeing.

All my life I have loved games. What did I want for Christmas when I was five? Monopoly. And not only did I get it: I won at it. And trust me, nobody let me win. I remember one victory against my dad that was probably the biggest gamble to pay off in Monopoly history. I don't know what year this would have been, but we were living at the first house I remember. I had $1,005 on hand, and I had a Monopoly of the dark blues (Park Place and Boardwalk). My dad owned most of the other board, but he didn't have that many houses on any of them because I owned all the railroads, and that kept his cash on hand to a minimum. I decided to build up on my dark blues, giving me hotels on both, leaving me with just five dollars cash. I did this because my dad was seven spots away from Boardwalk, and I don't know how I knew this at the time, but I knew seven is the most frequent dice roll, so I took the gamble, and what would you know, a seven was rolled, giving me victory.

That was just one example of my gaming mind. I live for the game. As I tell people on Xbox Live, it is not winning or losing that's important, it's the game itself. Through the game I am temporarily free of my mind. Free of Linda, free of Emily, and all the other mental anguish. Also, there's no better feeling than the unpredictability of a game set with predictable rules. Like that Monopoly game the expected unexpected happened. It's quite hard to explain, I know, but with a game comes so much more than that which is played out.

With my friends in Indianapolis I have probably spent over two hundred hours playing various games. Scrabble, Monopoly, and Trivial Pursuit are among the vast line of games we have played. And I get shaky just thinking about the pleasure I experience while within a game. In January of 2003, I went to their house and stayed the night. They were all busy, and in the twenty-seven hours I was there, there was just enough time for one game of Monopoly. But that one game was quite worth the travel time up and back and the other stagnant hours. One game was so freeing and exhilarating.

Is it the competition of the game? I would say yes and no, because I am impartial to whether I win or lose. The primary thing I want is for a game to go down to the wire. When playing video games, and especially racing games, I will attempt to put the game as close as possible 'til the very end. I live for the games that are decided at the buzzer. Win or lose it doesn't matter. The feeling that I get in the waning moments of any given game are of such that I don't know how to explain it. I have actually lost many a game trying to make it close. Now, granted, in a real-life race I want nothing more than to lap the field fifteen times. But for board games and video games I need them to be close.

Back to the point that I'm different in a game situation, I believe that to be a true statement. The chains that make me not talk and make me overanalyze life are gone. I become so absorbed in the game that all of the rest of the world becomes irrelevant. If in the middle of a fierce game of Monopoly I was told that their was a major calamity on the news, I would not care because I would be considering how to trade property A to person B to have trading power with person C to get property D. Also, I am much more talkative in a game. But why is this? What is it about a game that makes me who I think I really am?

In the warm months, I am the chief starter/race director for the St. Louis Karting Association, and at the track I command my post with authority. I have a much better posture about myself, and I move with precision and power. Well, I move with power because I do have power. I have the same way about me when I race, but that's another topic. While I take my duties at the track quite seriously, for me it's nothing more than being an emcee of sorts for a game. I'm sort of the game show host for a game that involves people hurling their bodies at breakneck speeds. So, in a nutshell, it's all a game at the track—a game that I am in control of, and I act according to what the rules say.

What the rules say. That's the key sentence in this piece so far: the rules. In all games there are rules. And within rules come knowledge of boundaries and limits. For instance, Scrabble can only be played up and sideways, but not backwards or diagonally. Monopoly must be moved clockwise, and it's fifty dollars to get out of jail. In a race, there are a set number of laps and many rules governing the way people drive. In bowling there are ten frames, ten pins, and a foul line that can't be crossed. Within rules comes safety. Within rules comes knowing what's going to happen next, to a certain extent. That's even a more important statement, knowing what is going to happen next.

In the "real" world there are few set rules except laws, and all other rules are determined by the individual. Such rules are: is it appropriate to talk to someone else for no reason; whether or not it's right or wrong to drink, and the list could go on and on. But in a game those elements are tossed out. My over-thinking and over-critical attitude of others is bypassed, because within a game all participants are playing by the same rules. This is Aaron's game theory. I believe my perception of the world differs from yours, but for the short time that a game is being played, the real world and my world coincide, and happiness is found through the medium of the game. So, therefore, winning and losing isn't important for me. It's the joy of that temporary coexistence with others that can't be found anywhere else.

So, in summary (I know I can be a bit confusing at times... okay, most the time), within a game everyone is within the same rules. When playing a board game and someone disagrees with a play, there is the magical book known as the "rule book." Life doesn't have a written rule book. So how can one that needs everything to have an "official" right or wrong operate in a world that has a gray area on rights and wrongs? Well, it's quite difficult, I can tell you that for sure. But for me, in the short times that I get to play a game, I am free because there are limits and there's a defined beginning and a defined end. In an open conversation, there is no predetermined end to a conversation. So in many instances, I'm thinking, Is this conversation over, or are they waiting for me to say something? But within games there are ends. In a race, it's when the predetermined laps come to a close; in Scrabble, it's when the last tile is played or when no words can be played; in Monopoly, it's when I've bankrupted... I mean it's when one player remains.

My mom has always asked me why I play so many games, and now I can tell her why. Maybe she'll understand when I can tell her why it was worth thirty-plus hours and five hundred miles of traveling just to play one game of Monopoly.

Just a note from Dad... As you will read below, the workplace is a real challenge for Aaron. The following quote is from a book entitled Asperger Syndrome Employment Workbook: An Employment Workbook for Adults, by Roger Meyer.

> Many adults with mild forms of AS do succeed at work. Many more do not. AS remains a "hidden disability" to others, but not to us. It is also a pervasive condition. This means we can't compartmentalize our lives with the hope that AS will be kept at bay. We may try to forget that 'it' is there, but under certain conditions our AS keeps popping up. Sometimes we can anticipate those conditions and avoid them. Other times our characteristics show up unanticipated and uninvited guests. Keeping our most challenging behaviors hidden or under control exact an enormous toll on your life outside of work.

WORK

This piece will be about my experiences and troubles in the workplace. As with all the other pieces I have written to this point, this too will be in chronological order.

If there was one thing more that I hated about the lulls in between my kart races, it was working on the kart. To touch any part of the kart outside of the driver's area was a guarantee that dirt or grease was to get on my hands, and I'm somewhat particular on having my hands be clean. So I had to be creative in finding a way to get out of that situation. Enter the eighty-year-old flagman whose name was Frankie. Frankie was in the waning years of his flagging career, and it showed. Sometimes a ten-lap race would be eight or fifteen, and sometimes, instead of giving the field the checkered flag, he would give the black flag (which means you've done something wrong and to pull into the pits because you have been disqualified). So my idea was to help him count the laps and hand him the right flag at the right time. I got my wish in the second half of my first season in 1995.

To be honest, I was after his job right away. I always wanted to be a flagman of some sorts. And at least now I was the "apprentice" waiting to take over the reins after Frankie retired. A couple of the heat races in '95 I got to do by myself when he had to use the restroom, and I did quite the job for only being twelve. I can't imagine what the drivers thought seeing a mere twelve-year-old being the head flagman.

Frankie was forced into retirement in 1997 due to fears he might die in the summer heat. The apprentice was now the main flagman. And all the while I was working for free. In fact, if I had had the money at the time, I would have paid them to let me flag. It's the ultimate power rush. I have the power to start the race, end the race, stop the race, and disqualify people. In other words, I'm in charge. At this point in time, I didn't have race director status, but I was still in control of on-track operations.

I finally started to get paid in 1998 (twenty-five dollars for the entire Sunday), but for timeliness not much has changed up 'til 2004 for that job. My pay has been tripled, and I am now, this season (being 2005), the head honcho for all on-track responsibilities. I talk about my flagging style in "game theory," so I won't touch upon any other flagging duties. Instead, I'll start on my jobs that were way out of my element.

My résumé, besides flagging, starts at a bowling alley. I had been bowling for one season and wanted to be able to bowl for cheap, and I needed money to buy all the good video games that were coming out on the market. So during one day at bowling, my dad talked to the manager and instantly I had a job.

My duties weren't of the highest jobs in America, but at the time I didn't care about making minimum wage, and now instead of a practice game of bowling costing two dollars, it was a mere fifty cents. But there was some anxiety going into my second night of work, and that anxiety came from the lady I would be working with.

Before starting there, I always hated going in on any night except Monday because the lady that worked the counter was, well, somewhat mean with the clients. Her name was Carol, and she had no tolerance for stupidity or ignorance. So going into my second night of work, which was a Wednesday, was of such high anxiety that it ranks up there with my first race. Would she yell at me? I had heard stories that she made other lane attendants cry and walk off the job. So how was she going to treat me?

Right off the bat she was a completely different person than what the legend of Carol was. She showed me everything that Kevin (the Monday night guy) forgot to show me. She told me that if I got tired I could take a rest and that on her nights I could have all the free soda I wanted. This was Carol the Terrible? I was thinking at this point in time, Okay, when is the nuclear bomb going to go off?

It didn't the first night working with her, and I was cautious of everything I said. Not knowing much about a work environment, I made sure that everything on the checklist was done. I don't know why or how, but Carol the Terrible was actually nice to me on that first night. Time would not change that.

I started at the bowling alley in September of 1999, while I was still talking to Linda, and every night was five hours of boredom that I pondered about her. This was the start of the beginning of the end of our relationship. Even though I was very efficient and active in the workplace, there was no escape from outside thoughts. I know that holds true for most people, probably, but for me, being on the job just made me reflect upon events more so than when I was doing some other activity. Fortunately for me, Carol the Terrible had no hesitation of telling me how stupid other people were.

These moments were bright spots on what was beginning to be the start of a long, dark period. Carol was full of stories about incompetent people whom she couldn't stand. Maybe she liked me because I wasn't a "phony." I did what she said when she said it, and I never made anyone mad, so maybe that's why we got along. Still, at the same time, other lane attendants told me about how much they hated her because she was so mean to them, but she got me to talk. We talked and made fun of the stupidity of certain bowlers for most of every night. I think she may be the only person who has a more bitter taste for the average person than I do. And maybe it was for that reason that Carol the Terrible was, for me, the best person I have ever worked with.

I was still content with $5.15 an hour, and it didn't matter, because working Wednesday nights was so much fun that even through the Linda incident that ended our communication, I still looked forward to Wednesday evenings. I still would dwell on Linda, but it was Carol's constant mocking of people who deserved to be mocked that kept me interested in keeping those alleys as clean as possible so I could stay at the counter as long as possible. She had a hard time, though, keeping her disdain for people to herself, as constantly she would tell people of their idiocies. Ownership got a lot of complaints about her, but the owner liked her because she dealt with drunks exceptionally well.

As the weather heated up and summer began, my schedule was cut back. They didn't need my services on Monday or on the occasional

Friday. But I did get to keep the Wednesday that I so loved. During the summer leagues, the first part of the night was an adult/child league and then a cosmic bowling session. There were maybe ten teams in the league, and then the cosmic bowling session normally looked like a ghost town. Sure, there was the normal fog and the ear-pounding music and the black lights, but at most there were maybe at a maximum ten people there. So Carol let me bowl while working. And bowl I did. On one night I had amassed twenty-seven games in less than three hours. And late in the summer I would bowl three games that would change my life forever.

It was the penultimate night of cosmic bowling on Wednesday night before the fall/winter leagues started. And on this night the lanes were perfect for my shot. As usual, Carol let me bowl while working, and on this night of fate I would have a three-game series like no other. My first game out of the box was a perfect 300. Then in the next game I had a 258, and my third game matched my first game for a three-game total of 858. I was astonished, and so was everyone else that saw it. (Author's note: Since this wasn't in a league, I got no awards for it. And still to the day I write this I have not had an official 300 game.) Word got around quickly of the employee who had an 858 while on the clock. The word must have been strong enough for the owner in Florida to hear it.

I missed the following week because I was somewhere out of town, and the first night of the normal schedule had me working a Wednesday. It was finally back to normal, or so I thought. I called the alley to let them know that I would be ten minutes late because my ride was running late, and when the line was picked up on the other end, I heard something odd, for it was not Carol who had picked up the phone, but instead it was Vera who had worked in the snack bar. I asked her if Carol was there, and then I was handed the most devastating thing I could have heard at that point in time, "Carol is no longer with this company."

The person who broke my workplace shyness was gone. But why? She handled drunks properly, and sure, she could be harsh with idiots, but they deserved it. So I asked myself all these questions on the way to the alley, and then I found out the real reason. The owner liked her and knew that there were a lot of complaints, but he could not get over the fact that she let someone that he was paying bowl on the clock for free. So my great series of 858 was instantly internally nullified because it destroyed my happy workplace.

I got along with Vera in a casual manner, and the person who worked Mondays was just downright stupid. It was no longer fun, and I started to look for other options. Thankfully, my dad did business with a video duplicator and again, as before, I instantly had a job and a pay increase to go along with it. I was up to seven dollars an hour. But at the same time I held on to my Wednesday-night position at the bowling alley.

I started at the duplicator during October of 2000, and to say the least, the job was repetition. Here's a typical scenario: put many VHS tapes in many VCRs, wait until program has ended. Then take said tapes out, label them, put them in sleeves, box them, and repeat process until you go insane … ahem, I mean, until the quota has been met. With the events going on in my life at this time (the still gaping wound of Linda and now meeting Emily), this was probably the worst possible job I could have. I got to do the same thing over and over and watch some of the worst programs in American history being duplicated.

But I still had my Wednesdays to look forward to. I left the duplicator's place at 2:30 to make it in time for my 3:30 league and after that I started work. At least on this night I had some escape. That is, until a new hire started working. This person started the week before I went to Las Vegas to attend the Derek Daly Academy. I had no idea what was in store.

When I returned from Vegas, I was temporarily on top of the world. I was told by my instructors that I "had it," and while driving those cars, my mundane job and Linda were not on my mind. It was an escape of sorts. But my routine at home was about to change late in November, because this new hire was quite flamboyant about his homosexuality. He said things I won't repeat, nor care to ponder upon, but I'm the type of person who can't even look at another person without feeling some sort of guilt, and now here's this guy who jabs about stuff that I won't even say. It took two weeks of that and I was out of there. I didn't need to hear those things or be subjected to them. So my Wednesday nights were gone, but I still had the video duplicator.

The money from working at the duplicator was nice, but the internal grief of having eight hours of monotony was taking its toll. I don't know if Emily would have stayed with me for as long she did had it not been for working at the duplicator. While working there, I had minimal human interaction (which is not necessarily a bad thing), but the people I did interact with had their problems.

I was a model employee (okay, the only primary non-family employee), and one day in the middle of July there was a bad storm that knocked out the power in the middle of the night; therefore, my alarm clock was blinking 12:00 when I woke up. I instantly turned the television to the Weather Channel to see the current time. It was 8:40. I was always to be at work by 9:00, and the duplicator's establishment was at the least thirty minutes away, and that's with no traffic. And there was never a situation where traffic was light. And this day would prove no different, even at the later time. My then-to-be future step-brother was working there with me at the time, so he can account for everything that happened next.

I arrived at work at 9:25, a miracle within itself that I was only twenty-five minutes late considering I had gotten up only forty-five minutes prior, and there were two accidents on the interstates. But the owner's wife didn't seem to think that being twenty-five minutes late was acceptable. She gave me about a fifteen-minute lecture: "Aaron, we need responsible people here to work. We can't have people who are late." Okay, if I was always out partying and was always coming in to work late, I would agree with that statement. But I had told them that the power was knocked out and that were two accidents the second I walked through the door. As she gave me this responsibility lecture, I could see the owner just put his hands over his face.

That lecture stirred in my mind for about an hour, then I came to the conclusion that I had enough grief living at home with my mom that I didn't need this and that the wife was way out of line, and to prove a point, I quit right then and there. Emily frowned upon my decision, but my future stepmother applauded the move as she told me, "You gotta do what you feel is right." Like I said before, I had enough grief with my mom, who was going through her own depression, so I did not need another negative element in my life. It was already negative enough having eight hours to just think. If I had known at the time what I know now, something productive have might come from it, but at the time just wondering how that school play went and if I would ever get a random message from someone I used to know was bad enough. The lecture was the straw that broke that proverbial camel's back.

So now what? I was unemployed, minus the flagging, which paid barely anything. I had my trip to New Orleans in late July, so looking for a job in the week before I left was a waste of time.

When I got back I had no clue what to do. Emily asked if working at a video game store would be to my liking. I thought about it but dismissed it. Then I thought about it and considered it. When the yearly Madden football game was released, I asked the manager at the store I bought it from if there were any openings, and he said someone had just quit and that they were taking resumes. I took an application, filled it out, and returned it that day.

I hadn't heard from Babbage's (the name of the store now called GameStop) for three days, so I drove down to the mall to see if he had looked at my application. He said he had, and he was happy that I stopped by because he instantly gave me an interview for the position.

An interview? What was I to expect? Every job I'd had prior to this was dependent upon my dad knowing someone, and I had it locked up before I even met the manager or owner, but now an interview. To say the least, I was nervous, and I didn't give much more than a yes or no answer to all questions.

At the end of the interview, he said he would call me within three days and let me know if I had the job. It was only two days later that I got the call, and, indeed, I had the job. I have no idea why he hired me. I would not have hired me, because in the interview I appeared to only know two words, but whatever the case, I had the job.

On my first day he told me that I would be his experiment and that I had two weeks to prove to him that I could make it in the retail world. None of my other jobs had me selling any services, but here there was so much to sell. For one, we always had to push the "used" games. Also, there were extra warranties on game systems, and then there were also MST, or multiple sales transactions, which were transactions that had a person sell more than one item. All of these stats were kept track of in the back room on a big board. And then there was the Game Informer magazine subscriptions and discount card.

Little did I know how much effect this magazine would have on my sales performance.

Working at Babbage's was a bit of a pay cut. I went from $7.00 to $5.75 an hour, but the twenty percent discount offset that. It was very late August of 2001 when I had my first day, and on my very first transaction, I sold a subscription. Was it beginner's luck? How did I convince someone to buy something that I myself had just learned about thirty minutes prior? I was a completely different person when selling that magazine. There was a sense of confidence about me that under normal circumstances was lacking. For someone that was shy and quiet, how was I able to sell something to people? It was amazing. On my first day, a Wednesday, I sold four subscriptions in just a four-hour time span. To put it into perspective, the store on the whole had three for the entire business week leading up to the day I started. Mr. Manager's experiment seemed to be paying off. Ryan was his name, and he once described the gamble to hire me as, "It was sort of like putting a bet on a horse at a track that has odds of 100–1. You know you are going to lose, but yet there's just that slight chance it could pay off." As of now, it was paying off quite nicely.

The attack on 9/11 took place just a week and a half after I started my job. I was scheduled that day, but I did not go in. Just as well, though, as all malls were closed on that fateful day. But in the next few days, I'll never forget that the television in the store that was normally used for games was tuned to ABC for continuing coverage of what had happened. Working during that time at a store that sells fun was somewhat odd. People were different for a while. I felt bad trying to get people to buy extra things after such a tragedy, but it was the rules of the game. People were actually more willing to buy extra things after the tragedy. Maybe it's because they felt a full-out nuclear attack was imminent and that money would be no good, so they might as well spend it now. Whatever the case, the expert salesman in me was being well tuned.

Maybe it was my years of playing Monopoly and convincing people that the deal was good for them and not me that made me so good. Whatever the case, I routinely doubled what everyone else that worked there would sell. Whether it was reservations or subscriptions, I was light years ahead of everyone else. And I worked the fewest hours on top of that, so either everyone else didn't care, or they just sucked at selling things. It was probably a combination of the two, as I've come to learn that the vast majority of the population doesn't have the work ethic I have. When I work, it's a game, but it is a game of such that I cannot lose. I must win whatever the cost. If you've read "game theory," you know that in a game it isn't the winning or losing that's important, it's the game itself. In a work situation, however, I must win. I had to be top seller every week. I had to beat everyone else weekly to prove that I'm the best.

The game I was playing only had one competitor who knew there was even a game, and that was me. Nobody else cared if they sold ten magazines or zero. I did, and Corporate America loves people like me. I had a streak from November to March that every day I worked, I at least had one magazine sale. My obsession with the sale became so important that I did not care to put cases back where they belonged because I was studying potential customers before they even got to the counter. About two-thirds of the time, I knew if I had the sale before I got halfway through my spiel. And if I knew I was losing the potential victim—I mean, customer, I would instantly change my selling tactic. For being someone as oblivious to other people, I could look at the faces of customers and know if I had the sale. This somewhat falls under my game theory, because for me it was a game and the customer was an unknowing player.

I could see eye twitches or a brief glance when I said something, and I knew what path to take to get the sale. Granted, I didn't win all the time, or even half the time, but I always had the highest sales. My career high was ten in a six-hour time span. I only had twenty-three sales that day, so it was a very high percentage. Company quota was to have a five percent success rate for the day on magazines, so ten for twenty-three was much higher than the expected quota.

Not only was I selling like mad, but I was able to communicate somewhat with the coworkers. We were one of the smaller stores, so there was usually just a manager and one employee. This is the element I can talk in. Anytime there was one extra worker, my mouth shut. I simply couldn't talk. For whatever reason, I don't know, but it was so aggravating. One-on-one was fine. Throw one extra person in and it became practically impossible to start or take part in any conversation.

March turned into April, and April would not be forgotten. The store's shrink (amount of merchandise lost) was always higher than corporate expected. And sadly, for me being so trusted, I had a hint of why that was. On this one fateful Wednesday, the loss-prevention guy came in. He interviewed the two other employees, and then he called for me to go to the back room.

The back room at the store was crowded to say the least. In its thinnest part, it was maybe one-and-a-half persons wide. This is where the LP guy had me sit. There was also a manager from another store sitting no farther than three feet behind me. If I had claustrophobia, I would have been a nervous wreck, but, thankfully, that's something I don't suffer from.

He quickly asked me if I knew who he was, and I said that I remembered him from a time he did a false robbery in the store. He told me at the time that I did a good job of catching him. That must have thrown him off his questioning track because there was an awkward moment of silence. He stated that he was from loss prevention and asked if I knew why he was there. I stated that the manager always said the shrink was high, so that's why he probably was here. Trap! I don't know what school these loss-prevention people go to, but the second I mentioned that the manager said that it must have raised a red flag in his head because no more than .25 of a second after I mentioned that, he asked me, "Aaron, do you want to go to jail?"

Jail!? What was this man talking about? Was he insane? Or is this a trick? For the first time I said, "Come again?" This must have disarmed whatever suspicion he had at that point in time because he stated that stealing was a serious crime. I responded with the fact that I knew that was the law and it was to be followed. Again, there was an awkward moment of silence. It was probably only five seconds, but they were painful ones. What did this guy want with me? Why was he taking away from my time of selling things people really didn't need? Oh my goodness, I thought. It had to be the Xbox that management let me trade for a new one.

Just as I thought that, the guy mentioned if a certain guy's name sounded familiar. It did. He was a guy who always came in and bought a game just to bring it back an hour later. He had some sort of copying system, and he was bootlegging games, but I suspected management was also letting him take valid copies as compensation for the money he was paying the managers.

I told him what that name meant and who was involved. He asked me, "Aaron, why did you not tell me this fifteen minutes ago?"

I responded quite simply with, "You didn't ask." That must have made him mad because he said withholding information could be a sign of collaboration with the crooks. These crooks just happened to be the ones that I could talk to one-on-one.

I escaped the clutches of the menacing loss-prevention guy and returned to work. The assistant manager immediately asked me, "Dude, have you seen a ghost?" He was saying this because I was pale from the stress of the interrogation. If you have ever seen any police show where the detective is interviewing a suspect, I can tell you that television does a good job in showing how it really is. And this guy wasn't even with the police.

At this time, I didn't realize the ramifications of what I had revealed to the guy, but I realized that I left out that management let me have a new Xbox when mine broke. This broke me. Like a lost child wandering aimlessly, I wandered back to the clutches to reveal what management had let me do. I had no idea how severe the punishment was going to be. An Xbox at the time was still three hundred dollars, and that could be a severe punishment.

I sat back down in the interrogation chair, and he asked me, "Why are you back? I told you to leave!" I had interrupted his writing on his laptop. I instantly broke down for two reasons. For one, I knew my revelations to him were going to change lives, including mine, but secondly it was that Xbox. Like the beating heart in that poem, there were stacks of Xbox boxes on either side of me where I sat. I then told him the truth about my Xbox.

Something shocking happened next. He said, "Thank you." Thank you? Thank you for what? What did I do? Then he mentioned that the information I provided was vital to his information, and although that Xbox was given to me, it was the manager who did that and not me. Therefore I was just the recipient of someone else's wrongdoing. Then it hit me. Wrongdoing. People were going to pay dearly because of me.

It was a repeat of my 858. I had just destroyed my happy workplace, and this time people were going to pay dearly. And they might know who blew the whistle. Oh God! My overthinking mind thought of how big the third-party guy was and how he had threatened people if they ever told anyone. I had been told I could be on the receiving end of his threats. Oh no, oh no, oh no. Why did this guy make me tell him that was happening? My life in my mind was in jeopardy. This made me break down even more.

I had a box-cutter knife in my pocket, and I got it out then. I wasn't going to let the managers or the guy who didn't work for the company hurt me. If I had to, I would get them before they could get me. To say the least, I was a wreck in that small back room. I was stuttering and slurring all my words, and I kept repeating, "I'm a dead man. I'm dead. I'm so dead."

At this point in time, the guy started to talk me down to earth. He mentioned that everything said was confidential and that nothing bad would happen to me, he would make sure of it. I don't know why, but I believed him at the time, and nothing bad did happen to me because I'm writing this today.

I stayed another two months at that store, buy every day walking into that back room I was flooded with memories of that fateful April day. It became mandatory that there always be three employees on duty to keep everyone in check. This made me somewhat of a mute, and I wasn't talking that much, and that back room loomed there ominously, almost screaming at me, reminding me of the day that I was trapped. I did all that I could, but as I have cut off most relations in my life, I instantly said I could not take it and I quit. The new manager must have been somewhat informed about the previous situation because he said he would've done the same thing. To date, I've been back to that store just three times, and that was because no other store in the entire city had the game I was looking for. And on each of those times it was to the point of being one drop from being completely overwhelming.

So now I was unemployed again. I had destroyed two happy work environments. Of course, I wasn't one hundred percent responsible for the fall of the people who were fired, but I was a contributing factor. I never had worked for the money. People told me work equals survival. I never could and never have seen it that way. Where I had worked it was always a game. When the game became tedious or the extenuating factors of playing the game became overwhelming, I simply quit playing that game. For me, having no money isn't as bad as working in an uncomfortable environment. Like the Babbage's, I would have gone insane if I had been there for one more day. You see, my memory is way too good for its own good, so every time I was in that back room I could remember the tension to such precision that I could feel the adrenaline of fear I felt. I could not remember what the guy looked like, but the chair he sat in was still there, and that chair took on the image of the loss-prevention guy. Same thing happened at the video duplicator. Not only did I have the dwelling on Linda every day, but the tension of the conflicting spouses and then the lecture for no good reason made the game irrelevant. It did not outweigh the gains.

So would my third non-flagging job be the charm? It took three months of looking, but my dad knew a banker and asked him if he had any openings. At this guy's branch, he did not, but I went in and filled out an application. About two weeks later I got a call from the bank's main branch that, if interested, I would have an interview. I took it, and the following week I had an interview. In this interview I was much more prepared than at Babbage's. And because it was one-on-one, I commanded it. Maybe too much, but I got the job, so I must have said all the right things.

At the same time I started this job, I was taking my first semester of college. My school schedule had me going on Tuesdays and Thursdays. I worked at the bank on all five days of the week and then four to six on Tuesdays and Thursdays.

After training out at a branch that was way out of town, I moved to the main branch. They started me inside, but after just one week I was moved out to the drive-thru. Now I do have to explain something about said drive-thru. Since the bank was building a new branch next door, they had to tear down the current drive-thru. So now in the drive-thru were two independent booths. I jokingly called this my "sensory deprivation chamber." I called it that because it was about as long as a four-door car and about as wide as the length a grown man can extend his arms. Mix in a safe, a counter, and a computer, and it was crowded confines. Two people could not comfortably be in one at the same time.

As much as I said I disliked this "chamber," it was actually a paradise. It was locked from the inside, and I had bulletproof glass in front of me. I did not have to physically touch anybody, as a drawer folded in and out of the chamber. It was virtually a paradise, so long as people didn't drive up and ruin my train of thought or doing my homework (which the branch manager encouraged, me doing that homework, that is, but, of course, not while customers were there). I forgot to mention that I got a nice pay raise there. I was making the big bucks at $9.25 an hour. Everything was going good until a snowy January day.

The cash in my drawer was running low, so I had to make a run inside to the vault to get some more twenties. Four thousand dollars total! As I did that and proceeded on my way back to my booth, I slipped on some snow that was sitting at the point where the parking lot met the sidewalk. The fall was vicious, as I went over backwards a la a cartoon character slipping on a banana peel. My head and neck slammed to the sidewalk with enough force to stun me. A customer was right beside me when I fell, and luckily they did not happen to notice the four thousand dollars in my coat pocket. As I regained my ability to move, I was instantly told not to for fear of neck injury. The last thing the bank wanted was a nasty lawsuit. So I got to lie out on that sidewalk in the freezing snow until the ambulance arrived. The final diagnosis was a bump on the head and a severe cervical strain.

The severe cervical strain was a killer. It hurt to sit upright, and I missed three weeks' worth of work. I didn't file for any worker's comp or anything, so I simply wasn't making any money. When I made my return, they moved me back inside where I had the anxiety of being robbed and the small talk with coworkers. Late in my return day, the head teller told me, "You missed so much work because you just want money. You're too young to be hurt. You just want to own this bank." I don't know where her statement came from, but my neck hurt too badly, and the anxiety was too great working inside, and that was the end of this game. I called the manager's voice mail that night saying that my neck hurt too badly, and I didn't know when it would get better, so I thought it best for them to find a replacement.

Jobless again, I was off a job for four months. July 2003 I moved from my mom's house to my dad's. The day after I got back from my D.C. trip I went to the new GameStop by my house. As I entered, the manager recognized me from Babbage's (remember that these two stores were the same company) and instantly offered me a job. I took it, and the expert seller was back on the prowl with a whole new host of people who could not resist buying a magazine they may never read.

Three months after working there I got my dream job. I had been a student at the Derek Daly Academy in Las Vegas three separate times, but now they offered me a one-month guest instructorship. October of 2003 would be the best month of my life. I was making big money to play the game I most wanted to play. I was hesitant at first talking to students, but by the end I was in my element. As with all of my jobs, this one too had a tragic end with me knocking myself out on a Goodyear tire. Here's a tip to anyone. Never replace a ceiling tile while standing on the extreme edge of a table. I learned that lesson the hard way. The school has never invited me back.

I returned to GameStop when I got back, but that lasted just a month. The game of magazines had become perfected. There was no newness about it. It was too easy, and after making $225 a day in Vegas, six dollars an hour didn't seem relevant. About this time late in '03, Missy started to catch up with me, and my troubles with Emily and the memory of Linda and the new house all hit me at once. I became emotionally unable to have a job.

And here I sit, still unable to. I so dearly want to start a job, but I have trouble starting things. You'll read why in my future piece called either "Green" or "Start." It's not that I don't realize the importance of working for money, for that money equals survival in the real world. For me, though, if it's stressful and emotionally tolling, the lack of money does not outweigh the feeling of hopelessness I feel at a job.

SEE

This title itself could have many meanings. For one, it could be a sort of "I told you so" type of title. But that's not what it is. "See" is about what I see and how I see it.

I've always liked playing chess. I know all the moves and strategies, but one thing always gets me, and that's my lack of seeing what the other side does. This is an interesting analogy of how I am in an open social setting. Take for instance a chess match—white moves, and then black counters. That's how it's supposed to be. For me, however, in both chess and in an open social setting, I am so absorbed in my move that what black, or what the other person does, is lost. It's lost so much that it almost becomes to the point of irrelevancy because I'm so concerned with what I'm going to do that when my opponent moves, I pay no attention to what they have done.

The interesting thing about this is that it's identical for chess and a social setting, but in Monopoly I can easily calculate moves to win. It's not that I can see what the other person will do, but in that game I can influence what they want by implementing trades, and somehow I know exactly what to do to get exactly what I want. I know there's a difference between chess and Monopoly, but what is it about chess that makes me lose sight of my foe?

I've probably played over one thousand chess games, and I am still oblivious to the opposing player's moves. Logic would dictate that if someone loses by means of one way they will learn and they won't fall the same way again. For me, however, that does not hold true. Every time, just as in a social situation, I become blind. I do not see. I cannot calculate the other person's variable.

But what's truly interesting in calculating outcomes is that I'm great when watching a race on television. Let's take a NASCAR restrictor plate race for instance. Most all of the forty-three-car field will be in one big pack. It isn't surprising to have thirty cars on the television at any given point in time. I have a gift in watching these races, as I can see trouble before it happens. My mind so quickly calculates what car A and car B are doing, and I can see that there's going to be trouble before that has occurred to anyone else. Ask my dad about this. It must be so aggravating watching a race with me because I can so quickly process the information and predict movements that I know there's going to be a crash long before either driver knows it. This is what makes me good behind the wheel. My mind so quickly feels the car and those around me that I can make the right maneuver.

So what's the difference between calculating the movements of cars on a track and another person's chess moves? I am so intrigued by this whole chess thing. I'm pretty good at every game I play, but with chess there's this block of blindness that I can't shake.

I can see tension long before anyone else has awareness of the problem. Case in point is that on December 26, I was on a flight from Frankfurt, Germany, back to the States, and as the plane was taxiing from the walkway I knew something was wrong. For one, the beeping noise that is heard when someone calls a flight attendant was different. Secondly, as I looked behind me there was a small yellow light flashing. I have come to realize if there's a flashing yellow light in any situation, it's probably not a good thing. And finally, the kicker that I knew something was off the wire was that all the flight attendants were on the phone. As it turned out, there was a small electrical fire in an air conditioning unit and we had to get back to the terminal so that mechanics could figure out the problem and fix it if possible. But it was that overanalytical mind I have that can so quickly calculate my surroundings.

I have so many instances where I subconsciously figure out something is wrong and so many races of which I've predicted the outcome that it is still a mystery to me why I have trouble with talking to others in an open situation. Could it be that I'm overanalyzing other people when talking to them? That could be, but I'm not sure if that's completely accurate. I can say it's quite aggravating.

There's no amount of money I could wish to pay for just one day to have my gift of seeing be reversed. Life is a chess match. There's a move and a counter-move. Now, granted, in life people are normally not adversaries, but it's sort of like a dance. One moves, then another follows. With me, as I've said, I move _____ I move. There's a blank where the other person's move is. I try to predict what that blank space is or will be when it's my move, but ninety-nine percent of the time I'm wrong. I grossly miscalculated the way Linda would react to the e-mail I sent her. If I knew it would lead to the termination of all contact for what is now five-plus years, I never would have sent it.

That's true for most social predictions I make. I can see perfectly if I'm a third party. If I see two other people talking, I can easily tell what the mood is, if they like each other and stuff along those lines, but when it comes to the first person, I am blind.

I want to quit being able to see from the position of the third person and start seeing and functioning from the first.

FEAR

Fear is an emotion that most people are well afraid of. It's a powerful enough word that NBC has a show called "Fear Factor." Its ratings as of late have been subsiding, but people watch it to watch people's fears. On the show, they have the contestants dangling from a helicopter and then make them eat some hideous food. I wish that for me fear boiled down to eating something gross, but for me fear is so much deeper and scarier.

As my dad quoted to me earlier tonight, "As FDR said, 'The only thing we have to fear is fear itself.'" If that's the case, I've got fear of the fear of fear. The anticipation of the fear is enough to throw me in a tizzy.

But what's truly fearful is hopelessness. Can and will things ever get better for me? I can do so many things, but my internal prison is such that I have not found the key. That is fear. To realize a problem, to see the problem, but to be powerless to do anything about it is absolute fear. As mentioned in "See," I can see the problem, but I am blind to a solution. Logic would dictate that if one knows of a problem, they are able to fix the problem. Logic in this case has let me down.

Fear is what Emily dealt me at the bowling alley with the horrible quote, "You have Asperger's, and no one will like you." Think about that for a moment. I was having a hard enough time accepting myself for having that, and someone I had known for four years said no one will ever be able to like me because of it. That is cold.

Fear is the absence of the knowledge of what love is. I've been meaning to use that unknown "L" word for many writings, and it's been tough to write, let alone think. Emily was also implying this when she gave me that knife in my back. It's true, though, that I don't know what it is. I think I know about it when it comes to animals, but with people it's like that emotion isn't there, or at least to the state that I've heard others talk about. For me love is, "I'd miss you if you were gone." There is no needing that other person's love or approval, there's just my quote. I don't know if the emotion even exists in my head. The closest thing I could say is that for which I felt for Linda. But not at the time I saw her. I yearn for who she was in Minneapolis and not who she became. Which is it though—that I loved her in my memory, or is it that I loved being free?

Does freedom equal love? I wouldn't know the answer to that, as I've only been free (free, meaning being free of my own internal prison) twice. Maybe there's somebody I will meet someday who has the master key to unlock my mind from all its hideous overthinking, but my over-thinking mind will overthink so much that just getting into my mind and through all the swirling thoughts is so tough. In both instances where I have felt freedom, it's been a "perfect" scenario. An analogy is a tornado. If all the elements aren't in place, a tornado cannot spawn, but if the jet stream is right, and the lower level winds are right and mixed with the right pressure, then there's a "perfect scenario" and a tornado can spawn. Now, granted, anything with tornados isn't by any means "perfect" (except when they don't happen), but that's an analogy. So many elements have to be there for something to happen.

I do not have fear of the possibility of never being "normal." If I were normal, I might not be able to write the way I do or drive a car with the precision that I do. The fear lies in the possibility that this internal prison I'm in will remain in place. Fear is also Linda. Her existence in my brain is of such that the sheer mention of her name is painful. The secondary fear to that is if someone I saw in person has so much power over me, how can I ever deal with the power their absences have?

Now we are coming full circle to "the only thing we have to fear is fear itself." If I allow the fear of the fears to come dictate my life, there will never be much of a life. What is so odd is I have no fear of dying, no fear of hitting a wall while racing, but this one person I met in Minneapolis gives me so much fear that it is overwhelming.

Where does the fear lie in Linda? Fear in will I hear from her? Yes, I did say that. If I hear from her, what will she say? Fear is the unknown. Death is a given; therefore, it should not be feared. Pain has many variables; therefore, it is most fearful.

I'll combine titles now because I believe the two of these go hand in hand.

LOSS

Two titles in one paper is new for me, but I see it prudent now making the connection that loss and fear are one in the same for me. The fear of loss is also the loss of people, which brings fear. A cruel cycle it is.

I'm a person who can instantly become attached to someone or something for no apparent reason. Take, for instance, the legacy of the Minute Maid soda can.

I'm somewhat lazy when it comes to cleaning up if it's outside the "green" zone. The green zone is any of my gaming area, which has to be in precise order all the time. But back when I lived on Nottingham, my former friend Ryan finished a can of Minute Maid and put it on the right of my television on my dresser. That can sat that for a month in 1995, and it was still there in 1996. It became part of my room and in some way a connection with him. That can was there until my mom decided to clean my room in 2001. It was gone. This is going to sound pretty odd, but how many people do you know have shed a tear over a soda can? Well, whatever your number is, it just increased by one.

The loss of that can in the big scheme of things was a small one. People lose things all the time. They might lose their keys or maybe a twenty-dollar bill. But for me it only takes a second of thought and an irrelevant thing becomes important. Even if I still know the person, I can't get rid of it.

I made a major step a couple nights ago. When I was withEmily we played a game called "Escape from Monkey Island." We were so far in that game. But I started a new game, which required a lot of memory card space. I had to delete something, and I came to the conclusion that our saved file had to go. According to the memory card manager, the file had not been accessed since 1/2/02. It was now 2/6/05. Over three years I hung onto that file, but finally, finally I let it go. I am not ashamed to say that a tear did cross my eye. Maybe that was a symbolic sign that I may be moving past Emily.

I maybe have had a breakthrough dealing with Emily, but the wound Linda has left has not gotten any better. For me, I have lost her picture, which I promised her I would keep for all time, and now I have nothing. Absolute loss. And I have no one to blame but myself. With Emily it became easy to loathe her, but with Linda, she never did anything quite to the scale Emily did. Sure, being mad that I would call when my life was being threatened is a frownable offense but most certainly forgivable. But I cut her off, and now I have nothing to remember her by except her unused screen names and her phone number. Like I've mentioned in prior pieces, I can't remember people. Maybe this is why I become attached to what most would say are irrelevant things. For you, the normal reader, a soda can on a dresser wouldn't last two days; for me that can lasted many years.

Where did this sense of loss start? I remember when I was very young I cried and cried when the space shuttle Challenger blew up. I was born in 1983, and I don't recall the year it blew up, but I was young and I realized the ramifications of the events. I knew the shuttle was gone and the brave inhabitants were gone. I, at the time, used dead. Being a racing fan from a young age, I knew death. Maybe that started it. I was ten at the time, but my two favorite drivers died within months of each other. Alan Kulwicki died in a plane crash on April 1, 1993, and I'll never forget the phone call I got from my friend Tony.

"Aaron, did you hear?"

"Hear what?"

"Kulwicki died in a plane crash outside Bristol!"

Being the skeptic that I am, Tony sometimes goofed around, so I was disbelieving and replied, "This is April Fool's, isn't it?"

"No, Aaron, turn on ESPN," he responded, and as I did, I was horrified. This was no April Fool's joke. My favorite driver was killed in a fiery plane crash outside Bristol, Tennessee. I was an emotional wreck. I know I missed many days of school dealing with that loss.

Several months later my new favorite driver died in a helicopter crash at Talladega in Alabama. Davey Allison would have certainly given Jeff Gordon a run for his money on dominance in the nineties, but we will never know. My two favorite drivers both perished outside of a racecar. Since then I have had no favorites. With no favorites, it minimizes the emotional attachment, lessening the risk for pain.

Here's where fear and loss coincide. If I had that much pain over someone I never met, what's going to happen on that horrific day when someone close to me dies? I know I have pain for Missy the dog, but it is so wrapped up in an emotional file in my brain that it's unreachable. She is in what I call a jam. I'll write a paper about "jams" at a later time.

But if Kulwicki's death was so hard, how will I handle the future? As mentioned before, I have no fear of my own death. What I left out was the fact that the fear is in the death of others. With death comes change, and with change comes anxiety, and anxiety fuels pain and then we have a "perfect scenario." This time, though, instead of being positive, we have the ultimate emotional trap—one of which I'm extremely afraid.

There is no avoiding death. Every second that passes is another we lose. Every second that passes is another I know my chances of just knowing if Linda will forgive me diminishes. Every second passed is another that you, I, my animals are reaching their temporal end. So here's where fear comes in. With every second passed, I'm stuck here in my internal prison. I so wish I had Emily's external prison. I would much rather be afraid to move about than to be trapped internally by my own brain.

The trapping of my brain is the overthinking. Do I overthink because I simply don't understand what is being said? Interesting question. With a race (as mentioned in "See") I can instantly tell you the current situation and tell you where the "big one" is going to happen. But in those terrifying and frequent social situation in which I'm almost a mute is the fact that I simply don't know what to do, or is it that I don't understand what's going on? Very interesting questions I hope to elaborate on later.

My birthday is the roughest part of my year. It's another symbolic move toward everyone's fate. But with my birthday means everyone else is also getting there. Maybe this is where my disdain for change comes from, because maybe somewhere in my mind, if things never change then, well, things stay the same.

I remember as a four-year-old I must have cried for hours when my dad got a new van. Now why would I care about a change like that? At that age, one's supposed to care about what letter is debuting on "Sesame Street" the next day. So this proves that even from the earliest of ages, I became attached to things rather than people. Do the things that I get attached to represent the people whom I can't remember? Again, interesting theory.

If my memory cannot remember you in physical form, I can remember you through a can, or a letter, or, well, the picture I lost.

TRAPPED

The alternate title for this piece would be pain because the two go together. In fact, it's been a while since I wrote anything because I couldn't decide on the title, so I settled it with a coin toss. Trapped obviously won. The coin toss was best out of three.

All of my life things have remained with me. If you've read up to this point, then you know how good of a memory I have. I dearly wish that I wasn't gifted with such a memory.

In any given situation my eyes are constantly moving, soaking in all the surroundings, which then in turn get stored in my vast memory. Just as my eyes go so too does my hearing and smell. I believe this to be true with everyone, but from my experiences with the limited amount of people I've known, mine is somewhat intensified.

With such a memory there are so many triggers that can initiate a painful memory. Now keep in mind, it doesn't have to be a bad memory, because a good memory for me is just as depressing. Every day of my life I walk through a minefield hoping that I don't step on the proverbial mine that will make me very sad. And again, I think everyone has his or her own triggers, but mine are much smaller than yours probably.

What's different about mine is that they are sort of "webbed" together. If one mine goes off, the whole field goes up in spectacular fashion. It's sort of like the game where you have to pull sticks out and hope that the balls don't fall to the ground. For me those sticks are very fragile, and it doesn't take much to create an avalanche.

So what is it that creates an avalanche? It can be something as little as hearing the year "1999" mentioned. Or it could be the minor mention of the city of Baltimore. It even gets so narrow that the mention of the Playstation game of "Gran Turismo 2" can create an avalanche. I got that game December 26 and talked to Linda on the phone the second I got home with it. The call was short because I really wanted to play that game, but the two, the call and the game, became intertwined. This is the trap.

The trap is what my mind does with every memory. It literally traps them with a vice grip. I've been told that time heals all wounds and you have to tell your story a thousand times before you feel better. Neither holds true for me. It's as if the memories in my mind become a vortex that just keeps getting stronger, not letting anything out of its horrible clutches.

So what can I do about this? So far I've found nothing that helps. And if the trend continues, eventually the mention of any given word will start the avalanche. My mind remembers too much and can remember so fast that a trigger can be pulled, and before I realize the connection I'm horribly depressed and on the verge of hopelessness. Again, given enough time passage, anything and everything will become a trigger because everything becomes connected with someone or an event.

As I have said before, I don't remember people, but there is no problem remembering rooms, smells, or sounds. I can tell you everything about the lobby of the hotel that I stayed at in Lithuania, but I couldn't tell you one thing about the pastor that we were with. I can tell you that he drove a red VW Golf GTI that had no tachometer. I can easily describe to you what the terminal in the international concourse looks like at the Frankfurt airport, but sadly I can't remember a thing about the said pastor. I even saw the tape of the trip yesterday, and yet I can't think of one way to describe him. This is part two of the trap.

Since I cannot remember him, how I remember him is through the memory of the lobby. And a big "mine" right now is anytime I see a red Volkswagen Golf. Maybe I've solved why happy times for me are so sad. Maybe it's because I do not remember the people of the event. Interesting concept, isn't it? The lack of memory creates a vacuum. As I try to remember them, I end up in minefields that remind me of them but not them in form. In other words, I remember "things" about them but not them. (That took enough sentences to explain.) This could be the true trap.

Another almost pathetic land mine for me is St. Elmo, Illinois. What is so big about St. Elmo? Well, definitely not its size, as it's a small stop on Interstate 70 in the middle of the state. But one thing for the longest time set it apart. On the water tower was the town's name, and below it was "1988 I.H.S.A.A. Final Four." For me this was always a highlight on my many trips back and forth between Indianapolis and St. Louis. For one, going toward Indy I always knew seeing that water tower was one step closer on seeing my friends (see "Game Theory") in Indy. In other words, it sort of became an unofficial gateway. Also, I always wondered about the team that made it to the Final Four. I first saw the water tower in 1993, and they had it on for many years to come.

Then as Emily and I were coming back from the 2001 Brickyard 400, I noticed that the water tower had been repainted. Lost forever for the world to see was the small town's pride that their small town had made the Final Four. For me this was a bigger loss. I know it sounds downright stupid. I mean, how could a person associate a town's water tower with so many things? I wish I knew, trust me. But in that instance, one mine multiplied into many more. Now every time I pass St. Elmo I remember that water tower's former writings. Then my memory quickly will associate that with Emily, and then all the memories with Emily keep backtracking as far back as I can remember. So much pain caused by one water tower. How is that possible?

What also comes from that water tower is that it had stated that the year their feat was done, 1988. So in 2001 it was erased. I'm sure that the pictures from the event and banners remain at the high school, but for the outside world it is forgotten. Not with me.

The silly thing about it is that I've never met anyone from that town, and I don't believe that we have ever even stopped for gas in that town (Do they even have a gas station at the exit?), but for some reason the fact that the year was up there on that water tower triggered something in me. Not only was it a passing checkpoint for me on my many trips to Indy, but it was a reminder of the terminality of time.

All my mind's traps revolve around the "T" word. That evil word is "time." With time comes inevitable change, and change is bad. So with the exterior, visible memory of the 1988 basketball team erased from the water tower, it was a symbolic action that time moves on. For me there is no moving on. I live in a time loop, constantly remembering everything. With change comes disturbance in routine, thus creating new mines, making the trap's grip of my mind even greater.

I envy that water tower. It moved on. To make an analogy, in my opinion most people's memories are like a train station. People get on a train and move on to the next station. For me, however, I'm still at station one, and my bags have been piling up for many years. I'm still waiting for that train so I can at least drop some of that baggage at the next stop, but my train has yet to depart.

I think I'm becoming somewhat redundant on this topic, but I'm trying to express a certain thing that at this moment I'm unaware of how to describe.

The true trap is my mind's inability to move on. Furthermore, it's even worse when it comes to time. When my mind can't find a logical answer, the vortex grows even stronger. When I have calculated something in my mind, I think I know the outcome, and if that outcome doesn't happen a trap forms. I still to this day am shocked about the results of that e-mail I sent Linda. So with all this garbage in my mind circulating at light speed it's very difficult for normal stuff to be expressed. So much of my subconscious think power is used on trying to find this logic that doesn't exist. Once my mind consciously becomes aware of a logical dilemma that doesn't make sense, an avalanche warning is instantly issued. The really sad thing for me is that it's the same things over and over and over.

A really scary thing happened to me last week. My dad and I are headed to Africa later this month, so we were going to get our shots. If you knew me, you would already know something weird was about to happen. I'll tell you what I can of the events that unfolded ... I don't remember waking up on that day, I don't remember the drive to the place, and I have no clue where this place was that we got our shots. The last thing I remember before getting my shots was watching a movie the night before. Then my memory recalls getting my yellow fever shot and it burned a lot going in. I remember the nurse saying, "Yeah, that's the response I get from most…" Then, according to my dad, I passed out as fast as you can turn a light switch from on to off. I was gone. He said that my head dropped with such force that my glasses fell from my face and hit the floor. I guess I'm lucky that I was caught before I hit the floor.

I came around to the point that I can remember in full detail just a few seconds. My dad was saying, "Aaron, Aaron, Aaron," and he said it in a tone that was much like the way he wakes me up in the morning. So at the time I remembered that I had to get up for my shots, and then I realized that I had this horrific stomach pain. As I opened my eyes, I was dumbfounded. Here I am, thinking I need to get out of bed to get my shots, and then the thought of, Why am I dressed sitting in a chair in a room that obviously isn't my own? Instantly, I forgot everything about my life. I did recognize my dad, but I didn't know the year, the place, or even what country I was in. And all of these thoughts were coming within a millionth of a second. So I remember calmly asking my dad, "Where am I?"

The next thing I fully remember is coming to in the emergency room of the hospital and asking my dad the same question. He explained what happened, and it took some time to register. Now if you noticed, I used the term "fully" in the previous sentence. I believe I was in that half awake-half asleep phase, because I thought I had dreamed an ambulance ride. And what was so terrifying about the dream was that I remember that the EMT was asking me questions and I knew the answer and I thought I was giving him the answer, but he kept asking the same question. I thought I was screaming my answer, but there must have been nothing. This was truly one of the scariest experiences in my life.

As it turned out, I had a vesal vega syncopy, something that made my blood pressure drop really low that made me instantly pass out. It wasn't the fact that I had the most supreme exhaustion I have ever felt or the knowledge that my streak of being out of the hospital had ended. There are a few things that terrify me to the bone.

For one, the ambulance ride is a great analogy. The EMT was asking questions and I knew the answer, but the motor skills weren't there to convert the knowledge into words that could be understood. This is just like everyday life for me. There are many times I want to talk, or I know the answer to the question that someone asks, but I'm unable to express my answer or opinion.

Another thing so scary about it was, again, as I have mentioned in prior pieces, I have a fear of things happening suddenly. I don't think anything more sudden could happen to me like this. Imagine remembering a day and then all of a sudden you are in a hospital with more wires connected to you than a home-entertainment system. The initial fear and shock was so great that the memory of it is somewhere in an inaccessible place in my mind. It's much like my memories of Missy; I know they are there because I can feel them every once in a while. But this shock of waking up, or rather coming to, having no idea where I was or even what year it was created such a fear that it is truly indescribable. My first thoughts were, Where's Emily? Did I have a crash? That can't be, so I don't see any racing gear. Umm, I'm not paralyzed or in a cast, so it couldn't have been a crash. But where's Emily? Then, as everything flooded back into my brain, I became even worse. I then knew there would be no Emily checking in on me. In fact, outside my household no one even knew that I had one of the worst experiences in my life. This is the epitome of the trap.

The true mind trap that this points out is that I'm alone (excluding family), but for the most part it's been self-induced to a certain degree. The jam in logic is in the fact that most people don't measure up to my standards (gosh, that sounds overbearing), but I so dearly want someone just to care. I had no one to tell of my horrific day or the true mortal fear I felt waking up and not knowing what was happening. So the real trap is the conflict of the two sides fighting back and forth, vying for supremacy. And the two sides are in equilibrium. The sides are that people aren't worth knowing (and my memory backs this up), and the other half is the desire to know what that normality on the other side is like. In all my other misfortunes I had someone to tell, but on this fateful February day there was no one to tell. And that now has become the biggest mine of them all. It summarizes the past six years perfectly. If the trend continues like I said, will this be the way it is in twenty years? I so dearly, beyond words, hope it isn't. The trap must be broken, or emotionally I will be.

(I will edit this to further state the trap, but with this happening so soon it's hard to write about it because I am still in my time lapse of the event. It will catch up with me though, and when it does I should be able to explain this better.)

TOMORROW

I just finished "Trapped," and now I want to talk about one of the most fearsome words in the English dictionary in my opinion. There is nothing worse than "tomorrow." Just as Annie says, "There's always tomorrow"; for me I wish there wasn't. Tomorrow is uncontrollable. What could happen? Sure, I may get a racing ride and my life will finally start, but I could wake up to a horror like 9/11. Someone I know may die. Will my animals be okay through the night? Sleep is a scary time for me. So much so that getting to sleep is difficult.

I like and need to know what's going on at all times. While this is truly impossible, I want to be "in the know" at all times. I have to know what everything means. And while I'm asleep, nations could fall, the stocks could crash, space monkeys could enslave us all, and who knows what else could happen. That is true fear. During the transition from a today to a tomorrow one will dream. Dreams are hideously depressing for me. In my dreams I can see people. While awake I can't picture people, but while dreaming those people are remembered in their true form. When I wake up they are gone, and a tomorrow has become a today.

Back on topic with this "I need to know." I do indeed need to know. It's almost to an obsessive state. Case in point was an incident at the end of an ARCA race at Daytona in the middle of February 2005. On the final lap, there was a crash on the backstretch. The initial camera shot had one car spinning to the inside of the straight. Then the camera changed, and it was of a car upside down that then was hit viciously right on the roof. The car did some sickening barrel rolls. As that car came to a stop, the camera changed yet again to the camera where you can see the entire straight, and it was an image straight out of a war zone. For the brief moment that the angle was being used, another car was in the air upside down and cars were hitting each other with crushing blows and yet another car started flipping. It was one of the worst sights I have ever seen.

But what made it bad? It wasn't anywhere as devastating as Greg Moore's or Kenny Brack's crashes. What made it bad was that Speed channel never showed a replay and never mentioned the crash again the rest of the night. On "Speednews," they said that another crash had ended the race, totally ignoring the horrific crash that took place on the final lap. My mind went nuts. "Aaron, calm down," was what my dad kept telling me. But how could I? There were at least fifteen cars involved, and when networks ignore something, it must be bad. How bad was this? How many people had been hurt or killed? I taped the race, and I watched the sequence over and over to try and figure out why they were so mum on the fact that the wreck had happened. I could come to no logical conclusion, except the fact that a lot of people had to be dead.

This is what I feel every time I go to sleep. What's going to happen tomorrow? How many people are going to die? Will I know any of them? If someone I know passes, will I be able to remember them? I don't remember my grandma at all. I remember everything about her funeral, but the person herself is nowhere in my mind. So the crash at Daytona was just an extension of the tension I feel every day. In the end only one driver was hurt and it wasn't serious, but the twelve-plus hours it took them to release any details were twelve snail-crawling hours.

Tomorrow something good may happen, something bad may happen, but no matter how much I wish, tomorrow will come. There are so many things pending in my life that with each tomorrow comes more anger and anticipation. I'm twenty-two, and I want to race more than anyone alive. Racing is me. I may not be able to truly connect with people, but when I drive it's like the best dance in the world. The car and I are in harmony. I can feel every movement of the car, and the car does exactly what I want it to do. But with each tomorrow comes one more day that I age. There's a youth movement now, and in an owner's eyes I'm really old.

Tomorrow something terrible may happen. There are so many possibilities in the world, and my mind tries to calculate them all. How will I deal if I find my cat dead? What will happen if there's another attack on America? With tomorrow comes the unknown. While a lot of positive may come, I am unable to see that. I am oblivious to any notion that good will come tomorrow. The anger that manifests itself in this thing called tomorrow is indescribable in words. The rage of not knowing is horrible.

"We'll talk about it later" and "We have to talk" create so much fear in me that I want to keel over and just disappear. If someone says one of those things, something must be askew, but what could it be? What have I done? Or what happened?! The anxiety in the unknown is unbearable. And what makes it bad is that 99.9% of everything that happens is unexpected, and 99.9% of things don't go according to schedule. Tomorrow has no timetable of events. It's just a human-appointed time frame of twenty-four set hours. But within those hours, lives change, nations can fall, and my life could go haywire in a heartbeat. But in the next twenty-four hours I have no clue what will happen. I try to think ahead and predict how it will be, but the monkey wrench can be thrown in at any time.

While it is true that if tomorrow didn't exist, I never would have met Linda; it is also true that the pain of her not in my life wouldn't haunt me. So the unexpected will happen on any given tomorrow, but on which one? Anticipation for me is a killer. The thinking of it swirls around like leaves of a windy autumn afternoon. There is no end. For every time I deal with a tomorrow, another tomorrow awaits. As much as I wish it would, time will not freeze. A week ago, for just a few moments while regaining my awareness after passing out after that Yellow Fever shot, it was the first time the "T" word didn't exist. For the first time I cared about the now.

While I feel pain of the past, it's fear of the tomorrow that fuels the pains of the past. Being out of it for so long and then slowly piecing together what happened made me forget about tomorrow. Sure, it was a dramatic experience and one I wish never to experience again, but it did give me a momentary lapse in the focus and power I give tomorrow.

So in the end, tomorrow will come, but when tomorrow becomes today, there's another tomorrow to deal with. So many unknowns except for the fact that tomorrow I will once again have to deal with the next tomorrow and what joys or horrible pains may come with it. Hopefully I will be in the know.

NO ONE ...

Just a note from Dad... Like many children with autism and Asperger's, Aaron has elicited self-stimulatory behavior. This first evidence of this was before he was six months old. He had a blanket that his grandmother had made him. It was yarn ties every few inches. Aaron continually twirled one of those strings. He did that until we finally put the blanket up when he was twelve. After that his "stim" (self-stimulatory behavior) became twirling the belt loops on his pants. He could strip a pair of pants in no time. Fortunately, he refused to wear a belt. Although he was embarrassed by this behavior, he couldn't stop. It was just one of the things that he knew people could not understand.

No one can fully understand me. I have found this out in day-to-day activities. Emily showed me that even with prolonged exposure no one could understand me. This is the "first" that got burned into my thinking. I suspected that before, but that experience reiterated that fact, but then at the same time I could not understand her.

No one around me, outside my house, knows why I do what I do, and sometimes they don't understand either. The twirling of the belt loops, avoidance of eye contact, and hesitantly shaking hands are some examples of the things that people don't understand. For me this is harder than the other person because I can hear the change in voice or body gesture when I do what isn't normal. I see people turn around and look at me, perplexed, and there's nothing I can do about it, so I fit in.

I want to tell people about my experiences this year, but I have no one to tell. I bowled a near-perfect game but had no friends to tell of my achievement. I gave Emily a text message, not expecting to hear a response, and my premonition was correct. I had two experiences this year that could have resulted in death, but only a few people would have noticed my departure.

T + J = CUTOFF

If you've read my prior writings, you know this is the first time I've used more than one word for a title. This is my math formula for the results of what has happened. This piece will take a look at the dynamics of my relations and the tragic results each has had.

First, you are probably wondering what the heck the T and J stand for. The T is for the mind trap and the J is for the jam that is the result of the trap.

I don't think I've defined a jam, so I'll try my best now. A jam is a hideous feeling that can occur rather frequently for me. It's like having a song stuck in one's head, but the song isn't good nor does it have a positive feel to it. Another analogy would be the difference between dial-up and DSL on an Internet connection. If you were to try and download a big file, it would take a lot less time with DSL, and if you tried the same download on dial-up, then literally the line would be filled to capacity trying to relay the desired download to the computer. This is what a jam is like.

I would do anything to avoid a jam. Heck, being in a six-hour traffic jam beats a mind jam on any day, except, of course, if I'm having both happen at the same time. When a jam starts, the mind doesn't slow down. The same search for answers and logic takes over and all others are immediately discounted. I get into a state of true self-thought where everyone else doesn't matter. My mind becomes the only concentration point. With this overthought, though, comes severe anxiety and stress. In this state, the floodgates are opened, and every fear and possible outcome of every possible scenario is played out. In other words, while in a jam, I'm quite simply looking for answers—questions to which I may never be able to know the answer.

Let's now start with the first major jam that was the Linda incident. Of course, this would help if you have read "Linda," but let me break it down in a nutshell. A lot happened to me in a few short months, and a jam was inevitable. This jam-up was about life and death. The dilemma was, does a person say what they feel, or do they refrain from saying it? If a person says what they feel, that person may feel better, but the ramifications are hard to calculate. However, if a person does not say what they are thinking or want to say, then if a person or the one who wants to speak dies, the thought is never known. The fight between these two trains of thought is overwhelming. To use an over-used quote, it was much like when a person asks the proverbial question about the chicken and the egg. For me, I could care less about the chicken or the egg (unless they are on my dinner plate), but this fight between two equal thoughts was crippling.

Say it, or don't say it? Do I tell Linda that I like her, or do I just keep talking pleasant small talk? Then I watched a movie that shook my world and sealed the deal for the "say it before you die" side. I had to tell Linda that I liked her and that I would want to know her in the least as friends forever. The results from this I am still puzzled by. I don't know why this was considered an almost offensive statement on my part, but that's how she took it.

After that came her trip down wacky religion lane. Another mind jam had started. I, for some reason, have a good sense in knowing when someone's doctrine is wrong, and I knew one hundred percent that Linda's journey toward charismatic-hood wouldn't be fruitful. So here was the jam. Do I tell her that her religious beliefs are a bit off center and risk rocking the boat, or do I sit back and do nothing? If I do nothing and something bad happened in her life, she may stop believing in God. Why is that? She started thinking that she had to be perfect to be worthy of God's blessings. While on paper this seems to be a good plan, in reality it isn't true, and if one believes that they could be setting themselves up for a disaster, because what if something bad happens? In my opinion, if something bad were to happen to them they would question a few things: 1. Was I good enough? 2. Since I was good enough and something bad happened, there must be no God. A tricky situation indeed.

Down deep I knew the answer, but I didn't want to do it. Maybe the situation would rectify itself. A month went by and no such luck. So now what do I do? Do I lay down what I think, or do I sit back and let it play out and see what happens? I chose to say what I thought and tell her where she was wrong. My figuring in this jam was that because she knew how much she meant to me by my saying that she was wrong, she would obviously consider what I had said. I debated this for weeks and then I said it. Tragically, with all my possible outcomes, I did not see the one that had happened. It's sort of like playing chess and you have the perfect move to obtain checkmate only to be blindsided by a discovery check from your opponent. This is what happened. I was blindsided and haven't heard from her since that February 2000 e-mail. From that point on, I was cut off. Now there are so many mines that create traps that in turn create this jam that fights for which is more logical. I often wonder what would have happened if no e-mail was sent. Of course, everyone has a "what if" situation in his or her own life, but for me the jam never leaves. Did my e-mail help at all? Am I a non-point in her life, or am I hated for being some sort of heretic? So many questions with so many possibilities.

The next jam leading to cutoff was with Emily. I think I may have liked Emily, or maybe I didn't. This alone was a jam. And with jams come extensive self-anger. How am I able to express myself through this medium of writing if I am not able to in spoken words? At times I truly don't know if I like or dislike something. So, I had that jam with Emily and it never left. She kept stepping on mines by constantly being late (a pet peeve of mine) and not saying what she meant and then following up on it. I am a big believer of "you do what you say." With that rule comes security in the sense that if someone is reliable and they say something, it will be done. With Emily this was never the case. This specific jam with Emily took over four years. Yes, you read that right, four years. In that time I was powerless to do anything. Maybe this is where I get my disdain for time. If time doesn't pass, no new thoughts will have to be processed, lessening the odds of jams.

Emily, though, was always good for a jam. Is it okay for her to be late because she's my girlfriend, or is that disrespectful? That was just one of many jams of logic that would happen in my relationship with her. So, in essence, her being late was a mine and when that happened it would start the jam of the question stated above. For me there is no defined answer. Many other occasions with her, she would say one thing and then do the other. This too creates a jam. One thing I don't get is when people ask, "Hey, what's up?" They have no intention of hearing the answer. So why ask the question? That too within itself is a jam. Emily was a lot like that. Why say something and then have no intention of backing up your statement? As mentioned in another piece, I talked to her on December 31, and she said she would call me back after she got done eating. I never heard back from her, so two weeks later I sent her a text message just asking why she lied about saying she would call. Four weeks after I sent that text message I got one back simply saying that she did not lie (I so wanted to respond with the line "Yeah, and Richard Nixon wasn't a crook."), and she just didn't want to give me the wrong impression. I don't know what impression that would be. Maybe she thought that by us just talking I would think we'd be back together and then the sun would be out and bunny rabbits would be rejoicing and the world would be a happy place. I had no impression, though, of anything like this. I responded to her lie of a lie by stating that a lie is when someone says they will do one thing and then do something else. I have yet to receive a response from her on that one. Maybe I never will. Perhaps I could have used a lesser word than liar, but it's true that a lie is saying one thing and doing another.

That situation happened a lot during our relationship. And I guess it even happens after our relationship. But in the end, why did I decide to break up with her each time? You may think it's because she never did what she said she was going to do and that maybe I deserved better. If you think this, you are horribly mistaken. I didn't break up with her or send the e-mail to Linda because of each situation, but rather because if I do something like that, maybe I can free myself from the jam. And it works ... for fifteen minutes. Then the new jam moves in and then the jam is, "If I'm with someone, I may be jammed or hurt, but being alone is rather lonely." That prior sentence is debated in the high court of Aaron's brain every day. Unfortunately, for this writer, the jury is currently hung. Neither side can prevail. And that is the jam.

The formula goes like this: A trap creates a jam that then can create a cutoff from people that are in my life. I often wonder if normal people have these same jams. If so, how severe are they? Are they so severe that they can only cry and shake and cannot speak because the pain is too great? Maybe for normal people the biggest jam is whether to watch the channel 4 news or the channel 5 news. I don't know the answer to that question. I do know most people would not be able to handle the severity of pain that comes with a jam session because they can last so long. And the kicker that really bugs me is that the same jams I experienced a decade ago still persist. I so wish I could upgrade my mind from a 16.6k modem to DSL. I wish I could clear out my proverbial recycle bin because my mind just keeps the same garbage forever. And having such pain can create irrational actions. (Okay, so maybe I act irrationally on some minor occasions.) If I weren't in a jam on that fateful Christmas when I broke up with Emily, would the results still be the same? Bam! Another jam. It never ends. My life is like a web with everything so intertwined that the traps and jams are so close, it doesn't take much, and when it gets so severe, my life changes drastically.

I think the normal mind in the least can come to some conclusion of which side to take on any given mind debate. Mine can't, and it's cost me the friendship of two wonderful people who now probably hate me so much. That hurts so badly because if only they knew. If only they knew the pain that went into my decision-making. If only they knew how much they truly meant to me. They couldn't, though, because I was lost in my mind, and for that I have been cut off from those whom I knew and remained jammed, in fact, of, "Was it worth it?" I may never know.

CRASH

Being the racecar driver I am, you'd assume that a crash would be something that I fear the most, and you are right. But the crash I'm talking about in this title is not of the metal-to-wall variety. This crash is far more devastating. It's the crash of my mind after a day of enjoyment.

It's the start of spring now, and the racing season is starting. I currently don't have a ride in anything, so I'm still flagging for the local kart club. The first practice was last Sunday. I waited all winter for this day, for on this day I was back in my element. I was in control of all on-track aspects on that day, and I was quite talkative. On these days at the track I am free. Memories are gone, fears are gone, and I can live and focus. Maybe, it's because all my mind's resources have to be on the task at hand. It's just like driving a racecar. When driving a racecar, my mind has to be completely focused on driving. But in both instances, my mind is so focused that I'm in a trance-like state. I can be completely focused and be thinking about the most oddball thing because all my actions become subconscious.

This is the best feeling in the world. On the weekends, I am free. My mind is so focused, nothing else matters. For me nothing else does matter because racing is everything. I enjoy the moment that I drive or flag like no one else enjoys anything else. I am free of all the chains and avalanches and traps and I am alive. Maybe it's for this reason that my memories of my time in Vegas hurt so badly because every day I knew I was going to be in my element.

Outside of my element, I am vulnerable to society. In my element, the only thing that matters is the task at hand. Whether it be to shave a tenth of a second off my time or to preside over a race and enforce the rules, I am alive. In my element, Emily, Linda, fears, anxieties, anger, memories, and bitterness are gone. Then the sun sets and the inevitable crash takes place.

There's nothing harder than the final checkered flag of a race day for me. This held true three days ago for the first practice session. As I flagged the last kart and said my goodbyes, I walked to my car, and the stressors mentioned above raced into my mind like a dam bursting. This happens every time, and I hate it. Once the crash happens, the mental anguish is multiplied by a factor of ten. I've never known why, though. Why is it that something so wonderful quickly flip-flops faster than John Kerry on any given political issue? Shouldn't my time at the track invigorate me for the upcoming week, for there's always next week, isn't there? Logic would say this would be, but it isn't so.

As the final kart crosses the line, it's another symbol that tomorrow is almost here. Another day gone by that I don't have a ride. As much as I like flagging, I don't want to be on that side for my entire life. I want to be the one getting the checkered and not giving the checkered. So, maybe, as every weekend goes by and I have my crash, it's due to the feeling that my clock is ticking. But if this is so, why does all the other stuff float in uninvited? If this was the case one hundred percent, then just my fear of tomorrow would bother me, but it isn't the case.

As I start my car and drive away from the track, the crash is normally in full swing. I relive my life every half second. It's of such pain I can't breathe or reflect upon the great day I just had. Maybe I crash because I get so mentally exhausted during the day that my defenses against pondering about any given subject are weakened, thus allowing everything to rush on in and get thought about.

The crash, though, is sudden. If it was the stock market, it would be illustrated with a day's trading session, and everything is going good, and then the line they use to show where the market is would just drop off straight down. And I wish my crash every week was of the premeditated kind, sort of like a self-fulfilling prophecy, because then I would be able to control it. But that's not the case. It's horrible to have what makes me most happy to be one of the things I fear the most. I can't wait for this weekend's practice sessions, but I know that there may be another crash come Sunday night. If I had a ride, I don't know if I would have a crash at the end of each weekend. That's something I won't know until I get the chance (hopefully) to find out. I know I had the ultimate crash when I came home from Vegas.

After my fall while working at the racing school, I knew I'd never get the chance to do that again. To make matters worse for me, I had an allergic reaction to the pain medicine, and that delayed my departure by two more days. I wanted nothing more than to get out of Vegas. So with severe cervical strain and all, I went to bed at 5:00 p.m. to get up at midnight to leave the town that never sleeps. The road to leave town that I needed just happens to pass by the Las Vegas Motor Speedway complex. The ultimate crash happened just as I passed the exit, because just like that time warp I mentioned earlier, it hit me with no warning. Instantly, my mom, Emily, and the feeling of hopelessness hit me with such force that I had trouble keeping my car on the road. Going past that exit was the hardest thing I have ever done. If you read my previous writings, you know I counted down the times I was going into my hotel room in Lithuania. This was a thousand times worse than the hotel room.

Going past that exit was as symbolic as it was painful. Driving past that exit 30 minutes past midnight was the true start of my current modern era. For me, my life was about to go to shambles, but just half a mile to the south was the happiest place I have ever known. But just like time, I had to keep going. As much as I wanted to take the exit to drive by the complex at the Derek Daly School, I knew that if I did I would be so overwhelmed by emotion that I wouldn't be able to drive the long drive I needed to drive. So I held my breath and made it past that exit. Then, just as I regained my breath, I lost it. As much as I described the pain about leaving Minneapolis in a prior writing, this was so much worse. My interaction between others does cause pain, but losing my connection with the cars I was driving was so much worse. I know that may sound weird, but driving a car is the most wonderful feeling I can feel. If given a chance to choose whether to relive my eleven hours with Linda in Minneapolis or any given time in a racecar, I would choose the racecar in half a heartbeat.

I was probably severely depressed after Vegas. Or, in my terms, I was in the crash to end all crashes and the proverbial cars just kept piling on. My time out there was somewhat of an escape, but I still felt the emotions in a way that didn't overwhelm me. I didn't care that Emily lied to me about seeing me, even though anytime I talked to her I asked her why. But it didn't bother me to an extent that I got depressed. Then, as I passed the LVMS exit, it all hit me. I did now care about how Emily treated me. I did as the lights of Vegas faded away in my rearview mirror. My time of extreme happiness was over. The first crash had happened. That was in October of 2003, and every kart race since then I've experienced a similar feeling like the "big one" I felt in Vegas. Maybe it's the fact that everything went down the tubes after I got back. I've only been in a big racecar once since then, and I know I'm better than at least ninety-five percent of those racing nationally. It's such a hole that it's no wonder I crash every race weekend. I shouldn't be the best flagman in the world; I should be the best driver in the world. But if that's the case, why does Emily sneak into the crash? Maybe in a crash it's like a feeding frenzy and every thought is invited.

With tomorrow comes the chance that I may finally get that call and be off somewhere to drive again. But also with tomorrow comes another day I age. And also with tomorrow it's another day toward happiness that will end in what could be a repeat of all the other kart weekends and be very depressing because I will have to drive home after giving that final checkered, and once again I will be forced to be brought back to my undesirable reality. For when I flag or race, that is living; outside of that, what's worth a tomorrow being a tomorrow? Racing is everything, but then why does everything else get in the way?

SCHOOL

Just a note from Dad … My oldest son had severe Attention Deficit Disorder with Hyperactivity. Every morning was a disaster. Every teacher's conference was a disaster. Every evening, as he tormented his sister, was a disaster. However, at least he went to school.
Getting Aaron to school, now that was an adventure.

There's nothing I hated more than going to school. The anxieties and stressors were always too much for me to handle, but it wasn't always that way.

I remember school wasn't that big of a deal in preschool and kindergarten. I differed from other kids in the sense that I would much rather talk to the teacher about something than talk to my peer group. I always knew I would learn more from the teacher than hearing about what type of shoes an individual kid wanted. Don't get me wrong, though; I didn't despise my age group, I just wanted to get more from a conversation. I remember in kindergarten the teacher telling me I would lose my recess if I didn't go play with the other kids. I had no idea why she did that, because we were discussing what math would be like in further grades and I was learning quite a bit, but then she essentially told me it was wrong to talk to her. This confused me greatly and was the start of my distaste for school.

First grade: The first day of the first grade for me didn't last long.

Maybe it was the fact that this grade had a number, or the fact that the teacher was laying down the rules of grades, but whatever the case, around 11:00 a.m. I threw up like I had never thrown up before. Thankfully, I got home in time to see the second half of "The Price Is Right." Maybe something else that bothered me and that I was unprepared for was the fact that school was now all day long. Prior to the first grade, school was just half a day. With that change came a change in the daily routine. I remember vividly that my apprehension for the first day of school wasn't the fact that I was going to ride a bus or actually have grades, but the fact that the timetable had changed. I know it sounds silly, but that was the initial fear.

For the first quarter of the year, I didn't mind school, and I stood out as a model student. However, as time went on, school started to wear on me. One thing that really got to me was syllables. The concept of syllables isn't too hard to grasp. All you've got to do is say a word and how many times you make a different sound is the amount of syllables in that word. Yes, it does sound easy, but this room of first-graders couldn't grasp the concept. I remember this one kid who got the answer wrong to how many syllables the word "word" has. He said three. Three! I had to endure this nonsense day after day. It was killing me. First off, I couldn't understand the incompetence because it's a simple thing to learn (or so I thought).

By no means was I a straight-A student. I didn't care about the grades. I may be somewhat of a perfectionist, but I'd rather play a game at home than study for a test. And in all my years of school, I think I studied less than an hour a month. With my memory all I have to do is hear or read it once and I'll retain it.

I was always ahead of the class in terms of knowledge. I don't want to sound overbearing, but while the teacher was trying in vain to teach these kids syllables, I was looking ahead in the various educational textbooks. Then about halfway through the first grade I asked my dad what multiplication was. He vaguely explained it to me, but I caught on, and by the next day I was working on multiplying numbers greater than four.

I felt on top of the world the hour before lunch when I figured out what 7x7 was, and I thought the teachers at lunch would be impressed. During lunch I told one of the other teachers that I figured out how to multiply numbers and that I knew what the total of 7x7 was. Was she impressed that a student knew how to multiply before he even was doing two-digit subtraction? A big no was the answer, and she told me that I wasn't supposed to know that and she revoked my recess for that day. I was crushed. I had the same punishment that the dumb kids and the misbehaving kids had, but what had I done? This planted the seed of my hatred of school.

During the latter quarter of the first grade, the city had their annual science spectacular at the Wayne Township Middle School. The teacher picked me to represent her class in the subject of general knowledge, and then she appointed me as team captain (the team was comprised of four). This would be the first official competition that I would ever compete in.

The format was two rounds. The first round each student would answer a question without help from the other students on his or her team. The second round the team captain would be able to overrule a teammate's decision. In the first round, I accounted for three of the five points with twelve being the maximum. We were batting below .500, and we were down by six points. There was about a twenty-minute intermission between rounds, and that's when I became aware of the captain's overruling option. I was elated because I had known the answer to all but one of the round-one questions.

At the start of round two we were down by six points from the leader, and we were sitting last. The second round would be sixteen questions per team. We needed a miracle to have any chance at winning. They had shown us the prize (a gold-looking medal with the competition's logo on it), and I wasn't going to settle for anything else. Thank goodness for the overrule option because if it weren't for that we wouldn't have had a chance. My team got a bit better on getting things right in the second round, but that option was our only hope. The lead teams started to falter a little bit, and with two questions to go my team was sitting in third, just two points out of the lead. The two teams tied for the lead missed the next-to-last question, and my teammate got her question right. It was time for the final question. To add drama, the emcee reversed order and went from fourth to first in asking the questions. The fourth-place team's question was irrelevant because they were four points behind, but my team's question was most certainly relevant. However, we still needed a miracle to take a share of the win, and this time the question was mine so there would be no overrule. It was all up to me, and I nailed the question, and the miracle happened as the two teams that were tied for the lead had missed their questions, which meant that the contest ended in a three-way tie. That was probably my favorite memory of school, even though it wasn't at the school I attended; it was the competition that I loved.

Second grade: You might have noticed that in my first-grade summary there wasn't much talk of other students or at least in a positive light. That's because, just like in kindergarten, I would much rather talk to the teacher than listen to the immature talk of the other students. I know that sounds snobbish, but that's the way I was.

I probably had my best teacher in second grade. Mrs. Jander quickly saw my intelligence and she gave me challenges. When other students would be adding numbers like 10+15 on the chalkboard, I was given problems of 457,292+876,890. In all my years of school, I was never bullied or called a teacher's pet. I don't know why that was because I had all the makings of one, but the other students for the most part left me alone.

One thing I loved about the second grade was the introduction to geography. One of the goals that were on the year's schedule sheet was that each student would know their states and capitols. I liked this because I had already memorized them from the flash cards my parents had gotten me. Then we played the states and capitols game. The game was sort of like Jeopardy in the sense that the winner continued playing and the loser sat back down. In the process of the game, because the winner traveled from desk to desk, people would be sitting at other people's desks. The first time the game was played and it was my turn to take on the winner, I knew it was going to be fun.

The way the game was played was the teacher would flip a flash card and it would have either a picture of a state or a picture of a state with a star on it. First one to yell out the answer would be the winner. If the person was wrong, the other person automatically was the winner of that bout. As it came to my turn, I immediately shouted the answer before the other person probably had the chance to visually read what the state was. It stayed that way for three trips around the room. There were about twenty-five kids in the class, so that meant that I had approximately seventy-five straight wins. I loved it because this was a game and I love games. In addition, it gave me a medium to talk because I never once had my name on the board for talking. But tragically I was cut down in my prime. I was "retired" as champion. The game was played weekly but without me. The teacher probably knew my dismay, and I became the one to flash the cards.

Later in the year, it was multiplication flash card time and history repeated itself. I went on another Ken Jennings streak, and again I was "retired" as champion because nobody could keep up with my reflexes on coming up with the answer. Again, as before, I became the giver of the cards. But I didn't want to be the emcee; I wanted to be playing the game. This sealed the deal on my dislike of school.

Third grade: We had moved during the second-grade year, but I finished my year at the original school, but now in third grade I was headed to another school. The anxiety was high again because there were going to be many new things, most of which were new students.

I forgot to mention that the second grade was the start of my poor attendance. The noise level of students talking endlessly drove me up a wall. There was never silence. There was always someone yelling, or even sometimes someone hitting another. It was foreign to me because I had no concept of why anyone would want to talk when they could get their work done in the here and now. The noise was as if an anchor was tied to my head, and it wouldn't let me get my head up and do anything. If I thought the second grade was bad, the third was worse.

For some odd reason I was able to make what could be called friendships in the third grade. They weren't much of anything, but I was a bit more communicative than in grades past.

The new game that this teacher had was the "T" drills. It was a game in which you would draw a T and put a number on the top left-hand side of the T, and then the teacher would read off six numbers to put on the lower left-hand side. The winner was the one who completed it first and had all the answers correct. You've probably heard the term that history repeats itself, and it did here again, as I was once again retired from the game for being too good. I can't tell you how irritating this was. The games played were the only reason school was bearable for me, and each time it was cruelly taken away from me. Socializing wasn't my strong suit, nor was participating in class discussions, but when it came to the game, I was a completely different person. Each time the game was taken away from me. I couldn't understand it. Why punish something that's good? I guess one could make the argument that retiring me gave other kids a chance to be the winner, but at the same time it took away the only thing I really had. Sure, I talked to other kids at lunch and recess, but I still could care less about what happened on last night's television shows or what songs were hip.

The kicker for my disdain of school happened late in the year. It was during the last day of the standardized testing week, and three of the people around me were arguing about who was going to use what pencil. The pencil was at first being handed around, and then it was being thrown around. It landed on my desk. I placed it on the person to my right's desk, and in the end the teacher saw that there were now three flying pencils being thrown about. The teacher immediately asked what was going on, and she then had three of the kids put their name on the board with a check mark (which meant a fifteen-minute loss of recess instead of five). Then one of the students asked why my name wasn't on the board, and without questioning him she told me to put my name on the board. The result was devastation. I had never had to do that, and now I did because my name had been mentioned. Where's the justice in that? Writing this now, I'm still agitated at that event. This event occurred after that day's recess, so the penalty would be served the next day.

I was not going to serve a sentence I didn't deserve, so I was conveniently sick the next day, and the day after that, and then the day after that. I did everything I could not to go back, but I was forced into going, but thankfully the board had been wiped down and the incident forgotten by most.

Fourth grade: I'd have to say that this year was the smoothest year I ever had. It was probably due to the teacher I had and that she noticed and rewarded smart students. Every day was sort of like a game, and she had the patience to hear the daily weather report from me in the morning. Because of her acknowledging me in that way, it sort of made a connection that made the school experience not as isolating as years past. Fourth grade probably has my highest attendance percentage of any grade. Even though I was once again banned from any math or state games, the teacher let me give the games, but she also let me grade some of the papers. Maybe that's because she knew I was honest and smart enough to grade the papers, or maybe it was to lighten her workload. Whatever the case, that added chore offset the anger of being banned from the game because at the same time it created a new game.

Fifth grade, Indianapolis: This was a miserable experience because the teacher was formally the school counselor, and now she was being moved to her first classroom. Every day sounded like a sporting event in the terms of the decibel level. Thankfully for me, we rotated classrooms for two other classes, so it wasn't like that all day. The math teacher I had told me I didn't have to do the normal curriculum, and I got to do some hard math and a bunch of logic problems. Regardless of how much I did, I would get an automatic A. I don't remember how I got such an accord, but it gave me an hour a day to just relax and work on some impossible brainteasers.

About midway through the school year, we moved to St. Louis. This was bad for many reasons. First off was the simple fact of change and newness. But at the same time the day I found out I was moving would be the same day I got the lead role in the fifth-grade school play/musical. My time in the spotlight would never happen, and we made the move.

Fifth grade, St. Louis: The change between schools took a great toll on me. Not only was I in a new house, but the students' attitudes and personalities in Saint Louis were very different from Indianapolis. In addition, this school was the type of school that if you weren't on the sports team, the students were very condescending to you. I never could figure out how being on a sports team made someone somewhat of an aristocrat.

Once again we played the states and capitols game, and once again I went around the room with ease, but this time I realized that if I wanted to play again, I would have to lose. I didn't want to give someone the satisfaction of beating me, so I let the kid with Down's syndrome to win. The teacher (Mrs. Nafzger is the teacher who wrote the letter at the beginning of the book) thanked me later for giving him the chance to win, but my driving force was that I didn't want to become retired.

The teacher I had for this half of my fifth grade wasn't bad at all, but the class seemed very much snobbish toward me. I don't know if they really were, because I have a hard time interpreting attitudes, but it appeared as if they were. Therefore I took offense to most everything. My attendance percentage was on its way to where it would stay, and that's very low.

Sixth grade: In the sixth grade, I was in the same class of people. They hadn't grown up, and they still were as obnoxious and annoying as ever. If anything, the summer had made them more annoying. Added on top of that I had a teacher that would talk for hours at a time. Now I don't mind a talking teacher, but when you are giving a lecture on the basics of fishing when the subject is math, something is obviously askew. And the lectures went on and on and on with no logic to any of them. Halfway through the year I'd had enough of school in general, and I saw to it by any means necessary that I was not going back. I got my wish, and we went to home schooling.

Sixth/seventh/eighth grade-home: Home schooling was wonderful. There were no annoying idiots in the class (except for my cat, who was all too eager to dive into my books ... literally), and for once I got to work at my own pace. The only downside was that my mom was the teacher. Don't get me wrong, I love my mom, but she isn't the person I would most want to do what she says to do. I still did the work but not at the pace she wanted me to. Besides, I knew I could learn more by watching CNN than reading any given book.

Even with my stellar memory, I can't remember much about this time period. I did actually get somewhat lonely, and over time, with the encouragement of someone I knew from church, I decided to give the ole school system another shot.

Seventh grade: For starters, you should know that age-wise I should have been in the eighth grade, but that class was a terror, and I knew some people in the seventh so I decided to go the seventh-grade route. The teacher was somewhat new, and the class a lot of times was a bit on the out-of-control side. But thankfully for me there was so much work to be done that I could concentrate on that and not on the loudness of the classroom.

I entered the grade during December, and on my first day I met the teacher who would make me hate school forever. She was currently the sixth-grade teacher and the science teacher. I was exempt from taking the science test on the first day, but as she was giving the test, she did things that weren't very teacher-like. As the other students were taking the test, she kept verbally complaining about the squirrels that were barking at her from outside the window. Also, she had a coffee cup that would play loud holiday music every time she would pick it up. I knew she was going to be trouble, but thankfully it was just the science period.

During this time, I just talked to my one friend from church. Sure, I talked to others, but for the most part I kept to myself. It was a new school and new people, but the conversations were still irrelevant in my eyes. Again, who cares about what movie star is doing what and who cares about the latest trends in shoes. My focus was on the NYSE going above 8,000, but none of my other classmates shared my interest in current affairs.

I survived the school year and was ready for the eighth grade, but on the last day of school we all found out that the science teacher was moving up to the eighth grade. The anxiety over the summer was horrifying.

Eighth grade: The official title was the eighth grade, but for me it might have well been the grade from hell. Not only was the terrifying annoying teacher there, but my diminished social abilities were coming to the forefront.

Also in the mix was the pastor of the church (this was a Lutheran school). During this year of school was the year that we would get confirmed. The pastor pointed out that everyone must attend "a" church service and take notes. Now notice that he didn't specifically mention his church. I had trouble making his Sunday services because they conflicted with my racing schedule. Luckily for me, another church in the area had Monday-night services. For many weeks in a row I was unable to go on Sunday because a number of races had been rained out early in the season, and we were racing every weekend to make them up.

This pastor was an egomaniac. He knew that I had missed three straight weeks, and his contempt for me going to another church was obvious. On this particular Monday he was going to make an example of me, or at least try.

As normal on Mondays, he took a show of hands of those who did not attend Sunday services at his church. He was already looking in my direction before I even had a chance to hear him finish the question. As I raised my hand with the half-dozen other students, he asked me as he did every week, "And Mr. Likens, where might you have been, sleeping perhaps?" I responded with the fact that we had a race the prior weekend and that I was the flagman and could not deviate from my duties. He replied, "So Mr. Likens, do you think that by missing church you will have a favorable look in God's eyes?" Then he proceeded with the dumbest thing I have ever heard in my life by saying, "Thou shalt not go to the racetrack on Sundays. Thou must attend my church on Sundays."

This was a high-stress situation, and maybe it's the most stressful thing I have ever experienced in a classroom, or for that matter anywhere, but I did muster the response, "But, Pastor, did you not say one could attend a church other than yours if they are unable to on Sunday?"

His blood boiled at that comeback as again he asked, "Aaron, do you pray?"

I said, "Of course I do, and especially before every race"

"But Aaron, if you do not attend my church, God will not hear your prayer since I have instructed you to attend my church on Sunday," he responded in anger. Looking back, if I was as quick to the gun as I am now on calling people out when they are wrong; it would've been a great theological duel (and I probably would've been expelled), but in the end I became silent, and for the rest of the day I had no energy. It was too much of an overstimulating experience.

Ironically, the next week, as the pastor predicted, my prayers went unheeded, and I had the worst crash of my life. In the crash I was temporarily stunned, and when I came to it was pain of which I have never felt. In the end, the injuries weren't life threatening, but the pain was immobilizing. I was unable to walk for a week and a half. Two weeks later when I went back to school there was a bit of resentment I felt from the teacher and the other students for missing so much school. At least I felt it was anger and resentment. Of course, it wasn't right away; the first reaction was asking me how I was, but then it seemed to quickly turn to bitterness. My assumption was that the other students were mad that I got to stay home for two weeks. Whatever the case, it was to overpowering for me, and with the conflict with the insane pastor and the fact that the teacher was insane herself, I simply said to my parents that it was time to go back to home schooling. Thankfully, they agreed.

Home schooling: This go-round of home schooling was different. Mary, who would be my future stepmother, worked with my dad in the Lutheran video department. She found a retired teacher who was willing to be my tutor. She was great. We talked more than anything. She came over just twice a week for two hours each, and on one day I did an entire year's worth of spelling. The next day she came I completed half a year of social studies. I was moving so fast that we got to material that she didn't know, so she said she didn't want to tutor me anymore because she couldn't be paid to teach things she didn't know.

About this time, I had been seeing a counselor, and he had been giving me many tests. At the time I was fifteen, and when the tests were complete I had tested as a sophomore in college. Therefore, he said it would be criminal to send me to high school. I am so thankful he said that, because not only would high school of taken up four years, but socially and mentally I would have been a wreck. His suggestion was that when I turned sixteen to just quit the home schooling and get my GED. We did that, and when I got my test results back, I'd had the third-highest score ever recorded in the state.

If I had been motivated to be anything besides a racecar driver, I could already be in a grad school by now. I did do one semester of college, and I had better results than in my prior experiences, but there was no motivation. In addition, I have a bleak look on time matters, and four years of college sends shivers up my spine. I know, I know, if I had attended college right after I got my GED I'd be done now, but my hatred of school in general persists.

In the end, I don't know what the most stressful thing about school was. It could've been a combination of things. For one thing there were many times that the teachers said one thing and did another. Also, I could not stand for it when teachers would teach something that in reality was wrong. And then, of course, there's this matter of time. For me, there's nothing worse than the passage of time, and if you add upon that stress with the anxiety of the other students and the noise level it makes for one bad experience.

What pains me the most is realizing how smart I am and knowing what positive things I could do in the world, but this hatred of school will block any major thing that I might want to accomplish outside of racing. My hatred of school runs down to the core matter of college itself. It could be so much faster, but in my eyes it's all about the colleges making money and letting professors teach whatever beliefs they have and not teaching truth. This thought I hold about the education system is clear-cut; there is no exception. I hate that about myself, but maybe with all the bad experiences and anxieties you too would hold school in a very negative light.

SCREAM

In so many instances in my life the title of this piece could be used to describe what I want to do. However, since I am not one to raise my voice, the scream is what happens inside my mind. It's not a pleasant feeling at all, so in this piece I will cover the various things that make me scream.

Social settings: To most people I am not what I seem in a public setting. I may appear to be disinterested, self-absorbed, and/or just plain stupid. In many situations, I am only able to muster up one-word answers. This pains me so, because I know what I want to say, but I am unable to verbalize what I am thinking. On the outside I appear to be emotionless, like in a coma, but on the inside I am very conscious of what is going on and the scream that is deafening and consumes my thoughts. This creates internal anger because I know what I want to say, but I am unable to convey it.

So the question is why am I unable to say anything besides a yes or no. On paper it seems rather easy; I know what I want to say, so why not just say it? If it were that easy, I wouldn't be writing this. The pain that is felt inside me is so draining.

This is different for me when I'm one-on-one with someone, but throw in one extra element and I shut down. My answers become short, and I do not start any new conversation threads. I am a completely different person, and if you're talking to me and someone else joins in you will see my change. On the outside I may look calm or a tad bit on the uneasy side, but inside my mind there's a storm of an F-5 category. But why is that? I mean, if I'm talking to someone and one other person joins in, what's the difference? To most people there probably isn't a difference, but for me it's doubling how much I have to think. You see, in everything I do or say I calculate the various possibilities and the outcomes. If a conversation goes from one to two, that doubles the outcomes of what I say and throws my mind track off its rails. When I look at the two moments in my life where time stood still, they both were when it was one-on-one. One of course was Linda, and the other was with my friend's sister Ashley. In both situations the conversation flow was fluent. I had no hesitations, and my calculating mind was turned off. I yearn very deeply to experience that feeling of freedom again.

Freedom is a powerful word. Countries have gone to war and civilians have toppled governments for freedom. I live in a free country, but through my mind I am not free. It's like being a dog chained to a tree. Sure, with a ten-foot chain the dog is able to travel, but there is no way to go ten feet and one inch. That's how it is with me most of the time. The exceptions are when I race and the two times I've felt truly comfortable in a social setting. I can experience the ground around the tree I'm chained to, but I do not know what it's like to live without that chain. The chain in this case is my own mind.

So I ask the question: Was it the people in those two instances or was it myself who temporarily set me free? I know for the others it was probably business as usual, a regular conversation with someone, but for me it was a time when my rigid privacy and lack of using non-fact opinions were nullified. My conclusion on this is that it probably was a combination of things that allowed the chains to be unlocked. Now I'm sure everyone has his or her personal chains. However, while the average person's chains may allow them to go fifty feet, mine are a fraction of that. So imagine if for your entire life you were unable to feel connected to anyone, but for a brief moment, for just a very brief moment, you experienced that. How do you think you would feel? It would be like tasting ice cream for the first time at the age of forty. Then, as you consume the ice cream, it is gone, and there are no refills. That's how it is for me. I know what it feels like, but it can't be duplicated.

The concept of feeling a connection with someone is enough to make me want to scream inside. I think others feel that more frequently and are able to make connections more readily than I can. In addition, what really hurts is what's a common feeling for others can be a life-changing moment for me. I'm pretty sure that Linda doesn't know what impact she had on me, and I'm pretty sure Ashley also has no idea of the impact that she had on me. So here's the jam; was it them that I miss, or is it simply that for that brief moment in time I felt as if I wasn't alone?

Most of the time I do feel alone. My mind is so wrapped up in thinking about any given topic that it's hard for someone to get through the static. I'm not so much alone in a family setting, but that isn't the type of loneliness I am talking about, because a family will listen most of the time (unless it's a bad family). Take for instance my time with Emily. She would listen to me, and I would listen to her (or at least appear to listen; who wants to hear about what new tricks her dog learned one hundred times over?), but it was like eating a meal and not feeling full. The final thing that made me break up with Emily was my talk with Ashley. (You'll read more about her later.)

I don't think I've written about that yet, probably because it is still quite painful. Just like Minnesota, it was a perfect scenario while in Indianapolis. I had been talking to Matt about my disdain for Emily, and Ashley had overheard it. Matt and I proceeded talking about various Monopoly strategies and other non-serious topics. As he went to bed, Ashley started talking to me about Emily. This was a shock to me because I didn't know she had heard the conversation, and furthermore I wondered why she would care. At first my privacy guards went up and I asked her a question about Germany to change the subject. She was quick with the response, and I thought that she would forget the topic of Emily. I was wrong, because right after a lengthy answer she asked me again about her. If it were chess, I was checkmated. I had run out of topics to change to, and if I got up and left that would just be rude, and I was just unable to say that I didn't want to talk about the subject. In all truthfulness I would talk about Emily to anyone who was willing to listen, but normally I was the one bringing it up and not someone else.

I told my story, and Ashley quite frankly said I should get rid of her like yesterday's garbage (not quite an exact quote, but it was somewhat along those lines). It was about 9:30 p.m. then, and for only the second time in my life the conversation flow was fluent. It flowed like a river. She talked about Germany and her not knowing if she would want to pursue art or German, and she listened to my worries about world politics, then she talked about what 9/11 was like in Germany. It was one of those two-sided conversations and only the second time in my life that I really cared about what the other person was saying. Then it was over.

Yes, then it was over. Moreover, for me it's been over for fifteen months. I can recall the conversation and feel how I felt, but that only leads to an internal scream, because I don't know if something like that will happen again. Both instances were like a tornado. For a tornado to occur there needs to be so many elements to interact to form one. Therefore, I'm the same way, always looking for the right elements, but all I hear is the scream. And since a moment like those two has only happened twice in my lifetime, I am worried that something like that won't happen again, and with that fear comes the ultimate scream, but on the outside you would never know it.

Decision making/starting: I was going to write a piece entitled "Start," but ironically I had trouble starting it. Sad, but true. Anyway, these two concepts are two of the toughest things known to Aaron. Here's an example … I love playing video games, or for that matter games in general, but video games suffice when there is no one else to play with. However, there can be a problem before I even play a video game and that's deciding which one to play. Call it a jam, call it a scream, call it what you will, because in the end it's just downright stupid. What's so stupid, you ask? It's the lockup I feel when deciding which game to play. How bad is this lockup? I hate to admit this, but one time I was staring at my pile of games for two hours with no resolution. In that time span I could have played most of my games for five minutes, but I wanted to play the right game at the right time. Yes, just to repeat it because you probably still can't fathom the concept this, but it's true that I sat motionless, staring at a pile of games for two hours. Think about how many constructive things a person can do in a two-hour time span. Albeit I wasn't mad in that time span; in fact, it was almost a state of meditation, but looking back it's so stupid.

It's not that hard (in theory) to play a video game. All you have to do is take a case, open it, put the disc in the machine, flick the power button, and just like that you are playing the game. However, was it the right game? Did you really want to play that game at that time? Think about the ramifications of not playing the other games! Those are thoughts and questions I'm sure 99.9% of the human population wouldn't think or ask. Sadly, I do. It doesn't affect me when I'm in my state of limbo trying to decide, but afterwards I scream so loud in my mind and I feel so helpless. We aren't talking about making a decision that could induce a nuclear holocaust; we are talking about just playing one simple game. The fear for me is that if I have such a hard time making a decision about starting a game, how hard will it be for me to make other more important decisions?

Making a decision has never been my strong suit. Currently, I am the assistant race director and practice day director for the St. Louis Karting Association. On practice days I call all the shots. The club is growing rapidly, and on practice days we split the on-track time among different classes of karts. Last week we had twenty-one rookie/junior karts (rookies are eight- to eleven-year-olds and juniors are twelve to fifteen) lined up on the grid. There's sort of an unspoken rule that on practice days for safety's sake there's an on-track maximum of twenty. Now we had twenty-one. Some of the parents came up to ask me what the plan was. As I mentioned in a previous sentence, it was an unspoken rule of twenty. It wasn't set in stone. So now I was operating in the most God-awful territory of all... the gray area.

Racing is all about black and white, or at least who can get there first. Now I had a dilemma on my hands. There are twenty-one karts with an unspoken rule of twenty. All twenty-one have their motors going, and they are all ready to hit the track. The question is, do I split them up, or do I let them all run at once? I was completely frozen considering the pros and cons of each. Then, while considering the options, I had the saddest scream my mind has ever had. It's one thing to look back on something and think, Boy, was that stupid, but it's a completely different thing to realize at the moment it's happening to realize just how stupid you really are. I'm supposed to be the director. If I wanted it, the rule could be a maximum of ten, fifteen, or nineteen. In my position I should be able to fire an answer to the parents inquiries on what the plan is. It took me one long, agonizing minute to finally make my mind up, and I sent all twenty-one karts on track. The next time that group was up I split them, but while operating in the gray area I froze. If the rule were set in stone, I would've had no trouble making the call. That's how life is though, a bunch of gray areas.

Starting anything is a gray area. Whether it is a conversation, or deciding which game to play, it's still all a gray area. On Sundays at the track all the rules are set in stone, or rather a rulebook. I operate flawlessly within those rules because I know every option that's at my disposal for penalties and what's legal and what's not. Life doesn't have a rulebook though. Life is much like Saturdays at the track where a split decision needs to be made. If you take one minute to make a decision, life can pass you by. There's probably been at least a hundred times that I could've said something or done something that would've made my life a little bit better. But while in the gray zone what should be a split-second decision can take a minute or sometimes two hours.

What happens a lot to me in a social setting of more than two people is a time lapse. It's much like watching a news interview via satellite, but instead of a one-second delay it's more like a couple hours for me. Take for instance what happens to me quite frequently at bowling. There will be a conversation, and I will hear it and start thinking about how to respond, but in the decision-making process all my possible responses are drowned out by the my mind's inability to have an instantaneous response due to the fact that it's trying to think of the outcome. So later I'll come up with the perfect response only to find out that I'm driving home from the bowling alley.

So in essence the "scream" is the self-realization of my shortcomings. I often wonder if my keen sense of self-awareness is a good or bad thing. One thing that causes a huge scream is this self-awareness.

Self-awareness/Kenya: While writing this piece, I should mention that I'm writing this while in Kenya. Three days ago we were in Kibera, a suburb of Nairobi. Now take everything you know about a suburb and throw it out the window. The suburbia life of America is nothing like this suburb. This suburb is the slum of the metropolis. The stench is one I will never forget. Trash is piled up on the ground in no particular fashion. While it is the slums, it seemed to be its own economy. For all of the mud huts and houses that would be honored to be called a shack, there were many vendors. I saw two sellers operating out of the back of a former trailer of a semi-truck. So while it may be the slums, the mood wasn't of one of dire straits. There was music playing by those selling audio equipment, and when passing by one pub it sounded like a karaoke contest was going on. It was almost surreal. Here is a place where most houses, if you would call them houses, are just one room with no electricity, and people are doing karaoke. There were kids in the streets obviously starving, but yet there were people smiling. Even the kids who appeared to be three pounds away from starving to death politely asked, "How are you?" as we passed them. There was so much contrast there. Kibera is a place that has no equal to it in the United States, but in the air was a sense of happiness.

I could not figure this out. To tell you the truth, I was scared senseless and quite confused. Well, the truly scary thing was the fact that I saw at least a dozen kids under the age of eight wielding machetes. However, in a place of constant sadness there was happiness and a sense of pride. This was most confusing to me. It almost depressed me. Of course, I had the empathy of hating for any human being to live in those conditions, but the depression actually came in the fact that these people looked to be happier than I did.

Don't get me wrong or think I'm selfish. I just couldn't fathom how these people had a sense of hope about them, and here I am living in the most civilized country in the world and I am not happy. Talk about an inner scream. I feel like I am chained to the wall of my mind, a prison, so to speak, and I am missing out on the world. But there have been instances where I am free, so I know what it feels like. For a majority of people in the slums, the slum life is all they know, so one cannot miss something they do not know. So if the slums are all they know, how could they know or miss what they have never experienced? They can't, and that's how they get by. If the average American was thrown into the slums and lived as they did, they would be consumed within a week, if not sooner. So the point of the matter is one cannot miss something they do not know. In my keen sense of myself, I unfortunately do realize my shortcomings. And unlike those people in the slums, I do not feel hope. And just that fact makes me scream. I have it an insurmountable amount times better in America, and here in Kenya in the slums there is more hope than I have.

If I would not have met Linda nor talked to Ashley, would I even have a second thought about my social skills? My thought is that I would not. As with the paragraph above, one can't miss what they don't know. That being true for as much grief as Linda has caused me, I could've been content with Emily even though she drove me crazy, but that would be okay because I wouldn't know that there could be better. I would've been content with someone that half the time talks about irrelevant stuff not knowing that I could feel connected with someone. So maybe in the long run as much grief as those two experiences have caused me, maybe they are preparing me for something. Maybe that's true, but I hope that if that comes I don't think of the right thing to say while driving home an hour later.

MISCELLANEOUS

It's been a while since I last typed, so I am now backlogged on topics to write about, so this title will be an umbrella of several topics. I may, in the future, expand upon something I write about in this.

My last written piece was written in Kenya three days before the most traumatic experience of my life happened. Written below is an account I wrote about the ordeal on the St. Louis Karting Association's Web site.

For those of you who didn't know, I left for Africa the day after race one. It had been a good trip so far, but my memories of Africa will not be a good one after today's events: My dad is here doing some film work about missionaries and various other things about Kenya. One of the subjects is the high amount of homeless kids in the lake city of Kisumu. As we were riding today and he was taking video, this mob of kids spotted the camera (to them, cameras are a good sign that the holder of the camera has money) and rushed toward us. Within seconds, the car we were in could not move as we were surrounded. It started calmly, as they just wanted money, but as the driver tried slowly to get away, the tension escalated. About five minutes after we were first spotted, there were probably fifty to seventy-five kids (ages from eight to eighteen) around our car. The front windows were rolled down, and if it weren't for my dad wielding his Swiss Army knife every time someone reached for him, they could have easily gotten him. At the same time, this mob was trying to get into my door and drag me out. Their intentions were, in the end, to stone us. The driver, who knew the area, talked patiently, and he eventually got a clearing and we made a break for it. As we made this break, the mob threw anything they could find, and one of the big rocks destroyed a taillight. I was in the backseat, and had that rock hit the window, this message might be completely different.

During the siege, I have never prayed so hard in my life, and if it weren't for the coolheaded driver, we might have been killed today. The whole ordeal was around twenty minutes, and though this isn't the type of hostage taking that goes on in the Middle East, but during it, it was just as dangerous.

I can't wait to get back to the States on Friday, and I will see everyone at the track this weekend. With the given events, this weekend might not be a good weekend to yell at the flagman.

I wrote that within three hours of it happening. I had such a shaking in my body that words can't describe the feeling I felt. The emotional trauma was such that I do not remember anything immediately after the crisis. I remember rounding a corner in the car, then another, then another, then finally we were in safety and then my mind went blank until we were having lunch at the hotel. I survived, but that fear and shock I felt that day is still in me somewhere and has yet to be felt again.

I guess this segment of this miscellaneous page will be about my travels to Kenya. What's interesting about that ordeal is when I recall my trip to Kenya, what pains me the most is, of all things, the airport in Amsterdam. In fact, in just writing that last sentence I am tearing up. I guess I'll start from the top and write about the whole experience … Kenya

All my life I have heard my dad's tales of epic escapades of his experiences the previous times he visited Africa. Granted, he was caught in a coup in Liberia, but nevertheless, I still walked into this trip naive to the fact that anywhere in Africa is a dangerous place, and I walked into this trip with open arms. I mean, come on, you never hear of anything bad happening in Kenya. Or so I thought at least. I should have known something was up when while getting my yellow fever shot I had a vassal vega syncope. In laymen terms, that's fainting. And that faint broke my streak of staying out of the hospital for a year.

Moving ahead, I survived the next round of shots and it was time for the big trip. Ironically for me, we had a layover in the most sacred and fearful ground I could ever go. If you have read all my prior writings, you already know what that is; if you haven't read, then you need to read to understand how Minneapolis can be the most depressing spot in the world.

Our plane had a bit of a delay, and we flew in circles for about fifteen minutes, but then it was time for the approach that took a lifetime. We were sitting on the left side of the plane, and we were flying from west to east; the airport there is situated on the south side of town. This gave me a bird's-eye view of downtown. I saw the convention center that had changed my life forever. What was probably less than three minutes of being able to see everything seemed to be forever as I experienced all of those fateful fourteen hours and the disaster that was to come all over again, and again, and again.

The plane, mercifully, finally landed, and the pain was instantly lifted. I don't know if it was the trip at hand that gave me the energy or the Red Bull, but all that was temporarily forgotten. Added on top of that, I found an arcade on the concourse and they had pinball tables, all of which were in good enough condition that I played as soon as the change machine accepted my dollar. My dad got coffee and was reading his book as I played "The Simpsons" pinball table. I am very experienced at this table, as this is the same table that's at the pizza place where Emily and I ate at least two times a week. Playing that machine up there was very bittersweet, as instantly I thought about Emily and what she would think if she knew I was going to such an exotic place, or if she would even care anymore. Anyways, all that was once again forgotten instantly because I had a killer game. There is no better way to kill a four-hour layover than to have a pinball game that lasts three-quarters of an hour. I set a high score in that game (if you are ever at that airport, check to see if AML still has high score).

After that I remembered I had not eaten a thing, so my dad and I ate at the Pizza Hut Express that was nearby. Then we prepared for the long trans-Atlantic flight to Amsterdam.

The flight over was uneventful. I tried to sleep as much as I could, but at the same time I was trying to calculate when I would need to be awake and asleep so I could better adjust to the change in time zones. Whatever I did, I would later find out it was horribly wrong.

It was about 6:30 in the morning when we stepped off the plane and walked into the Amsterdam airport. The international terminal of the airport is much like a potpourri of world culture. People from all walks of life walk the concourse. The shops are in pristine order, and there's always some announcement being made.

One memorable line is of the lady over the intercom. In Amsterdam, they have no tolerance for tardiness for a flight. Constantly heard was an announcement like the one that follows, "Would John Doe flying on Flight 99 to Istanbul please report to the gate. You are holding up the flight. Your luggage will then be offloaded." The accent of the lady was so sharp that it made Anne Robinson, former host of "The Weakest Link," seem to be a nice second-grade teacher.

As early morning turned into midmorning, my dad and I ate at the McDonald's there, and during the dinner, or breakfast, or whatever meal it was, he took a picture of me. I had somewhat of a look of disdain, or rather a look of just being fed up. If he had taken it five hours after, I would've had that look for a good reason.

As 11:00 approached, we headed to our flight. We boarded and sat. Then we sat and sat. Eleven thirty passed, 11:45, then noon. Around noon, the captain informed the passengers that the plane's proximity radar was not working and that the ground crew and mechanics would look at it. Two hours passed and still there wasn't a resolution. In the end, they could not fix it, and at first it looked as if they weren't going to be able to find a replacement plane. At the last minute, however, one was found, and after another two-hour delay, we were on our new plane.

The trip from Amsterdam to Nairobi seemed to last forever. It didn't help that in the latter half, we were flying over the desolate parts of Sudan, so scenery was sparse to say the least, especially since it was night.

I was so tired when we landed that the only thing I could think of was getting to sleep. Lost in my tiredness was the fact that I was in Africa. The luggage seemed to take forever to get out, and finally, finally, after such a long day, we were outside in the fresh air, or rather the fresh air heavily polluted with diesel fuel fumes. Nevertheless, the hotel was just fifteen minutes away.

As we pulled up to the hotel, I was flabbergasted that a hotel of these standards would be in a place like Kenya. This place was immaculate in every sense. After a lengthy check-in, we were finally off to our rooms. It was a long walk, as we had room 626. When we opened the door to our room, there wasn't a word we could utter that described what we were looking at. It was a room fit for royalty. It had two levels, was very spacious, a bathtub like no other, and the best-feeling bed I have ever felt. It would be worth anyone's troubles to travel there just to sleep in that bed because sleeping in it was like being in heaven.

Neither of us could sleep due to the fact that our body clocks were so confused that they literally could not tell night from day. And added on top of that was the fact that we had not eaten for some seventeen hours, so at 3:00 a.m. local Kenyan time, we ordered room service. Once again, I was speechless as I tasted the hamburger. Maybe it was the fact that their cows aren't fed growth hormones, or maybe more so the fact that I was so hungry. Whatever the case may be, it was the best-tasting hamburger I can recollect ever having. After that impressive meal I was finally ready for bed, but I could never be prepared for what was to come ... Two days later we flew to the town of Kissumu on the shores of Lake Victoria. I don't know if it was a reaction to the pain medicine, or if I picked up some funky virus in the slums of Nairobi, but in any event, I had a mouth sore like I never had before. It was bad enough to keep me at the hotel for most the time. This was very aggravating because I wanted to see as much of anywhere as I possibly could. During this five-day stint at this hotel, my dad was to be gone for two-and-a-half days. My plan was to write a lot on his laptop, but it decided to be a dork and not work but long enough for me to write two papers. So to keep me company was the television. Thankfully, they had a movie channel that primarily showed American movies (albeit bad ones; ever see Glitter? My goodness, that was bad!), but they also had CNN International, and the channel I would end up watching the most, Eurosport3. During my three days of solitude, I saw plenty of soccer matches. There was this one with Manchester United and I think the other team was the Bolton Wanderers. What a game that was; there was scoring, yellow cards, corner kicks, and the game kept going back and forth and … okay, enough about my temporary soccer kick (pun intended).

As my dad got back from the bush, I was finally feeling better and the mouth sore had started to reside, so the next day I was finally able to go out and see some of the landscape and do what I actually was getting paid to do and take pictures. The first day back, we went out to where these camels were. This was a most interesting drive, as in a span of fifty miles we went from what looked like Kansas to what looked like the rolling hills of Kentucky, then to the rocky mesas of Utah and then, finally, to the bareness or harshness of the Nevada desert. I never thought I would touch a live, wild camel, but that naive thought was put to shame as I got up close and personal with a camel. And if you don't believe me, I do have the picture that I actually put my hand on a camel's neck, albeit, reluctantly.

We got back late that night and we had one day left in Kissumu and two days left in the country of Kenya. The next morning, we checked out of the hotel and went to where the fishing boats come in. After that, my dad needed scenery shots of the town, so we drove around. This drive would change my life, or rather how I perceive life.

I've always heard to stay on the beaten path. We, however, didn't heed that call and went just one street west of Main Street. As written by my description earlier, this would be a time of great drama. If you ever have been held in a mob with the mob having the look of death, these words will mean nothing to you. In life we all strive for control. Control over money; control over health; control over relationships; control over anything and everything. When control is lost, chaos reigns. And in this great drama, chaos ran rampant like the running of the bulls in Pamplona. These kids didn't care about anything but money. If they had to kill for it, so be it. What started out as one kid by the side window turned to ten, then twenty, then forty, and there wasn't an organized headcount, but we agreed that there were maybe around seventy-five kids when the mob reached its maximum amount.

Now imagine if you have always had control for the most part, or in the least felt as if there were some control, and now your life is in the hands of an angry mob. I was so terrified that I didn't even know I was terrified. The only word that comes to mind is shock.

There were kids on the hood, the roof, and the trunk. There were kids reaching in and even one kid in the car.

The ordeal went on and on and on. For nearly thirty to forty minutes, the driver, who was from that town, was talking in their native dialect to try and ease the tension. Whatever he said must have worked because I'm writing this today.

There were about five kids who had put their knees below the front bumper that impeded our chance to escape. After much talking, the driver got one of them to go to his window, the other kids then parted ways and, like a running back finding a hole to the end zone, we were gone. Granted, it wasn't like a top-fuel dragster. After all, how fast can a 1985 Toyota Corolla that's seen its better days go? As mentioned before, it was a thrilling escape that should be put into a movie, but what I didn't put in that description was the internal aftermath that followed.

Pure hatred, pure fury, and pure dismay were what I felt afterwards. It was one thing to have nearly had the chance to be in the seats where the wheel of an Indy car had landed in 1999, and it's another thing to nearly be killed by a tornado. But this episode was the result of other human beings and that bothered me. I had never had a firsthand experience of absolute desperation, and now I had an account that will haunt me forever. There was more that went on in my head, but I will cover that in my next piece.

That night we got on a plane, and you could have told me that the plane had an eighty percent chance of going down and I still would have boarded it just to get the heck out of that town.

We got back to Nairobi, and a big temporary healer was the fact that we got the same elaborate hotel room with that bed that could let me sleep for a month straight. We didn't do much the next day, and on that night we got back on a plane and headed for Amsterdam.

Our flight arrived at about four in the morning, and the airport was a ghost town, a big contrast to what was seen on our last visit. In a way, it was eerie as weary-eyed travelers slept anywhere they could and most shops were closed. I tried to sleep, but the sporadic noise of a suitcase being wheeled made sleep elusive. Within two hours, the airport that was a ghost town quickly became that bustling world village I knew from my prior visit. I don't know what it is about an international airport, but there is something so freeing in being in that type of atmosphere.

This time when our plane was called and we boarded, there were no problems and we were back on our way to the States.

We got into Detroit and had a layover scheduled for four hours. If you've read my previous writings, please reread the prior sentence to look for that ever-important key word. If you saw and deciphered the word "scheduled," you're right and you win the knowledge of knowing what happens next. What was scheduled for a four-hour layover was extended because the plane coming out of St. Louis had broken down. So add another four hours and that was the official time of that layover. During the extra time, my dad and I recounted our experiences to this marching band from Webster Groves, Missouri, and they were ever intent on listening to our harrowing experience from the escape of the natives. What seemed like a month finally was over and we were finally, finally, on our way home. It was midafternoon, and when we got back to my hometown, the sun was just going down. This was a fitting end that the sun would be going down, because I, too, was headed down for a lot of sleep, but also internally I lost a lot of myself on that trip. Little did I know at the time, but time would show the wounds that were incurred in my ordeal.

Since then I've heard rumblings that there's a small chance I may go to Sudan. If you follow world events at all, you know that a quarter-century civil war was just concluded and that it still remains a place of turmoil. With my luck, I've thought on whether or not I should go, and I've come to the conclusion that if I went, nuclear war would likely break out, or at least their equivalent to a nuclear war, so I think it best if I just stay here in the States ... that is, unless, of course, the price is right.

DESIRE

I'm writing this after writing "Kenya," and I feel bad that I didn't recall that trip in more detail, but I feel it more important to write this at the present time.

I know if you've read all my prior stuff (and why shouldn't you; I do write with almost a recurring theme and you'll pick up on things if you know the prior story), you are already perplexed by the title of this. All my other writings are of events or theories; however, this title is bold. For the sake of clarity, imagine that this is the next episode of a "to be continued" television show.

Before I went to Kenya, I was scheduled to work for the Lingner Production Group at the Indy Racing League race in St. Petersburg, Florida. The Lingner Group provided the production team for ABC's coverage of IRL races. This, however, conflicted with my overseas excursion, so it was planned that my first work would be at the Indy 500, or rather the events proceeding up to the big race and including the race itself. April came and went with just one hospital visit for a sprained ankle I suffered at the racetrack, but other than that it was a boring month.

Then the much-anticipated month of May approached. In less than two weeks, I would be at the world's most famous racecourse ... with credentials! But, as things normally turn out for me, things went awry. On May 2, I received a phone call simply stating that ABC had taken over the responsibility of the production group, so the long and short of it was that the much-anticipated month was now the biggest letdown. There would be no credentials, there would be no working with television professionals and meeting the drivers, there would be nothing.

Four days prior to what would've been my first day of work, I felt this big sore on the back of my neck. At the time, it wasn't anything out of the ordinary, except for its mass. I passed it off as just a pimple and thought nothing of it. Silly me, the way 2005 had been a-running, I should've known that something ominous was looming around the bend.

The next morning, I was in an almost trancelike state of pain, and my fever climbed to a staggering 104.5. My dad took no hesitancy in taking me to the ER; within fifteen minutes of him getting out of bed, I was in the ER.

The mass was now a bulging mass. The best way for me to describe it would be to say that this was a pimple on steroids. The ER doc lanced it but then thought it best to give me IV antibiotics and admit me overnight. As he lanced it, he also took a culture to see what caused this enormous mass of pain and puss.

The first night wasn't bad, except for constantly being woken up for my vital signs. The pain was lingering enough not to make me to uncomfortable, and the pain medicine made sure I was asleep when not bothered by the nurses.

However, the next morning during a shift change, my medicine was overlooked and the words "excruciating pain" got a whole new meaning. I was supposed to take the strong painkillers every four hours, but it had been eight and the pain was of such that I could not blink without feeling that pain in the neck.

I kept hitting the nurse call button and they said they would be right there, but their sayings were fallacies. Add on top of that, it was the middle of the night and I had no one to talk to. And then it hit me like a freight train that's lost its brakes rolling down a Virginia hill. Not only was I hurting physically from the unknown cause of this mass in my neck, but now I truly felt just how alone I was. If I had perished in Africa, not too many people would've known, minus immediate family. Now I was in the hospital with what at the time was an unknown mass and not one person outside my immediate family knew. What used to be a life filled with others (okay, maybe one other) was now filled with emptiness. During this thought process, the fact of time became all too clear in my mind. What dawned on me was that I have Asperger's, and there's nothing that can be done, and that I may have to be in the hospital again and history will repeat itself and there will be no one (excluding parents, of course).

In the end, I had that mass taken out surgically and it turned out that it was a MRSA staph infection. The remnant of the surgery was a hole about an inch deep with the circumference of a U.S. quarter. Needless to say, it hurt, but nothing could have hurt more than the internal storm brewing inside my head.

Two thousand and five has not been a good year. Three hospital visits, three life-threatening events, and what hurts the most is that I had no one to tell the story to.

So what is desire? If given the choice between a relationship and a racing career, a racing career would win out without a second thought. But as of now there is no career, just emptiness. So what do I want? There's only one thing that comes to my mind: understanding. I want people to know of the pain I feel. I want people to experience just once what I go through. Sadly, I have no one I know to do this with. I don't even know how many people will read this, but I wish a multitude would, so maybe, just maybe I would feel like someone knows and won't look down on me for me being myself.

Is it too much to ask for someone with the luck of mine to ask for just one experience where I am free? I would give almost anything to have some random person read all my writings, and even if it's just for a millisecond, I'd give the world if they could have just a spilt-second thought of what my world is like. My world is not much different, but this world is much like a space shuttle. The space shuttle has over one million parts, and if just one part malfunctions, it can cause a catastrophe that cannot be corrected. The space shuttle has one million or so parts, but the world has six billion parts (parts being people), and within each part is a story, a life, and probably ten million internal parts. I'm good with math, but six billion times ten million is a number I don't want to type out. This is my life, and I yearn for it to be different, just if it's one more day.

There have been a few experiences when the world and I have existed in harmony, but just five days out of twenty-two years isn't much. The thing about it is that a relationship can't be forced, can't be induced, and, in my case, can't be initiated. For something to happen it's almost like a tornado, i.e. conditions have to be favorable for something to happen.

So I don't know; maybe people reading this and maybe coming to or having some idea of what my life is like will give me a temporary respite from the pain I feel day in and day out. All I want before my end comes is to have another experience like I had in Minneapolis or Indianapolis during Christmas of 2003. I know that's not asking a lot for a normal person, but for me, those mind-freeing things don't come like the rains in April.

The desire doesn't mean love in the least; what this desire is, is simply the desire to have a moment where I feel like someone understands. This is the purpose of the writing medium. Maybe you the reader can relate or have empathy or sympathy, or even to the point of almost truly knowing what's it's like to have this dreaded syndrome.

Having this is like being in a soundproof phone booth. In reality, I seem all right, usually there's not a look of disdain on my face, but on the inside of that booth I'm screaming, wanting out. I am truly trapped between a phone and a door, sorry, a rock and a hard place.

All I want is someone to care enough to read this and to understand, even if not fully. The problem is that when professionals read this, they dissect it and look for psychological reasoning. I'm sorry to tell them that there is no reasoning as to why I am what I am.

Again, there've been two instances outside of driving that I've been free, and I sure pray every day that maybe I'll get a random e-mail from someone I know, or maybe someone out there will get my writings and maybe, just maybe, for a brief moment, I will be free and the desire will turn into a brief moment of contentment.

LAS VEGAS

I've written snippets of my experience in October 2003 in other pieces, but I've decided to write a stand-alone piece that will describe the events of that roller-coaster month.

Two thousand and three had been a rough year. I had a serious knee injury in May, I had my dog put to sleep in June, I hadn't driven a racecar in over a year, and my mom had gone temporarily insane and I had moved to my dad's house. This move took a toll on all my friendships and relationships. The move was sort of like pausing a CD, in the sense that when the move was made all relationships were frozen. Time moved on like it always does, but for me all relationships were frozen. Don't get me wrong, I still interacted, but I did nothing to gain or lose anything, as I was unable to assess the gains and losses.

Enter the month of September. My dad had formerly done advertisements for the Derek Daly Driving Academy in Las Vegas. So on a long shot he called out and asked if there were any openings for instructors. In a bizarre turn of events, luck was on my side, and there was in the month of October when they were going to have a bunch of corporate parties out. I was invited to become an instructor for a month, and needless to say, that made my year.

My girlfriend at the time seemed to have mixed emotions about it. From what I deduced it seemed to be jealousy. My belief is she got mad that I was going to be making quite a bit of money, but I never had gone to college, so I didn't really deserve it. Whatever the case may have been, our relationship started to take that left turn behind the wall (racing analogy) at that point in time. As mentioned in prior writings, she did everything she could to avoid seeing me. And in some instances, she flat out lied about seeing me (see "Emily"). I would go into details about that, but it's been covered and I don't really feel like typing it out once more.

October 4 was upon me, and it was time to start my journey. This was going to be my first trip away from home by myself away from family for more than two days. Also this would be the first time I was in excess of three hundred miles away from any family. Add on top all of that and the family I was staying with I had never met. It was truly a journey into the unknown.

The morning of the fourth was an odd one. I got up around four in the morning so I could make as many miles as I could before needing that all-important sleep. Before I left, my stepmom and dad talked to me in the living room. The conversation was one like one would have if they were off to war. I was in a half awake and half-asleep state that I don't remember the exact words, but after a lengthy goodbye it was off to the gas station for a Red Bull. Any time I drive anywhere of great distance I have the routine of drinking a Red Bull. The can says energy drink, and I don't know if it works or if it's just a sugar pill, but it is required for me to start a journey.

By the time I got about two miles from my house the trip started to sink in, or rather it was sort of like waking up from a nap and having no idea where you're going or why you are even in a car. I quickly called my dad and asked him, "Umm, where am I going again?" Of course I knew the destination, but to get there I was blank. He told me, and I quickly regained my bearings and it was to Interstate 70 for what would be the most triumphant drive of my life.

The sun hadn't cracked yet as I pulled on to I-70, as the time was about 4:50. My fuel was full and many a mile of road lay ahead. I noticed something on this first leg of my journey, and that was the fact that time flies when it's dark. The sun started to become pronounced as I entered Columbia, Missouri. While driving through Columbia, I had a flashback of my prior experiences there.

My first unofficial girlfriend, Michelle (I never really have written about her because there wasn't much to say, as she didn't really say much), was attending college at Mizzou. I recalled the time I bowled in the travel league there. Ironically, that's the first time I saw Emily when I saw her at the hotel. How could I forget the other teams throwing chicken into the swimming pool?

Just as fast as my mind thought of that I was through Columbia and had knocked down ninety of 1,600 miles. My goal for the day would be to get to at least the Colorado border.

Traffic got really heavy as I crossed Kansas City and entered the west side of town. That same day a NASCAR Busch series race was going to be run at the Kansas speedway. After about twenty miles of going twenty miles an hour I was "green" again and back up to speed.

My first refuel stop came past Kansas City right before the turnpike. What was very peculiar was the fact that the three cars I had been following all stopped at this same gas station. I remember that trio of cars well because one was a Ford Taurus with US GOVT. license plates, and the person who refilled the car looked to be a highly decorated airman. It hit me at that point that I would probably never see this person again. I don't know how or why, but instantly, like film, that person and car were imposed into my brain like film (title of "film" coming soon). I realized that everything I was going to see and drive through I may not pass through again, and then I was reminded of this song that was sung in second grade. I don't remember most of the words or melodies, but the finale line of each verse was, "Friend, I'll say goodbye because I may not pass this way again."

After my little bout of emotions, it was time to trudge on. I had always heard that Kansas was boring, and people don't lie. No offense to anyone in Kansas, but I salute you because to see such dull scenery day in and day out would have to drive you to the brink of insanity.

I refueled somewhere before the Colorado border, and by this time it was about 2:00 p.m. I was getting a bit weary eyed, but I had to keep going to make it just a one-night drive.

To keep me up, I stopped early for fuel and at the same time got another Red Bull (just for your knowledge, this isn't an advertisement or testimonial about Red Bull) and food. I bought some shelled sunflower seeds and a Wild Cherry Pepsi. The clerk lady asked me where I was headed, and I responded that my destination was Vegas and that I had left St. Louis some eleven hours prior. She was rather impressed that someone at my age would be making that trek. She wished me good luck, and as I walked through the door once, I knew I'd never be there again. As I entered my car and drove away, it finally hit me what I was actually doing, and the trigger of all things were those sunflower seeds.

Every time I remember my family going to the panhandle of Nebraska, my dad would get shelled seeds. So when I got them, I realized that I was writing my own chapter in my life and that I was doing it by myself. It was the first time that I actually felt independent of all others.

Now a couple of paragraphs ago I gave a condemnation to people who live in Kansas. I now have to give a recommendation to those poor souls who live in the eastern half of Colorado. Why would I do this? In Kansas, there are wheat and sunflower fields, so in the least there's something to look at. In the first part of Colorado, the land is barren, the traffic is sparse, and the Rocky Mountains loom in the distance, barely visible, and there is nothing else around. Even the truck stops were barren and boring compared to others around the country. If I lived there, I would go insane, and for no reason whatsoever I would move to Buenos Aires, Argentina.

As those Rocky Mountains in the distance remained in the distance hour after hour, my reflexes were slipping rapidly. The Red Bull may increase awareness in a normal person, but to one who has been driving for twelve-plus hours, its effects are minimal. I had passed Limon and after that the next stop of significance was Denver, so I was pretty much committed regardless of sleep to make it to Denver.

At about six o'clock in the evening I finally reached Denver, and those mountains were now not too far off. I had an inkling to drive farther, but thankfully my senses prevailed and I stopped at the American Inn due north of downtown. This would be my first experience in actually stopping at a hotel and ordering a room by myself. I did this process perfectly (well, can someone screw it up?), and I immediately headed for my room.

My intentions were to go to sleep right away, but the hotel had Speed channel, and they had a USAC Sprint Car race from Indianapolis Raceway Park on. I watched that and went to sleep shortly thereafter around 7:30.

My banking institution inquiring as to why my ATM card was being used all across Missouri, Kansas, and Colorado rudely awakened me at 9:00 p.m. I talked rather angrily toward the person, saying that I was on a trip. After that I was right back asleep.

About 2:00 in the morning I woke up wide-awake. By the way my body was refreshed I thought it was eight or nine. I looked at my cell phone and was shocked that it was just two in the morning. I tried but failed on returning to sleep, so I packed up and headed to my car to check out.

While driving away from the hotel and back onto the Interstate, I decided to refuel. This refueling for some reason gave me a special feeling inside. I don't know if it's because I was now less than fourteen hours away from Vegas, or if it was because I was where I was by myself and I was doing it with no fear. I didn't think about that for too long, and after the car was full I went in and got myself some ... you guessed it, Red Bull.

Very quickly, there was great contrast between the wasteland of eastern Colorado and what was to come. It started quickly by seeing a horrible roadside crash in the eastbound lanes. After that, it was much like being at the top of a roller coaster about to descend into excitement.

Within an hour I was in the most scenic part of America I had ever seen, and this was at 3:00 in the morning. I could tell that the hills on each side of the road were staggeringly high. As each small resort town passed, the roads became windier and the mountains higher. This was the most fun bit of road I had ever driven on by far.

I did exceed the speed limits in places, and I was making excellent time because in that part of the country in the middle of night, there is virtually no one to be seen. In fact, the only people I saw were two workers in a tunnel washing the tiles on the side of the tunnel.

Time once again was going by fast and right as the sun broke, I was at the Utah- Colorado border. As the sun shone over the hills, I saw the vast mesas and mountains of this region. It was so beautiful that I nearly drove my Maxima right off the road. I wish I had a camera then so I could describe to you just how awe-inspiring that sight was.

Because I had gotten up at such a wee hour, my body was getting tired, so somewhere near Green River, Utah, I pulled off onto one of the scenic lookouts and took a nap. I couldn't believe I was doing this. I felt so alive while taking that nap because that was something I never thought I would do.

Two hours later, it was go time once again, and I'm thankful I refueled there, because for the next what seemed to be one thousand miles the only exits were labeled "ranch exits." Then, after a while, I would get to one of the most depressing interchanges of my life.

All my life I have lived on or near I-70. That interstate runs through my former hometown of Indianapolis, and it is a main thoroughfare of St. Louis. On numerous occasions we have taken that road east to see my aunt in Washington D.C. But now, on this October 5 day, I was reaching the end of this interstate. I guess for the normal person this would be a moot point and just a transition from I-70 to I-15, but for me it was almost like losing a friend. I had been on I-70 for nearly one thousand miles, and we were almost like buddies, and now it was the end. And when I say end, it's a very abrupt end as if you were to bypass the exits you would end up in the side of a rock face.

As choked up as I was, I made that turn to the south and got on I-15. This would be the road that would lead me to my destination. I was good on fuel until just after the Nevada- Arizona border, and as I got out I still had my leather jacket on. What a surprise I found when the air temperature was a steamy one hundred. It was definitely a stark contrast to the fall-like weather of Denver.

It was now about 1:00 p.m. when finally, finally I had completed my 1,660-mile quest. Because it was only 1:00 p.m. Vegas time, I decided to stop by the office of the Academy just to see if anyone was home. I had been there on two previous occasions, so I knew where it was and I knew the layout. I asked one of the mechanics, whom I had never seen before, if Jeff, the manager guy, was around. He replied that he was with two special clients on the Inner Road Course. The facilities at the Las Vegas Motor Speedway have many tracks and the Academy uses two of them, the Inner Road Course, which lies within the oval that NASCAR uses, and an Outer Road Course, which, when NASCAR runs there, is used as a parking lot and heliport.

Because of the fact I had never been on the IRC, I wasn't about to just drive to the infield and say hello. I was just going to wait for them to come back to the office. It wasn't like I had anything else to do. The family I was staying with wasn't getting back to their home in Henderson (which is about thirty-five miles south of the track which lies about fifteen miles north of the famous Strip) until 5:00 p.m.

During my wait, I was listening to the NASCAR race on the radio, and about an hour later Jeff came back to the office. I got out of my car, and he instantly remembered me and said, "Ah, Mr. Likens, I see you've made it!" I had made it indeed.

That day there were just two students, and I went with them to the IRC just to watch and wait. As that day concluded, my nerves started to get frazzled as I realized that I was less than an hour from meeting the family with whom I would be staying for three weeks. As I left the track, I asked when I would be needed and they said not officially until the fifteenth, but I could come to the track and help out if I'd like. This was different from what I had understood, because I thought I was going to be needed right away, but I wasn't going to complain.

As I made my way from the track and to the house where I would be staying, anxiety took over. Would these people be freaks? Would they have some sort of strange eating habits or play loud music? The only thing I knew for sure was that the lady's name was Sundance, her husband's, Frankie, and that Sundance was a church secretary. Other than that, I knew nothing. Would I have my own room and/or television? There were so many unknowns that would be known in less than an hour.

I drove cautiously as I approached Horizon Ridge Road, and I exited the I-215 and got off. I had a map my dad had made me, but it was outdated and I was having a heck of a time finding Snowgoose Drive. When I finally found it, they were just getting home themselves. I helped them unload the groceries they had bought and introduced myself. They introduced themselves, and I instantly felt welcomed. I was shown my room, which had its own television and a fish tank. They had bought bed covers for me and a pillowcase (which I still use to this day!). I set up my video games and then it was time for dinner. Now, mind you, I'm a picky eater, and on the first night in this new household they were having tacos, and I despise tacos with a passion, but it would be rude to turn it down, so for the first time in my life I ate tacos. They weren't bad, but I wouldn't care to have them again, unless, of course, Frankie was to make them again.

After Sundance showed me her cats, I went straight to bed, as I wanted to get to the Academy early to learn everything I could about what I would be doing. So on Monday, October 6, I was at the track for the first time in a non-student role. I was performing duties of an instructor on that day and all of that week but wasn't being paid for it. It didn't matter, as I was around the cars and was driving a BMW Z3 every once in a while and also serving as flagman, so I didn't care a bit about pay. In fact, to be honest with you, I would have paid them to do what I was doing.

That week passed, and it started out a bit rocky with me being overguarded and shy, but as the week went on, I slowly crept into my element. At week's end, another instructor whose name is b.c. went out with me and we drove around in separate Z3s and he helped me learn the optimal lines in a GT car. Then he drove me around, and then rode with me, and it really helped me in that he was willing to help me out and talk to me. After that, I was right at home at the Derek Daly Academy.

The atmosphere at the house was great. Our sleep schedules were off, so it was as if it was my house. I rarely saw Sundance, Frankie, or their daughter, Illana. But nagging at me at the same time were thoughts of home. Not homesickness mind you, but what to do with Emily, but because that's covered in another paper it will be left blank on this one.

The day before I officially started working, I went to the Boulder City public golf course to play, and this course was class "A" fabulous. If you have ever seen the movie Casino, you've seen this course. What was really odd about this round of golf was the fact that I was paired with someone else, and for the first time I didn't mind it. The guy who drove the golf cart was a retired machinist, and I heard all about Boulder City and the surrounding areas and the difference in people from Boulder City and Los Angeles. And do you want to know the weird part about this? It was weird because I actually listened. For once in my life, I cared about some irrelevant old man's talk. Forever before this, I hated being paired with someone while playing golf because the last thing I wanted to hear was small talk, but now because I was in my element, I actually was enjoying it. It didn't hurt that I started the round with four consecutive birdies.

Later that day, I went to the mall by the Sundance Station Casino and actually talked to a couple of random people. One person I talked to for about an hour and a half while she worked the Dippin Dots stand. I learned and asked what there was to do in the surrounding areas but was even more shocked that I, Aaron Likens, was talking to people and actually starting the conversations. I had started on the drug Lexapro a week prior to coming out to Vegas, but I doubt that was the reason why I was opening up. My hypothesis was, for the first time in my life I was happy. I was happy because I knew that tomorrow, and the next day, and the day after that I was going to go really fast in a racecar and that was all that mattered.

The thirteenth to the seventeenth was a corporate event, and I worked about ten hours each day, arriving at the track at about five in the morning and staying till 3:00 p.m. or later. I didn't mind, though, because this was paradise. It was all I ever wanted and more. After each day's work, I either stopped at the Petro station and ordered a T-bone for $9.99, or I got a pizza from Villa Pizza when I got back home. Whatever I did, it was the best!

The weekend saw another short session, and then on Monday I was off. I knew my tenure was running thin by this point, so I went to play another round of golf. I didn't shoot as well, but I had fun and that's all that matters. On this day, I also made my one and only trip to the Strip.

When I had been there previously as a student, my dad and I stayed at Circus Circus, so I decided to go there. It didn't hurt that they have a good arcade. When I got there and parked, I was overwhelmed with emotion. Memories started to flood back into my mind as if a levee had broken. Even though the year was 2003, for me and my video-graphic mind, it was 2000 and 2001 and my dad was with me. I could see as I walked by the Steak House my dad and me sitting at this certain table talking about the successful day I had, and I could see as I walked through the Adventuredome the miniature golf course my dad played mini golf at and the holes he got his holes in one at. To say the least, it was overwhelming and after just one dollar spent on a game of "Dance Dance Revolution," I got out of there very hastily.

With that behind me, I went back to the house and went to bed early, as the next two days were going to be long ones once more.

Those days passed and it was now the twenty-third and I had just one day left scheduled to work and that was just going to be a half-day school. As celebration of my achievements, Sundance and her family took me out for a prime rib dinner.

I get down a lot about people, and I often forget the kindness of people like Sundance. I was just a kid from St. Louis, and she was nice enough to change out a room so I had one, and now she was taking me out for a prime rib dinner. People like that come few and far between.

The dinner was over, and once again I went to bed early so I could get up early and work my final day. I wanted to be perfect on this day so I would be called upon again because, as I mentioned before, this was paradise. I mean, I had never had so much energy before. This trip would be like a person who is a great piano player, but all their life they've played on a small piano that was out of tune, but now they're getting to go to a great cathedral and play on a great organ for a month.

But, as you should very well know, something weird should be happening soon. I mean, I've written now nearly seven pages and nothing horrific, terrifying, or bad has really happened. I feel some people may read this for the same reason people watch auto racing, and that's waiting for the big one, and my big one was about to happen, but not in the way you're going to think it's going to happen.

As soon as I got to the track, I went to set up the half-day course. I got the cones in place and the cars washed and I was set to go. About forty minutes before the students were set to arrive, I was asked to replace these two ceiling tiles in the classroom. I said no problem, as I didn't want to disappoint anyone, so I went to the classroom to tackle this ceiling tile issue. The ceiling tiles, though, were, of course, on the ceiling, so to get to them, I stood on the table. I managed to get one in right, but the other one wasn't fitting properly. I struggled for about five minutes and then it came down on me. The last thing I wanted was to break it, so I attempted to catch it and in the process I stepped off the table and onto what I thought was the back of a chair I had placed by me. Big mistake! I didn't step on the back, but rather the arm, and it flipped over faster than a spinning SUV and I took a head dive.

I don't know exactly what my head hit, but all signs pointed to a Goodyear tire used for demonstrations. I was out for an unknown amount of time until another instructor found me. They instantly called the LVMS crash response team and, before I knew what was going on, I was loaded in an ambulance and headed to some hospital I had never heard of. This was very scary because I was coming in and out of consciousness and I'm 1600 miles away from home and no one knows that I'm going to the hospital and all in all it was bad.

Because of the neck injury, I was admitted to the ER right away and was given pain medication right away. I really wish they had mentioned the whole "take with food" catch because I hadn't eaten anything prior to this. Within thirty minutes, I was throwing up. Mind you, I was throwing up while in a cervical collar. I was so alone.

Beside me was a victim of a car accident (you would've thought of all things, that's why, if any, I would go to the hospital), and her mother actually attended to me while I threw up.

A couple hours passed and the nice mother's daughter was discharged, so I was alone, but not for long, as Sundance made her way to the hospital to stay with me. I was in the hospital a total of nearly six hours as they lost my CAT scan a couple times and in the process I threw up a personal record of fifteen times. After the hospital, Sundance had some work to finish up at the church where she worked, so we went there.

I slept in the pastor's office, and not too long after we were headed back up to the speedway to get my car. By this time, Frankie had joined us, and he drove my car back to the house. Sadly, the bizarre world I live in would get worse for me.

The doctors prescribed Soma for my pain, and little did I know that I was allergic to it. So, on Sunday, the twenty-sixth, while heading to church, I lost control of my bodily movements and slowly turned into a vegetable. This necessitated another trip to the hospital where they gave me some IVs, and within three hours I was back to normal but was told not to take the Soma again (wow, who'da thunk that advice?).

By this time I knew I was never going to be an instructor again, and I had no idea what other horrible stuff lay in store for me, so I rested on Monday and on that day I told Sundance I was going to head back to St. Louis the next day. She said I should wait at least a week to let my severe cervical strain and possible slight concussion have more time to heal, but I was so frustrated with the turn of events, I just wanted to be home in my own bed. I knew emotionally I was going to be unable to stand the goodbyes, so I had to leave quickly.

So, on that Monday, I went to sleep at 4:00 p.m. and woke up at midnight. I woke Frankie, as he told me to, so he could lock the door behind me. As we headed toward the door, he gave me his keychain thing that has the text and colors of his native Guam. He told me that I was a joy to have around the house and that he and Sundance would miss me. I held back and simply stated the same thing but in reverse and got in my car and left Snowgoose Drive.

Once again, I had Red Bull, and I knew that driving past the exit of the LVMS was going to be tough. I passed the track at 12:45 a.m. and was headed home. I made great time once again in the dark and made it past Denver, but Limon was going to be my limit. Once again I got myself a hotel room and then went to dinner at the Fireside Grill, and, boy, was that one of the best steaks I have ever had. For one, it was a steak of achievement as this was the start of the end of my journey, and secondly, it was just really good.

I went back to the hotel room and went to sleep, and at 3:00 a.m. I was back on the road. Within four hours, though, I got tired, so once again I slept at a rest stop and within an hour and a half, I would start the final journey home.

If I had been able to feel emotion at that time, the entire drive probably would've had tears. But it didn't, and I drove and drove and drove. I made it from Limon to Saint Louis with nothing out of the ordinary happening, minus the fact that my neck hurt so badly, and by the time I was home, I could not turn it one way or the other.

I kept in contact with my dad on my way home and he was waiting on the front porch, and as I rounded the corner and pulled onto my street, he waved a checkered flag, which was a great symbolic gesture that I had finished my first great journey by myself.

Sadly, though, after that my memory goes rather blank. I remember a snippet here and a snippet there. I know I attended Handel's Messiah, because I have two ticket stubs in my car, so I'm assuming I took Emily, but I don't remember. The Lexapro really messed me up after that trip, and except for one experience in Indianapolis with a friend (I still can't write about that!) my memory is totally blank up until April of 2004.

I do remember driving home from Vegas, and I rethought it again after my conversation that Christmas night that it is true that, "Friend, let me say goodbye, because I may not pass this way again." How true that is.

FILM THEORY

This will be the second installment of the "Theory" series. These theory pieces aren't intended to focus on one subject of my life, but having no idea where the text will take me, I have no idea what will come ... I have done a lot of thinking while writing all these papers, and something always is out in the forefront of my mind: Everything in life that is a major is a "first." Everything, whether it be Linda, Vegas, 1999, the Challenger exploding, or Emily, everything was a first. I'm not haunted by any of the seconds, but just the "firsts." Why is this? Enter the film theory.

Film is an interesting item. It is a sheet of plastic (polyester, nitrocellulose, or cellulose acetate) coated with an emulsion containing light-sensitive silver halide salts (bonded by gelatin) with variable crystal sizes that determine the sensitivity, contrast, and resolution of the film. When it is exposed to light, it captures an image for life and can then be developed into a picture of any size. So too I believe my mind is like my film. Once film captures an image, it can't be changed. It is like a computer that is locked and cannot be re-programmed. It is, in essence, stuck with that image.

So what if this is true? What if my mind is like a roll of film and every "first" I experience becomes imprinted on this very long roll of film that is life? That could answer a lot of questions, such as the reason why Linda and Emily haunt me. Even though I didn't particularly care for either one, because each was a unique "first," my mind could not handle or comprehend the missing of that first from my life. You see, once something happens in my life, it becomes sort of like a snapshot. You can take a picture of a hillside, and ten, twenty, and even forty years from now, that picture will remain the same. While in real life that hillside will be subject to drought, floods, fires, and meteor landings, so what is in the snapshot may not reflect what it will be like X amount of time from when you took it. This is where I differ; when a snapshot is made, it is there for life, and change of it in reality is very hard, if not impossible to comprehend.

This could be the most important thing I have written about because it could be the key to so many padlocked doors. Time and time again, I have stated that time is of great mystery and fear to me, and if this film theory is true, then it would mean that my mind is almost operating on a different concept of time than everyone else. If that is true, this is the reason why there is such difficulty.

If this is true, every characteristic I have could probably be traced to a cause for having it. Take, for instance, bad language. I remember way back when I was maybe two or three, a bad word was said on the Letterman Show and my brother repeated it, and my dad instantly said that type of language was inappropriate and bam! a snapshot was made, and in my mind, foul language was off limits. Think about that; if every little thing like that would be taken a picture of, or rather programmed into the brain, just think how many micro programs there would be!

So if every time I heard a rule or experienced something for the first time, it instantly became exposed to the film. There is not a chance for a second exposure. Once it's taken, it is done. With that type of mindset, I can see why life would be scary for me. I don't know when or how racing became part of the film roll, but since there are no seconds, I literally can't comprehend life without racing.

I probably need to do more writing or thinking on this matter to fully understand it, but I think I am on the right track on this.

The other day I found an interesting and depressing thing. I came to the realization that embedded in the film are all other types of memories. Call it captions of the time, if you will. Take for instance this VHS tape I came across four days ago.

I love the winter Olympics. There is no other multiple-day sporting event that has more drama and danger than the winter games. I remember each one like they were yesterday. In 1998, I taped the final day of the Nagano games and CBS had a recap in video then the credits rolled for about fifteen minutes. To most people, this would be nothing, but for me it was an emotional bulldozer that leveled me and incapacitated me. How could something so simple be so devastating? Reenter the film and add the captions and I believe we have the answer. You see, 1998 was the start of the end of the first half of my life to this point. So much happened during the games, though, that watching the end of the games makes me remember the end of that time span that February. During the games, it was the last time I had Paul and Josh over to my house. Dale Earnhardt won his only Daytona 500, and a no-name came out of nowhere to win gold in the figure skating. So many events happened, and in those credits come the captions of the times. This event differs on that it was multi-day, but with all the major events come these captions and tie-ins.

For Linda, captions of the times are anything associated with Sears Point Raceway, Tony Hawk's skateboarding feat of a 900, and JuJubees. When something major or minor happens that gets on the film, everything in life gets on the roll. To make yet another analogy, imagine a memory on steroids and that's what we have here.

For Emily, because it was such a prolonged relationship, there are too many things to mention, but what I just thought of is that these "triggers" I have mentioned would be better suited to be called captions or images from the pictures and snapshots. And to make these snapshots of life worse is that I don't remember the other person.

This paragraph I'm going to write next will probably be the hardest and deepest part of me I have ever exposed, but now I understand why it is the way it is ... In my most recent paper, I wrote that I could not write about my experience in Indianapolis in 2003. The shear mention of this will send shockwaves through every nerve in my entire body. What on earth, you are probably thinking, could cause such a commotion in me? Well, let me tell you. On that evening (one of the few evenings I remember during my bout, or rather consumption of Lexapro) I played a game of "Risk." Oh sure, you're thinking, everyone's problem is that darned "Risk" game, but there's more to this than trying to conquer Kamchatka. The people playing this game were of course me, and my friends Christopher, Matt, Kim, and Ashley. I've known each and every one of them for as far back as I can remember, and I want you to remember this sentence.

It was a great game, and Ashley and I worked great in taking over the game, and when it came down to just her and me, we decided to declare both of us winners. During the entire game, we never attacked each other once, and this was baffling to me at the time. Forever it had been that we were sort of rivals when it came to games. It was the classic Yankees vs. Red Sox clash that would always come down right to the wire. But in this instance, there was no Game 7, and, in fact, we worked together.

Later that evening, their mother, Anna, asked me how my relationship with Emily was going. I stated that things weren't going all that well and that I didn't actually care for Emily too much. Before I could finish that sentence, Ashley would not let me finish the sentence before telling me to get out of it then. She took over the conversation then and her mother went on to do other things, but then it left just me and her talking.

There was another sentence in that previous paragraph that is important to note, and that's the, "I don't particularly care for her." I always wanted Emily to be slightly different. Now if you use your imagination and think about what I have written so far, you might be able to deduce where I am going to go with this.

This was the first time in nearly five years that I actually spoke to Ashley because she was either at college or studying in Europe. We must have talked about all sorts of different matters for about two to three hours, and I had never felt so free. I usually would never let anyone know what I was thinking. I could go on about what I was thinking at the instance, but it would take me one hundred pages to finally use the right words to grasp the true power of the moment. So I won't try and describe the internal feelings, but rather why they were there. If you read that line that I wrote about "I knew them all my life," that answers it right there. If the film theory is true, and I believe it to be, then this family, and Ashley, in particular, was the first family I remember outside my own. Now, add on top of that the fact that I had never had a bad experience at any age there, so no bad pictures had been exposed on the film. When you add together my families (a first) with their family (a first) and no bad experiences (a first), then you really get a "first."

Yes, a first. Since she was the first girl I ever knew, all others, no matter who, would be compared to her. Regardless, if I like Ashley or not, she was the first one I knew. So from being four on to my current age, she was the "film" for girls. So, now, in this instance, on this fateful Christmas 2003, I was talking to her and was completely open. It was so seamless and easy because since the film was already there, I already was in my comfort zone. Another sentence you should've taken note of was that I had not spoken to her in five years. But for me, time doesn't work like it does for most people. Five years was nothing, and it was like those some 1600 days never existed and I was right back in the most recent snapshot I had.

When it was time for me to be picked up, it was over, but that snapshot was taken, and today it is sort of like the Pulitzer Prize-winning photo that is shown over and over. There is no respite from it, and there are so many captions that go along with that picture.

I don't know if there can be any erasing of the film. If there is, I do not know of it or how it would be possible. This theory may answer a lot of things, but it sure makes the future scary because, if it is true, losing things will be really hard. Even though I believe time is different for me, I haven't lost too many things in my life. The only things I can think of are three houses I lived in, contact with Emily, Linda, and Ashley, and Missy the Maltese. Other than that, though, my experience of loss has been minimal. How will I be able to live, though, thirty years from now?

Everything is about routine and sameness. If my theory is true, it is necessary to duplicate the film, whatever that film may be, each time and every time in exactly the same way. For me to find someone to know for a long time will be difficult because if they don't fit in the framework of previous films, compatibility will be quite difficult. This is a scary notion for me because to realize there's a difference or problem and to be unable to rectify it is downright terrifying.

Think about it. What if every small snippet of your childhood was fused into your brain and the hard drive couldn't be cleaned? Everything you learned that was a rule was added to the list of film and there was no compromise on any of it and the world would truly be a scary place. What one is taught in school is nowhere near what the real world is. Bad language is used, but why? I was told it was inappropriate, so then why do people use it? I was told that people don't do bad things, so then why do I hear on the news that a suicide bomber killed twenty-three people in the Middle East? What I was told and what film was developed and what is in the real world clash. But were the people who told me these things that I took to heart at fault? Of course not! How was anyone to know that every word they said was taken to heart by me and would be what I expected forever? There was no way anyone could have thought that something like that would happen. I always hear that people have a "coming of age" experience where they learn about the real world. I may never have one of those. Maybe my talk with Ashley, which was one hundred times more powerful than my talk with Linda, could classify as one you could say. But no, since she was a first, there was nothing new.

I don't think I've explained the film in my mind well enough. I truly mean it to be a literal term. Call it a photographic memory if you will. That could be where I get my hypervigilance because I remember every event every time, and if it's off by just a proverbial degree, I will pick up on it.

With the photographic nature of my mind, I do remember all events when not medicinally hindered. Therefore, my mind is constantly taking snapshots, but the mind film hasn't been taking as many photos as before. This is important.

I've read that some people with Asperger's don't find out, like me, until about age sixteen to twenty-two. Why is this? If film theory is correct, it's because normal people are erasing and throwing away old photos while the person with Asperger's is hanging onto the old photos. This is why there's a separation at that age. Around that age is the time that independence is attempted to be formed and rebellion against the norm is the norm. That rebellion is quite simply their mind producing new film and with new film comes new thought processes.

A stick in the mud is often referred to as someone who is stuck in his or her ways. Sadly, I qualify to be that proverbial stick. With my film, every friend should be like Matt, every girl that I would have the possibility to like would have to be like Ashley, every career I would want would have to be like racing, every time I go anywhere far I have to have a Red Bull, every time the Indy 500 rolls around I must go to a bookstore the day before the race, every time I write a piece the headline must be in eighteen-point. The list could go on and on, and each of the things mentioned above are film-related items. Maybe film is also a cause of OCD.

Whatever it may be, a person like me is completely petrified anytime someone tells me that everything is different and everyone is different, because for me if it isn't like I first knew it to be, it is downright terrifying. So with that said, maybe now the others can maybe understand just how scary the world is and how dire it can look from my eyes, because where you see change for the better, I see what was there before and always will.

THE DARK ROOM

(A supplement to "Film Theory")

This piece is written on the high chance that my "film theory" is true.

Somewhere in everyone's mind there is a dark room. A dark room is a room where film is developed and a picture is made. Before a dark room, the film is just on a roll, but after the transformation, it can be enlarged to any size. So what's the point of this mind dark room? People every day take mental snapshots of their days and a lot of film is simply thrown out. For me, however, my rolls of film have forty-eight exposures compared to the normal twenty-four. Now here's the important part: Every one of my exposures stays with me, and the entire context of the photo can be relived in a heartbeat.

I'm sure everyone has photos in their mind that stay with them, but does it affect them? Here is where I think I'm different. My photos are relived day in and day out in my routine. The photos have to be relived because they are almost burned into my vision of life.

This is a very complicated thing to put into words. I have found out that, for some unbeknownst reason, I have the ability to translate my unspeakable feelings into text, but this subject is quite difficult. It makes perfect sense it my head, but it will take time and paragraphs to get it perfect.

In "Film Theory," I mentioned that I believe my mind takes a photo of important events, and that photo is then etched in stone as law. I mentioned the bad language as one example, but there are more examples. I can remember when I was maybe four, and we (my dad and I) drove by a Big Lots and at the time I wanted candy so I asked if we could stop. My dad told me no because Big Lots has sticky floors. Now whether or not they do or don't is immaterial. What is important is that the photo of that sunny day back in 1987 I was told something and to this day it remains as law.

So this raises a question, is there a me? Have I ever made a photo by myself, or have they all have been influenced by third parties? At this point in time, I can only think of one and that is racing, and maybe that's why racing is so powerful to me.

Every time I go to a restaurant, I order the same thing. The origins of each food that I eat can be attested to someone choosing it for me, as I have never chosen a food for myself, and I believe me to be unable to do so. Food at a restaurant is such a minor thing compared to the workings of life; so if I have that sort of trouble at a restaurant, think about the fear of bigger choices.

The more I think about it, film theory must be true. But what makes it a major part of my life? Could it have been that from an early age my intellect understood the world too well but did not have the street knowledge to make sense of it all, so, therefore, my mind became reliant on these firsts to set the norm forever? Very well could be. And if it is, it makes for a difficult process ahead.

A lot was said in such few words in the prior paragraph. What if during the developmental cycle of my brain, part of me was more developed beyond what the processing side could handle, and therefore these photos and excessive laws came to be? This may be the origin of Aaron's dark room that's open 365 days a year and twenty-four hours a day.

My writing talents are best pronounced when telling a story, and right now I'm having trouble implementing a story. I could go on and on about little things on how I got my quirkiness in certain areas, and you know, that sounds like a good idea.

Since my dad was a pastor, I always heard about the right things. Bad things were just simply not allowed and that was that. There was no compromise when it came to things that weren't good, so that's how I assume I got so rigid in rules. As I always followed them, I could not understand why others would not. This was my main problem with

Emily. Granted, the rules in her situation weren't like cheating on me or anything, but rather simple things. But nowhere in my life was a line drawn and levels made of the severity of a rule break. To me a rule break is a rule break. There is no greater than another. I can see how this would make for an interesting and complicated relationship, because what I am essentially saying is perfection is required. The only thing that is perfect is God and the math formula 2+2=4. I'm pretty confident that no one will debate the two-plus-two part.

Where did perfection come about? To this I do not know the answer, but I think I can attest to the fact that in kindergarten and onward I was always the best at games and work so, therefore, if I could do it, why couldn't others? If I can be on time one hundred percent of the time, why couldn't Emily? How could she be tied up at work when I never had that problem?

Here's the main problem: If I wasn't exposed to something at an early age when the majority of film was being burned, I don't tolerate it. I lost at games when I was young (though not often) so, therefore, it is tolerated. What other things are kids given to make the body fight things? Vaccinations? While all the snapshots were being taken, if I didn't have one that "vaccinated" me for a situation, it simply is not tolerated.

If all of this is true, I have to say again that there are so many reasons why life would be so scary. How can one part of me realize that no one is perfect but expect perfection from others in the matter of timeliness and overall demeanor?

At my young age, all the "perfect" snapshots were taken. The epitomes of life were formed in my head and set in stone. These picturesque pieces of perfection are set for life in my head. What are these pictures? Here are a few that come to mind...

- Mediocrity is the end of life. To be on the mediocre spectrum of anything is not acceptable.

- Money is the key to happiness and also the root of all internal fears.

- Winning isn't required. Respect from the competition is the real way to win at a game.

Those are some things that come to mind that are on a podium, but at the same time, along my life, others photos were taken that aren't as positive (the money one up above may not necessarily be a good one) made their way onto that same podium, and they are ...

- I am completely unlikable for reasons unknown.

- Bad things happen to me by the bucketful (this one has been proven true).

- People in general aren't good; evil is everywhere because the rules aren't followed.

So, from that last line, if a rule is broken, that makes someone evil? Sadly, at times it does. If I hear someone use a bad word, I immediately lose all respect for him or her. There is no reason why one should use improper language, but yet time and time again people do, and this puzzles me.

If you did read my "Film Theory" then you read the story of how I know Matt, Christopher, Kim, and Ashley. Not once in my life has anything so slightly occurred that made me lose any respect for them, and, therefore, to me, that is the perfect environment. This is what makes that Christmas talk so strong and lingering. Whatever was going on in the conversation side between her and me was accompanied by the fallacy of my perception of perfection.

The conversation reminded me of my talks with Linda, and one thing that I learned for no logical reason from that was that I was never going to be able to have that sort of open conversation again. Once again, I believe that to be true.

I'm much like a mile-long train without brakes going down an infinite hill. Once the train is pushed, there is no stopping it; so too with my brain and its photos. Once something has been pushed off the side of the hill, it will go on forever. So, as a young one, when learning new things every day, just imagine how many mile-long trains were being pushed. Everything that I learned became a picture and got aboard a train and departed into the depths of an infinite trip. All it takes is one thing, one minor insignificant thing, to launch a train.

With a mind like mine it never stops. Thinking is always going on, and calculating of the future never ceases. With so much thought, one little thing can throw a wrench into the works of my mind, and a train with a photo is launched. Take, for example, a certain e-mail exchange. I e-mailed Ashley about travel advice before I went to Lithuania and thanked her in an e-mail when I got back. Now when I had that conversation back in 2003, I asked if we'd be able to have a talk like that sometime in the future and I got a positive response. But when I got back and sent her a thank-you letter and a little about the trip, I received no reply. Instantly, all was lost. Matt, her brother, had told me that she was always experiencing e-mail difficulty, but that was irrelevant. I could not think on the theory that she never received it, because my e-mail said it was sent, so instantly I knew that I would never hear from her again. Why this drastic thinking I do not know, but that's the way I have always been. I cannot trace back to why my thinking always leans toward the apocalyptic side of things, but that's the way I am. Somewhere in my life, there's a picture that tells me that good things never happen, therefore, think the worst. I can't comprehend that maybe it was accidentally deleted, or maybe it was lost in one of this world's many servers, but all I know is that there was no response and that will be the end of the story.

And, now, not to sound like a broken record, maybe the world can see why things are always gloomy for me. For me, if something is unknown, it is immediately filed under the "it's bad," or "it's never happening" files.

So back to this dark room … Most photographers throw out the bad photos and pick the best ones, but for me, all photos remain.

A photo is an event in my life that either happened to me or I heard about. These photos were then taken to heart and etched in stone. After that, they became my reality. In my mind, the big photos are not bound by the laws of time. If thought about, I instantly return to that time period. For the rules, photos are forever the templates of why I do what I do. Call them programs if you want, or photos, or experiences, but whatever they are, they are there, and they don't want to go anywhere. My dark room has a slot for the picture to go in, but the door is locked and there is no way to take photos out. With that being so, all the things that have gone bad stay and hope can't be found. I know this is why I am normally hopeless, and I will need to think more on the correlation between these two, but I am fairly confident that the two are most certainly related.

I will write more on this subject, but for now I am at a loss for words and don't want to repeat myself over and over, so I'll close by saying that I know one can't live a happy life when one can't see hope. Hope is what makes one get up in the morning. Hope is what sparked revolutions. Hope is the essence of happiness. And for me hope isn't in the dictionary. Maybe I should check the thesaurus.

OPEN LETTER

This is an open letter to whoever has met me and had a non-normal experience.

I start by saying I'm sorry. I'm sorry that I am not like you. At first, I know at times there may seem to be no difference, but trust me, inside I am thinking completely different thoughts. What's important to you may have no relevance to me, and things that I'm thinking about may never have crossed your mind. While you've been talking about what band merged with what, I've been considering the financial ramifications if North Korea launches a nuclear missile.

It's not that I'm not fully interested; it's just that what you're talking about is irrelevant. I know that sounds very harsh, but it is sadly true.

When at a store I may seem very stoic and almost catatonic, and in a way, I am. I have noticed my eyes are always down and to the left away from the person speaking to me. When I speak, however, eye contact is partially made, but in that in-between, it must seem to them that I am retarded or developmentally disabled. What makes me scream inside is I yearn to be able to go into a store and have no hesitation when I check out to make eye contact, but I simply can't. This is often taken that I'm looking down on them or that I don't care and that couldn't be further from the truth. It's just that there are so many thoughts going on at once, I simply cannot function.

When life becomes very stressful, I start to become more and more prone to being uncommunicative. Yesterday, as I walked into the kitchen, my dad asked me, "What's wrong?" I guess from looking at me, one would think something must be wrong, but my expression was just that of what I had at the store a week ago. It's a look of deep thought, but the expression can easily be mistaken for either not caring or being deeply depressed. As much as it is confusing for those around me, it is painful for me.

This is one of the problems Emily and I may have had. If my writings were ever turned into a book and she were to read this, this is what I would write to her in an open letter:

> Emily, I know things must've been confusing. I can't apologize enough for some of the wackiness that occurred. I know that just the slip of the tongue on your part could make me go into a tizzy, and while you must have been confused, I was screaming on the inside. If I had never known, officially, that I had Asperger's, I don't know if things would have been better or worse in the long run. You said I changed when I found out, and I probably did. At first, I had denial. Then there was a brief stint of anger and finally a long bout of anger and confusion.
>
> To get the answer of why one is the way they are when they've been wondering their entire life is an odd experience to say the least. I took this as a death sentence. It had been a year up until today that I saw you in person, as on my way to the movie theater I stopped in where you work and ordered some chicken noodle soup for lunch. I am unaware if you saw me, but after I entered, you disappeared, so I have to assume you saw me. While you may or may not have hidden, it was a milestone for me. It was like a passing of time that had to be done.
>
> I don't know how wacky I was during the Lexapro era, but I never have understood why you were talking to me around May to August of last year and now there's nothing. Granted, I have been unable to call you, and maybe my text messages have not gotten to you, but I wonder every day how you are.
>
> Emily, I don't think you or anyone without Asperger's

could understand the pain that is felt by the one who has it. I know it's the cards that life dealt, but I really wish that I wasn't stuck with the two and seven, off suit. What is it like to be you? What is it like to be able to get over somebody? What is it like to be in a social circle larger than four? How can you accept change? How can you move on? These questions get repeated daily, and I wish I could just ask you.

In the end, our relationship probably strengthened both of us, as now if I know anyone for more than a year I will under no circumstances do anything that may sever communication. I so miss dialing your phone number, but that's the way it is. Whether or not Asperger's played a roll in it is irrelevant. What is relevant is that regardless of what happened, a strong friendship was destroyed. Could it have been Asperger's or Lexapro? I don't have that answer, and I apologize for any oddities that happened. I am what I am, and I apologize for that. Maybe someday I'll get another call like the one you gave me on December 30 of last year just to tell me how you were. I know, though, that I will be unable to call you, as my mind has too many calculations of which way the conversation will go. I wish you the best, and again I hate the way things turned out.

That would be the sort of letter I would give her. There are a lot of things in that letter that have bigger ramifications. One of which is the extreme fear of loss. If I meet someone and they are horrible for me, but enough time passes, the fear of loss may create a trap. I partially had that after I severed my communication with Linda, but now that photo has been blown up and enlarged and is large enough to be a billboard on the side of the interstate.

The other thing is the big fear if a person with Asperger's can be accepted? I fear that answer because I am afraid that it is a very big no. How can anyone put up with someone who tries to be perfect and expects the same? How can someone accept someone who fears every possibility and calculates all the possibilities of any given scenario? Emily knew me for nearly four years, and as soon as that "A" word was mentioned she ran faster than the runners at the Running of the Bulls in Pamplona, Spain. Maybe it was just a scapegoat on her part, and then again maybe it wasn't, but for me, that was the reason it ended.

Imagine for a second you have a stable relationship, and years down the road you get a small skin discoloration that's not cancerous, it's just a different shade. Even though that different color pigment doesn't change who you are, or who you were, your friend takes off running and barely say goodbye with no understanding that the discoloration doesn't change a thing about you. This is what it was like for me.

Being diagnosed with anything doesn't change the person; it just gives them a label. If someone knows the person after they've been labeled, then they know that, but if someone knows the person before and then after there is, or rather there shouldn't be, any change, as the person doesn't change. Complicated sentence I know, but it is a really deep thought.

Maybe one problem is misunderstanding. Of people I come across, less than approximately five percent have ever heard of Asperger's. With the misunderstanding of the condition comes misunderstanding of the actions, with that comes friction, and then ultimately a termination of a connection.

With having such a photographic memory, I feel the pain of each of these every day. I always wonder if Emily truly forgives me for whatever reason. I know I've been angry at her since I broke up with her. (Yes, you read that last sentence correctly.)

Asperger's could easily be compared to a board game. Let's take my favorite, "Monopoly," as an example. If you play it more than once, you should have a general idea of what happens if you roll a seven from "Go." In that instance, you would land on "Chance." Then a ten from there takes you to "Community Chest." And then X takes you to Y and so forth and so on. But with Asperger's, it would be like playing Monopoly in the blind. I roll the dice, but I have no idea the results of the roll. This is a great example of my relationship with Emily. I took the roll and broke up with her, trying to get some emotion from her. And what I expected from the roll was to land on Boardwalk, thus completing my Monopoly, but instead I was way off and I landed on Free Parking (which is on the opposite side, in case you are Monopoly illiterate).

The scary thing is I know this will happen again, and again, and tragically again. This isn't a self-fulfilling prophecy, but rather what the odds show because history repeats itself. So I ask again, how can anyone accept a person with Asperger's? How can one accept a person who thinks they are driving on the interstate, but rather they are off in a cornfield in the middle of nowhere? It's almost as if I'm living in an alternate universe where all things, according to the odds and how I think they should go, should happen. Why? Because if I have concluded that the odds are better than fifty-one percent, things should happen. But when things don't go the way I expect them to go, everything ends up in limbo.

I don't know if Emily will ever truly understand how I felt about her and what she meant for me. She was why I took that semester of college. She is why I kept bowling. She is why I have to eat at Fortel's on Monday nights. She is why I cringe at the mention of her name, her place of work, and anything that is connected to her. But the thing is, I doubt she will ever realize that even though I was probably rather emotionless on the outside, on the inside I was so at ease.

As time went by with Linda, it kept getting worse. Much like a pendulum that's swing gets larger on each pass, so does the pain of the memory. I knew Linda for less than fifteen hours in person and less than a year overall, and the pain can be debilitating. I knew Emily for four years, and the pendulum has just started swinging. If Linda hurt so bad, yet I knew her for so short, how bad will Emily eventually get?

The thing about these two isn't that there was "love" there, but for brief moments, I was at ease on the inside. Almost as if I was understood, you could say. I don't know if love is in my emotional dictionary, but what was most important was that I was at ease, and to lose that stability due to my inducing it hurts beyond belief. This makes the future scary. History repeats itself; I am unable to learn from the past, and the question has got to be asked, Will I make the same mistake for a third time, and is there any preventing it?

INTERMISSION

Just a note from Dad... I think you are somewhere near the halfway point of this book. I also think it might be time to stretch a little. Aaron probably seems like a pretty depressed person; much of the time he is. But Aaron also has benefited from his depression. How? You are reading it.

These pages are a unique form of therapy that... that... well, that has done more than I think any therapist could have done. One of the goals of any therapist is to bring the client to a point of self-discovery and self-realization. Denial, avoidance, projection, transference are all mechanism that can stand in the way of effective, helpful therapy.

As Dr. Cameron said,

> I think it is important to note that unlike most current books on the subject of Asperger's, this is not a "how to" (treat symptoms, etc.), but a "how did" book. It is Aaron's intensely personal journey, begun half unconsciously, its "purpose" emerging intuitively. The process has been self-healing, but the product, like many literary "journeys"— from Homer and Dante to James Joyce's re-visitation of Homer's hero in "Ulysses"—Aaron's writings speak to us all. When he came to realize its potential value to others, he unselfishly decided to share it with others.

There is something else about Aaron. His willingness to confess his shortcomings, his ability to describe his pain, and his ability to construct theories has not only had an impact on me, his father, but also Dr. Cameron.

> One of the "changed lives" has been my own. Aaron's writings and our conversations have granted me clinical insights, a new understanding, and subsequently more effective care for my other clients with autistic-spectrum disorders.
>
> Much of the material about Asperger's is written by clinicians, therapists, and parents. All of this is based on observation of behaviors, or lack thereof, and an attempt to explain these aberrations. Some material has been written by those suffering from Asperger's and has offered much to the understanding of this disorder. But I believe there is something that sets Aaron's work in a field by itself.

Not only does Aaron talk about the "how did," as Dr. Cameron said, but he also explores the "whys." Several special education teachers read some of Aaron's compositions before the book was finished. All of them, really, all of them were amazed and said things like, "I've always wondered why my AS students did what they did. Aaron has answered the questions."

Dr. Cameron even took Aaron to the Missouri School for the Blind and utilized him to interpret the behavior of some of the students with autism. Dr. Cameron was amazed at Aaron's ability to understand the "why" of certain behaviors.

One of the biggest challenges I have had is that of learning how to communicate with Aaron at a deeper level than racing, games, or travel. I have learned that the best time to talk with Aaron is when he is depressed and racing on-line: both at the same time. When he is in his element of racing, the many barriers that stand in the way most of the time are not there.

I really don't understand how he can race against ten or fifteen other players, fighting to keep his number-one rank and still be able to talk about things that he normally can't. It is like something happens when he exists online.

What it makes me think of is that dog guy on cable. I'm not going to use his name or the cable channel because I have ADD and will probably not get around to getting permission, etc. Anyway, when he rehabilitates a dog that chases bicycles while on a walk, the dog guy will have someone ride by on a bike. The moment the dog starts to react to the bike, the dog guy reaches around with his foot and taps the dog on the fanny. Bam! The dog is looking around, trying to figure out what happened. The dog guy describes it as bringing the dog into the "now." While trying to figure out what hit him on the butt, he forgets that he is supposed to be chasing the bike.

When Aaron is racing on-line, or flagging at the track, or driving, he is living in the "now." When he is in the "now," the past and future do not have the power they normally do. He will tell me, especially when he is depressed, that he wants to talk. It has gotten to the point that I will only talk with him if he is racing on-line: in the now. This activity has the power to neutralize the power of those things that plague Aaron the most.

Well, enough from Dad. Get a drink. Go to the bathroom. Sit back, because the best is yet to come.

MAYBE ...

Maybe today will be the day. Maybe today will be the day that things are figured out. There are so many things that apply to what could be on any given day. Maybe something, anything will happen today. My existence is a hard one, and maybe today will be the day. Could today be the day I lose the painful memories? Or could today be the day that, out of the blue, I receive a phone call that changes my life forever?

There are so many things that could be and need to be. Perhaps maybe today is the day that the world may get a slight glimpse into the world of a person who has Asperger's. Maybe somebody somewhere will have an inkling of a notion on understanding it, and then they may share that with others and maybe, just maybe, over time, the pain and agony will be known.

But then again, maybe the pain and suffering don't have to be. Maybe I will just become normal. Likely not, but maybe it could happen. Maybe I will learn what life is about today, tomorrow, or this month. What makes the world tick? What does one have to do to know happiness? Maybe today I will find out.

There are so many maybes that it makes the mind boggle. Perhaps the maybes will be reduced today. I could live in a world of knowing and having no maybes, but yet I would find a way to look and live and be stuck in the maybes.

Maybe today is the day that the names of people won't send shivers up my spine. Could today be the day that the current becomes the past and the future becomes the now? The present has been so for nearly five years. What will it take to allow the future to come to the present? It's so difficult to be stuck like this, but maybe today will be the day that all that will change.

This is the world I live in. Like a car on the side of a highway with a flat, I'm not going anywhere fast. The only things I have right now are the maybes. A maybe has never been a safe bet, and it is not a fun world to be in. Every day I hope that just one maybe will become true. I wake up every day hoping, wishing that maybe that phone call or e-mail will come. Sadly for me, I go to sleep every day with the same wish I had the night before.

What is even more aggravating is the fact that for the most part I am powerless to change what is. And on top of that is the fact that little of the population has a clue about why I am the way I am. When people ask certain questions like, "Do you have a job, or do you work?" and I say no to both and then they look perplexed, I know that the next question is, "Well, what do you do?" To explain what I have is like trying to sell an ice cream machine in northern Alaska. In other words, they look at me like I'm speaking French and they speak Japanese.

So as the sun is four hours from breaking, maybe today will be the day that my life will start again. Maybe today is the day...

"MIRROR" AND/OR "FROZEN IN TIME"

A confusing title, I know, but for you, the reader, I envy you because the confusion of the title is nothing in comparison to the actual feeling.

When one looks in a mirror, what do they see? There are so many things to see and recall. One may have a scar from a childhood fall, or one may see the early signs of aging. When one looks in a mirror, they see themselves, but when do they see themselves? The reason I have the split titles is that they go hand in hand with the issue.

When I look in a mirror, I see an image of a twenty-two-year-old. Now reread that sentence. What I said I see and what I left out is important. What I said is that I see an image of a twenty-two-year-old. If things were normal, I would have said that I saw a twenty-two-year-old and not the image. For me, when looking in a mirror, I see what used to be, and by that I mean way back in time.

I know I have stated the whole time thing and how the concept of time is lost on me, but it is really present when I look in a mirror. I do not see myself as I am now but as I used to be. I don't know if it's like that for everyone, and maybe to a certain extent it is for people, but for me, it is very extreme.

The question can be asked though, "Well, Aaron, when do you see yourself?"

A very good question, but the answer is a difficult one.

I can narrow it down to the years 1994 to 1998. Somewhere in there I stopped something. What that something is I do not know. But in my mind, that is the time period I am supposed to be in. So when I look in the mirror, I am somewhat confused that there is this image of a twenty-two-year-old when there should be a fourteen-year-old. Maybe it's like this because inside that's what my equivalent age is.

An interesting occurrence happened over the last weekend. I was doing my flagging/race-directing duties, and there was an incident in which I had to black-flag someone. My first premonition in my mind was, I can't do this, and I have no power and am too young to make a call.

The last sentence in the previous paragraph can be used in so many instances in my life. I don't know if this is Asperger's-induced; I have to assume it is in some way, but it is a very perplexing thing to have. Why is it so weird? Well, since I have the authority at the track to make the calls, why would I think about my age? It has nothing to do with the fear of making the wrong call because I will never make that mistake. For me to bring out the black, I have to have a feeling of one hundred-percent conviction to do so. So, if that's the case, why do I have this age problem?

In the end, the guy ignored my flag and drove around four or five times before actually stopping on-track to ask why he was being black-flagged. I told him why, and naturally he was upset, and I was aggravated that it took him nearly twenty-five percent of the race distance to finally heed the flag. But the ramifications from this are greater than him endangering the lives of others on-track by stopping and ignoring me. The greater ramifications are that, in those minutes, I realized that I am frozen in time.

There is no more depressing song than the CBS Olympic Theme. I may have mentioned this before; if so, you'll hear so again. But how can a song for the Olympics on a television station cause such depression? During those minutes on-track, I finally had the answer. The years I mentioned earlier, 1994–1998, also coincide with the Winter Olympic Games. It might seem coincidental, but let's take a look at what was going on in those years.

The 1994 Games in Lillehammer were at or about the same time I started my life here in St. Louis. The school I was going to was a living nightmare, and getting acquainted with the new city and new way of the locals was very taxing. This could be the start of when I started to stop developing somewhere in the brain.

The 1998 Games in Nagano happened at the closing of the chapter of school. I have so many memories of these games, but not because of the games themselves, but rather surrounding events. During the 1998 games, I had Ryan over to my house two or three times, and I also had Josh and Paul over for two consecutive nights. So in a nutshell, during this time, the descriptor of "normality" could be applied.

Also occurring during the 1998 games was the conclusion of my school career; now, granted, it had been three months, but it was finally sinking in. So as 1994 was the start of an era, the 1998 games was the end of one. It was more than an end of an era, though. Something happened during this time period that made something change about me. Remember that the names of Emily and Linda aren't even in my realm of imagination at this point in time. So what happened in this time period that made everything change? Maybe I can write more and figure it out.

I was always ahead of my fellow students in school. Not in grades mind you, but in demeanor, overall logic, and knowledge of the over-all world, I was light years ahead. Again, as I said before, reread that sentence. Notice that I did not mention one thing about interpersonal relationships. All the way back as I can remember, relationships weren't an issue because they were deemed irrelevant. This may be a factor in why the games of 1998 are so relevant.

Why would they be relevant though? I think I have a good answer. One can go through their entire school career and not need relation-ships. School in my mind is much like prison, and the only objective is to do what you're told and nothing more. That was how I attacked that evil thing called school. Others used it as a means to socialize and what not, but for me socializing wasn't needed, as I always had one or, at the most, two friends I would do things with. That's great and all, but what about the 1998 games of Nagano being relevant? Hang on, I'm getting there.

Nineteen ninety-eight marked the year that I turned fifteen. People grow throughout their years, and the years between thirteen and twenty-one are very important. But what happens if someone like me gets left at the station? Take, for instance, a graph like a stock market. If overall socializing development were kept of a running graph with the far left being age zero and the end being the present, the results would be interesting. Let's say there's one line for me and another line for the average person. At around age ten, the lines would probably have been fairly close. But in 1998 something happened and my line went flat. I didn't lose my stock value, but it just remained the same while everyone else cashed in on a bull market as it continued to soar. This is frozen in time!

If development of something (I'm sorry, but I don't know exactly what it could be) stopped in any which way, I would be locked in the time when that stopped because that time period and all things surrounding it would be all I know.

Don't get me wrong, I have learned new things and have done different things, but have there been socializing developments? In my opinion, no. It may seem so in my previous writings, but everything that I wrote for the most part were new experiences; therefore, there can be no comparison to how I dealt with something than to how I reacted pre-1998. So the bottom line of this is that while the "first theory" still holds true, the things that I had experienced up until 1998 have not changed. The programming I was programmed with up until 1998 has not changed.

I often have to remind myself of my age. When asked my age, I often have a reflexive response that wants to respond with fifteen or eighteen, but twenty-two never comes to mind. It's much like that my life since 1998 has been nothing more than a dream. And maybe it has, or maybe it hasn't, but whatever the case, I am here in the now writing this as confused as can be.

If my "frozen in time" theory holds true, it will back up the first theory because, developmentally, if I had a freeze on that, I would have all the previous firsts intact. This isn't necessarily that big of an issue in most cases, but for me it is. All the beliefs and wants I had at the time in 1998 have remained just the same to this day. This answers a lot of questions about why certain things are the way they are with me. This may also be a key somehow, someway in unlocking Asperger's.

Think about it for a second. From the little stuff I have read about the syndrome, the symptoms are sometimes not noticed until later in life. Why would that be? I think it is because they get frozen in a time period. If this is true, it would answer a lot of questions about me. I know that.

Back to the actual games of 1998 for a moment. On the last night of the games, I taped it so I could hear that song and preserve memories of the thrills and spills of that Olympiad. In the programming that was taped, CBS ran their fifteen minutes worth of credits. During this, they had many of the production assistants, cameramen, and various other personnel on camera. They did various things while talking to the camera. Many just said hello to loved ones, some goofed off, and others just did nothing much. Whatever each person did made me very sad. Those images and words or actions are frozen in time. The happiness that was shown on camera might not still be—some of them may be dead, others may have had a horrible time since—but on that tape for fifteen minutes, happiness and love abounded. It's very much like a world I wish existed in which things remain the same with no change except the threat of someone taping over it.

I don't think the 1998 Games in itself had anything to do with whatever happened in me, but it's just that it's the most significant milestone that happened around the time that things changed. For me, I am still in 1998. The big party that was the eve of 2000 never happened, my driving of a racecar never took place, and my international trips are still years away. It's rough living in two time periods, but that's the closest thing I can describe to you what this is like. Like I said at the start of this piece, this is confusing, and I envy you because however confused you are, I am one hundred times more so.

Don't get me wrong, all my memories about all the events that took place after 1998 are there. It's just that developmentally nothing has changed. The same fears are there, the same desires are there, and the same emotions are there. It's as if a flower was growing, and while it was halfway to being fully developed, all development was stopped, but it still lived. This isn't the most perfect example, because one would notice the defect with the flower, but with me, only if you look closely enough you will see the differences.

Something stopped on that fateful year of 1998. The year I write this is 2005. I am twenty-two years old in image only.

WHAT DOES
IT MEAN ...

Answers from My Point of View

... to survive? This is a tricky answer, because I do not know the complete answer. Emotionally speaking, survival is obtainable when the stressors are at a minimal state. Money issues play into that. To work to survive is not programmed into my brain. To make little by little to get to a point is way too stressful, so the actual work of making the little money is worse than having no money. It's sort of like a "go big or go home" attitude. That mode of thought is very discouraging because I realize my shortcomings.

... to love? My mom once asked me if I loved. She was speaking in general for that question, but other times it was more directed toward if I loved her. I never thought about the actual emotion of love before that though. It was always a reflexive response, because if person A says that, person B should respond with the same.

As I thought about my answer, I instantly became jammed. Five minutes passed. Ten minutes passed. As the minutes ticked away as painfully slow as a bad infomercial, I could not think of anything to say. Finally, I came up with the line, "I'd miss you if you were gone." That was it. This is all I know about love. There is nothing deeper.

Maybe when it comes to love, that's as good as it gets. I don't know really though. Of course I said I'd miss you if I were gone, but more so, because that would mean there would be a change in the world.

I can't put into words the deep sorrow this gives me. To see others who appear to be in love and knowing that quite possibly my deepest emotion of love I will ever feel is of an "I'd miss you if you were gone" variety is so, so sorrowful.

…be happy? Happiness for me is when I am completely disassociated with the world. I get this feeling when I'm driving a racecar. While driving, like I've mentioned now what must be one thousand times, it's just me and the car as one on a track. Relationships don't matter, living doesn't matter, and the only thing that matters is going .1 of a second faster. Even though I think about the rest of the world while driving, it actually for that time makes sense.

Happiness is also days that I flag. It is also sorrowful to think about those days because it could be used as an analogy of Asperger's. How so, you ask? Just as in a normal social situation, I am isolated. Most contact comes via the radios, which means that it isn't immediate personal contact. The key thing is that I am alone, yet functioning. What I do when flagging I do to the best of my ability, just like everything else I do, and just like everything else, it doesn't involve other people. So while flagging is one of my more happy times, it is still a stark reminder of what I have because the two are very similar if I look at it the right way.

Happiness comes in memories, which in turn causes sadness. My memories get turned around. For instance, I know for a fact that I wasn't too happy to be with Emily, and I'm even reminded about that from people, yet the happy memories are so overwhelming that I am so distraught that I do not know her anymore. This way of thinking goes down the board. Most eras of my life that were generally bad get turned around in the present and are made to look like they were really good. This way of my memories may go to prove my "stuck in time" theory. In any case, it is so very hard to know what happiness is in the present when happiness in memories is overwhelming, and, in fact, happiness in my memories wasn't really happiness at the time of the memory. So how can one be happy when they don't even know what it is on a whole?

To live, one must have a purpose and a reason. To drift from day to day, month to month, and year to year with no destination is not conducive to a happy state of being. Unlike others who have a driftwood state of being their entire lives, I know what I want. But right now I'm not doing what I want, which gives me a driftwood-like appearance. This is most aggravating, because I am not like that. When people ask me what I do, and why I'm not in school, I have no answer that they will understand. The general public would better understand thermodynamics than the ways of an Asperger's.

Think about that last line of the last paragraph for a second. To be where I am so distraught and sad, and to have most people having no understanding except the thoughts of, Well, maybe he's lazy, or, Maybe he's retarded? is so aggravating that it makes the arteries in my body pulse with extreme rage. There is no happiness here, and it happens day in and day out.

If I were told I had the chance to never leave the house again and that all food and services would be provided for in my house, I would not hesitate for a second to take a person up on that offer.

… to be good? To be good means to be the best. If one tries something, they should try and give it everything they've got. The ultimate goal in anything in my opinion is to be nothing short of number one. For me, if I can't be better than the average, then there is no reason to do it. I haven't found many things that aren't worth doing (except anything artistic).

This mode of thought clashes with the general public though. My mindset is the same in the workplace, and therefore I hate slackers. In every normal job I've had, eventually I get to the point of the realization that no matter how good I am it doesn't matter. Being the best in speed at the bank won't help me secure happiness. Selling a horde of magazines at the video game store won't help me get more of anything. In every workplace, I was typically overall the best performer, but what's the worth of it? Why be good? Why try like heck to sell the magazines when there is nothing in it for me? I would make the same if I just sat around and barely did enough to keep the job.

Those questions are what eventually make me go temporarily crazy. I must be the best, but why do I try so hard when it gets me nothing? One could argue with me that self-knowledge of being the best would be enough. I would make the counterpoint that unless it is shown or stated that I am the best, then I don't know it. I did "say" that I was the best earlier in this piece, but I am going on statistics alone. I never knew if I actually was the best.

This is another field that is so aggravating. This goes along with the survival question. If I didn't care, I could just do the job and cash my check on Fridays. Unfortunately for me though, I have all this other baggage. Unless it's big, then it isn't worth doing. Why be normal? Why conform to the status quo of society? If one is good, shouldn't they be rewarded for it?

... to be friends? A very painful question indeed, because I do not know what a "friend" is, nor do I know how to make them, what to do when the rank of "friend" is achieved, nor do I know who calls me friend.

... to be alone? This is much like a coin as this has two sides. On one side, I love it. There is no conflict minus the self-conflict, there are no added stressors, there is no worrying what the other person is thinking, and there is no need to be concerned about anything about anyone else.

However, I have known what it is like to not be alone. Life is more interesting with others. One would be unable to climb Mount Everest without a team. One would be unable to do much of anything without others. So is there no happy medium? Well, there isn't. This is very paradoxical. And living within a paradox is very confusing to say the least.

If others typically only let me down, then why know others? But without others, what is there to do for the rest of life that would make life not so mundane?

Others are unpredictable, but the predictability of being alone is so predictable that it is downright painful.

The point/counterpoint could go on forever, and for me the two are in equilibrium. Neither side has more of a pro or a con, so, therefore, as mentioned, I am living in a paradoxical world. Not fun in the least.

... to be the best at any given thing? This is sort of like the question about being good, but this question is about when the facts are clear that I am the best. I do have an easy and sad answer to say about when I know I am the best ... there's just emptiness. There's nothing. There's more substance in a book of blank pages than there is joy in my head when I know I am the best. When I got the number-one score overall in Forza, the jubilation I felt was non-existent.

So why do I strive to be the best and when it is achieved I feel nothing? It's much like a dog chasing its tail. While the dog has the goal to catch the tail, it won't know what to do with it once it catches that wagging tail. Much so like me. I chase and work and struggle to get to be the best, but when I get there, I don't know how or what to feel. The only thing I feel is something along the lines of, Well, that's where I should be. The emotion of joy simply doesn't exist for me.

... to know or want something and be unable to do anything about it? This question has a huge umbrella of topics it could pertain to, but the answer for the most part will be the same.

To know what I want and to see it pass me by is much like watching a train going down the tracks and seeing a car in the distance parked on the tracks. The only thing you'd be able to do is watch helplessly as the speeding train obliterates the parked car and any occupants. This happens to me every day, except in my case, I am in the parked car. Day in and day out I get hit by many speeding trains; trains symbolize many different things.

What various things? There are many. One is just the art of talking to others. To want to talk and to be powerless is much like stalling on the tracks. To want to talk to someone in particular and to be powerless is the most helpless, saddening feeling in the world. It's not that I don't want to talk to others (believe me, I really want to!), but it could be just as a blind person wishes to see ... they're unable.

... to be comfortable? The first answer, as predictable as it may be, is to be in a racecar. Outside of that, there aren't many. Well, now outside the walls of my home, there are none because I'll probably never be at my friend's house in Indianapolis because now he's married. I may be there at some point in time, but it certainly couldn't be the same. I have worried about the coming of that day since I was about ten and, until now, have felt nothing of it. Virtually, my only other place of comfort is somewhat gone now. And the thing is, they probably don't even know what they have meant for me.

I know I have sidetracked from the "comfortable" part of this question, but bear with me.

I have so many memories with that family, and, as I have written before, I don't remember people in my memories. Why is this relevant? Because I can only recognize someone if I see them in person. Once I recognize them, I remember everything that happened when I first saw them; for instance, three days ago I saw a police officer shooting a radar gun on a road. It's a rather slow road, so I was able to recognize him, and instantaneously I recalled that this same officer had been shooting radar about a mile down the road … six months earlier. He had been shooting radar when I was ordering at Steak and Shake and I was about a week or so from going to Africa.

Why is this relevant? Because things will never be the same in Indy, and for all I know I will only have memories, and without seeing them in person my memories will just include me and only blurred images of them. If I see a person, they get inserted perfectly into my memories, but ten minutes later they're a blur again.

… to be me? One word: painful!

WHAT WILL BECOME?

Just a note from Dad... When I was a young boy growing up in Oklahoma City, I developed a phobia of tornadoes. I'm pretty sure it began when I was five years old and saw The Wizard of Oz at the Yale Theater in the Capitol Hill shopping area. It didn't help that my father had the same phobia. My phobia came to an abrupt end one afternoon as I watched news crew from Wichita, Kansas, get caught on the interstate with a tornado bearing down on them. The reporter and cameraman got under an overpass, and the tornado went by and they didn't die. It was amazing.

For a number of years now, Aaron has been confronted with the reality that I will not always be here. On 9/11 I sat on the couch with him and we watched the two towers in Manhattan collapse. He sobbed. "What about all those children who won't have a dad or mom come home from work?"

This fear of losing me is a great burden for both him and me. I think that's one reason why I take him a lot of places with me when I shoot video. If I'm going to die in an accident, I want him with me. It seems that I couldn't live without him and he couldn't live without me.

What will become of the future? There are so many variables in life, and they are impossible to calculate. I apologize for my stating of the obvious, but for me variables are just gasoline to an already blazing inferno. After another night of very realistic dreams and hearing on the news that Al-Qaida may be planning an "American Hiroshima" by Christmas, the variables have been intensified.

So what do dreams at night and the threat of nuclear terrorism have in common? In their own, they have no common thread, but when I look at them, they are both reminders of the world I live in. That world would be the world in which I am unable to change my surroundings. I don't dwell on the threat of terrorism, so I won't cover that too much in this piece, but I will try and explain the thread between the two.

If I could have my wish, I would never dream another dream again. A dream is a powerful medium in which one can learn a lot about oneself. You can also see their shortcomings because in a dream a coward can be fearless, a deaf person can hear, a blind person can see, and a paralyzed person can once again walk. For me, nothing is as extreme as those mentioned in the prior sentence, but for me, in dreams I can talk, I can be fearless with other people, I can do the things that I can't on a normal basis, and most of all, during those dreams, the word of "variable" doesn't exist.

Take out the variables and I can function quite normally. Sadly for me, we live in a world with as many variables as there are stars in the sky. I get lost in the thought of the variables because my mind must try and know everything that's going on so I can properly prepare for any and all circumstances. This is where the timing of hearing about the possible attacks plays in. What will happen if they do happen? What changes in the world will occur? Will any people I know be directly affected? Those questions are just more endless variables, but with the timing of the dreams I had last night, it is a stark reminder that time is passing.

I feel as if I am someone caught in a time flux. I am aware of my surroundings, but because I am so wrapped up in my own mind, I am unable to see that time is passing by. Every once in a while, I will instantaneously become aware of what has happened since the last time I realized the concept of time. Case in point would be last June ... I was flagging a practice session, and someone gave me an opportunity to drive their kart. I took them up on the offer and later that day I was driving that kart. On about the tenth lap, the left rear tire came off in a very fast turn, and instead of thinking about the fact that this may really hurt, my only thought was, Oh my, it's 2004, and it's June. Where did the time go and who am I now?

It was the most surreal feeling I have ever felt. It was as if I suddenly reappeared in this world after being on autopilot. As the kart spun, it nearly rolled over, and while it was happening I was aware of it, but my only thoughts during the two-second ordeal was re-connecting with the past twelve months. And it was during that incident that I first realized in its fullest form that I wasn't talking to Emily anymore.

So what will become of all this? How can I live with all these variables and times where I don't even know what year it is? Time is passing, and before I know it, time may pass me by, but sadly I won't know time passed me by until ten years after it has, because I still will be contemplating the complexities of some Free Trade Accord or something else of the sort.

SMALL THINGS

I operate on the big level. If it isn't something out of the ordinary or a five hundred-foot home run, I'm not typically interested. This makes for an interesting contrast to the importance of irrelevant things.

As I think I have written earlier, there used to be a soda can on my dresser. It was there for over three years, and then when my mom cleaned my room it was gone. The level of sadness felt over the loss of that can was ridiculous, but even so the question has to be asked: Why is there so much sadness over a can?

There are so many things right now that could be compared to that can that I am keeping. The number of things is staggering. What would be just a piece of trash or an irrelevant instruction booklet from a game made sixteen years ago to you would be something I could not part with. Every little thing has a memory. Every little thing I keep, I keep because I can remember every small detail about it.

There's an interesting contrast here, in my opinion. I'm the type of person who, if given the chance, would travel the world years on end. But at the same time, I can't bear to get rid of an instruction booklet from a game I don't even own anymore or throw out a controller that doesn't work.

I haven't figured out how long something has to be in a certain locale before it obtains the status of "immovable," but, in either case, it shouldn't be there. How can one feel sadness over a can? To tell you the truth, I think I can honestly say I felt more lingering sadness over that can than I have for Missy the dog. How can that be?

Yes, how can one feel such sadness over a can that rivals, if not surpasses, that of a very loving dog? Here's my theory: That can represented more than the Minute Maid orange drink that was in it. The year it was originally placed on my dresser was 1998. The soda can was placed there while Ryan was over and we had just conquered "Final Fantasy 3." The next week, I went to North Carolina, and when I got back, just like my house, the can was still there. The can was there when I returned from Minneapolis and sat there, as it always had, looming with a hint of vagueness. It was there but not prominently.

The can was there as I went to Alaska in 2000, and when I returned, the can was still there to greet me. The can was there the day I first met Emily; then, tragically, a week later, the can that had sort of been a staple in my life was gone. Thrown out like a normal piece of trash. It was treated just like these four cans to my right as I write this will be. Terminated and/or recycled.

I know it sounds silly, but that can really meant something to me. There are, as I have mentioned, other things that have a similar being as that can. One thing that pops in my head is the defunct car freshener I have in my car.

I bought this car freshener in Las Vegas just to buy something at a store in the mall in Las Vegas as a means just talk to someone. This was bought back in late 2003, and it's freshness-producing capabilities have long since passed, but there's no way you could get me to throw it out. That car freshener was with me my entire time out there after I bought it. It was with me all the way to Florida, D.C., and countless trips to Indianapolis. It was with me on a number of dates with Emily and what would be the last date I would have with her.

So, is it so much the actual item, or the memories that are tied to it? If I were one hundred percent crazy, I would say the item itself, but logic would dictate that it is the memories. In this piece alone, I have rattled off how one irrelevant piece of trash or a used car freshener can invoke so many memories.

This is a scary thought when thought about long enough. Why so? Think about it; if a can or a used car freshener can bring me to the brink of tears, what will happen when something major happens? This has already happened somewhat with Missy, and tragically for me I think, I have had more sadness for the can. Really think about that last sentence and the sadness about that. I should feel a deep sadness for what we called "the sweetest little puppy in the whole wide world" than a product of the Coca-Cola Corporation. And what hurts for me is that I do know that I should feel the sadness for the dog, but in the long term since, it's been that darn can. Even worse is, as written previously, I think I have even had more sadness every time I drive through Saint Elmo, Illinois, and see their new water tower.

Such simple things to you are items of monumental proportion to me. And what is so aggravating and irking is that I realize the near stupidity of it all, but it's like trying to reprogram a computer virus to go good instead of evil when you know nothing about computers. In other words, it's impossible for me not to get attached to small items. But what's weird is that I don't get attached to semi-relevant items like keepsakes or collectors' items. I always despised Emily's "Cherished Teddies" collection. I could see no value in those irrelevant items. Why spend upwards of fifty dollars on a depiction of what normally is a cruel and vicious animal being a cute and huggable bear doing something like holding hands with another bear? Yup, why spend fifty dollars to get attached to something when all you need to do is drink a soda, place it on your dresser, and enjoy!

With that logic, I always was on Emily about the stupidity of spending the massive amounts of dollars on such irrelevant items. Maybe relevancy is in the eye of the beholder, and if it is so, then I may never fully understand it.

There are other small things that I don't get to enjoy that don't relate to cans or bears. The small things are simple conversations. Outside my family there are minimal occurrences that a conversation takes place. Sure, I talk at the racetrack, but for the most part, I'm either giving orders or answering yes-or-no questions. In other words, everything is skin deep. It's been one and a half years since I had a conversation outside this house like what normal people experience on a normal day, and that is a conversation that is just that, a conversation. Unscripted, unrehearsed, and unplanned is what this conversation was.

Normally, I am prepared in every conversation for every possible response. It is sort of like being a defensive coordinator for an NFL team and having to know every play of the opposing offense. Such is how I am in a conversation. What for most people is a conversation that flows like a river, I am guarded and play the conversation much like a chess match. A chess match, you ask? In chess, if one is black, they start by countering white's moves, and the number-one goal is not to get trapped early in the game. That is my conversation goal, normally. I just give a simple response, so I don't get trapped in an area that I don't know or don't want to talk about. But on this night that I have mentioned before, all the rules I live by were thrown out.

On paper, a conversation between two people is a common occurrence that doesn't require much fanfare, or someone writing about it five times. (Can you tell I am stalling in mentioning what exactly this conversation is?) On this fateful Christmas night of 2003, I would experience a taste of normality. What is a small thing for the common person, I got to experience for just the second time in my entire life. That's not to say that I have never talked before, but this conversation wasn't played like a chess match. Much like the can, though, what is significant for me is just another thing for the other person. What was the only shining spot of the second half of 2003 (minus Las Vegas) for me was probably just another day for her.

Looking back, I don't know if I would have wanted to have that conversation. That two-hour talking session then was great, but now, since there's nothing, there's only the knowledge of what I am missing. That brings up the question, "Is it better to have experienced something once than never experience it at all?" Right now, I can easily answer that question by saying I wish I didn't know, because one can't miss something they are oblivious to.

I can justify my yearning for that conversation by saying that was one of my few tastes of normality, but what about the irrelevant items? I still am at a loss for words when it comes to defending how I can miss a light piece of decorated aluminum.

Anyone who has ever moved anything of mine can say that I get a bit testy when I find it moved. Take, for instance, race days when I flag. We have the start line about eighty yards toward turn one, so the speeds are lower in the interest of safety. If there is someone on the straight to help slow them down, they will normally grab a flag out of my holder to signal to the drivers to slow down. But when they go to put back the flag in the holder, they never put it in the right spot. They will always put it in the wrong holder. You see, I have a scientific process in the way I have my flags, but I always have to rearrange back to perfection when someone tampers with it. This, too, is how my rooms are at home.

While they look like a mess and look like everything was thrown together haphazardly, everything, in my eye, is in its proper place. While there's a pile of wires and controllers, I know where everything is and what the order of it all is, that is, until someone slightly moves it. Or there's always the dreaded "cleaning day." Nothing's worse than cleaning day, because if I'm not around for it, I never know if I'm going to lose something like that ole can.

But still, for the life of me, I can't understand how items with no substance other than the fact that they're there can have any effect over me. Small things to me are anything but. What is a can to you is a beacon of hope and a staple in my life. What was two hours to the person I talked to was two hours that changed my life. I guess to make an analogy, it is sort of like going to the middle of Africa into the bush with U.S. currency. While to you, the American, that one hundred dollar-bill is the legal tender to buy food and such, in middle of nowhere Africa, that one hundred dollar-bill is about as useful as firewood in a forest fire. While one party understands the relevance, the other party doesn't recognize the relevancy of the said bill. That's very much how I am. That conversation with Ashley in Indy may just be a footnote in the index that is life for her, but for me it was life changing. That can, in the scheme of things, is the cycle that is the process of recyclable materials, but for me, it will always be on my dresser in my memories, always there rain or shine, sitting there as it has been since day one.

TWO HUNDRED FORTY-FIVE BOXES

This piece is written for all the people I wish I could tell my story to.

An interesting title is the first thing that caught your eye. What could 245 boxes mean? If you're a warehouse worker, it may mean your worst nightmare. Then again, if it's Christmas, it may be that you are really loved or come from a really big family. But in this case, it deals with the calendar. The time span this piece covers is 245 days, and as my journal is in box form via a calendar, that is how I came up with the name. What is one box (or one day) to a normal person is just another day gone by, but these past 245 have been memorable for many different reasons, and the word "normal" can't be used to describe any of it, so here we go.

I hope if you are reading this you have read all my prior writings; if not, that's okay in this piece because there won't be too many references to prior events, and if you have read my writings before, some things that happened in 2005 will be rehashed.

We start with December 15, 2004. Besides the fact that my calendar mentions that Hanukkah ends on that date, it is the start of the 245. On that day, I had what you could call a date with a girl by the name of Rachel. I had met her on the Internet, and the day prior, I spent six hours talking to her via the Internet. On this Wednesday, I met her at my favorite pizza place and we talked, then I went bowling in my late league. This date was noteworthy because it was my first date in over a year and even more noteworthy because I actually initiated the contact.

The story of Rachel only lasts five boxes, as she was a bit too out there for me. As she put it, "Beer has killed too many of my brain cells." But the end of that story leads me to the start of the Winter Solstice and the start of my overseas travel.

December 21 is the date that I will remember forever because one of my life's dreams was fulfilled. I finally was going to travel beyond the borders of America. My fifteen minutes in the fifty-first state, ahem, I mean, Canada, doesn't count (just kidding, Canada!). With my great memory I cannot recall what time we left, but I do know we flew from Lambert to O'Hare in Chicago. I wasn't in the least apprehensive about any of the travels, but in O'Hare for a short time, I didn't know the whereabouts of my dad. I quickly became panicked, as I did not have my cell phone on me, and my brain started to think of every bad scenario that may have taken place. It wasn't long before I found him, but for some reason, he was a bit on edge, which, in turn, put me on edge, and then we disagreed on something, so at the start of this trip, there was a bit of tension. Oh, I forgot to put where we were going. Not too many people are traveling out of the country for Christmas unless it's family related, so I guess I should mention where we were going and why.

My dad is a film producer/director/writer type of person, and he had a project to do in Lithuania. For those of you geographically challenged, Lithuania is east of England and was part of the former Soviet Union.

The tension quickly died down, not because we resolved it, but just because there was so much to think about and to prepare for. For me everything was a new experience, and I wanted to take it all in. In fact, I can't even remember what we disagreed about, but whatever the case may have been, after the four-hour layover, it was off to Frankfurt, Germany.

The plane ride was a peaceful one, probably because of the destination than air currents. Traveling anywhere, when it leads to what one wants, always tends to be smoother.

We arrived in Frankfurt as the sun was rising, and while looking out of the plane on approach and taxiing, there was only one thing on my mind, Which way is the Nurburgring? The Nurburgring is a famous track in Germany that the public can drive around at any speed for a certain price (I think about twenty dollars a lap). As much as I pondered that, it was time to get off the plane. I was shocked and almost afraid, as we had to exit the plane and get off on the tarmac and get into a bus that would take us to the terminal. It was a very eerie feeling exiting the plane and being so close to the massive turbine engines. I conquered that short fear and entered the bus, and we were headed toward a place that in my mind is one of the most compelling in the entire world, and that is an international terminal.

Writer's note: There are many different stories or pieces that could be written by themselves in this time period, but this will just be one long one with everything being covered that happened in that time period. I may write more about one topic or another and may provide more insight on something, but I will not be throwing anything out like a "game theory" or something of the sort.

On that Wednesday, the twenty-first of December, I got my first taste of an international terminal. It was almost to the point of sensory overload for many reasons. There were shops that had products I had never seen before, there were at least a dozen dialects being spoken, and the sheer size of the terminal was almost breathtaking. But what really struck me was the sense of goodwill in the air. My experience was, that it is a place of peacefulness even through the chaos of hurried and weary-eyed travelers.

After the layover there, it was time to fly to our final airport destination—Vilnuis. As we taxied toward the runway to take off and leave Germany, my thoughts were on that for the short while I was in the same country as a friend I used to know, Ashley. But as much as I dwelled on that, I had a book to get back to and it was a short flight (well, short if you consider the length of the flight from O'Hare).

We got to our destination, and what first struck me while we were taxing toward the terminal was the coldness of the airport. What I mean is that at the end of the runway, it looked like a prison. The architecture of the surroundings had as much life as a cemetery. The wall between the airport and the road was a three and a half feet-thick concrete wall with enough barbed wire on top to kill an elephant. This was a definite sign that this country was once under Soviet rule.

As we got off the plane, we met the pastor that would be our guide of sorts, and thankfully for me, he spoke English quite well and was more than eager during the stay to answer my questions about Lithuania.

That first day we spent in the capitol city and my dad did a couple of interviews, one being the head bishop of the Lutheran church of Lithuania. The church that this bishop was at was in the middle of a very highly populated area, and the density was astounding. The roads are small and packed, and the last place you'd expect a church to be, there it was. What was even odder, there was a beauty salon connected to it and was essentially part of the basement.

We didn't stay there at that church too long, but long enough to hear the story of how the Soviets had trashed it during the Soviet era and how it was, and still is, being rebuilt to its former glory. I also tasted coffee for the first time, and I can tell you, I'm never trying it again. Even though my dad said it was a very strong brew, I'm still not going to try it again.

From there, we drove around the city for a short while, and it was during this short while that all the day's travels finally caught up with me. I started to fall like a brick from a high-flying plane. I was awake long enough to be scared to death a thousand times by psychotic European drivers (trust me on this, if you think Chicago is bad, you haven't seen anything). So psychotic, in fact, that in a thirty-minute time span, we saw the aftermath of no less than five fender benders.

From Vilnuis, we had to drive about five hours to the city where we would be staying. I don't remember that ride because I was fast asleep once we left the city, but my dad said I didn't miss much except a drunk driver that nearly killed us.

After that drive, it was finally time to sleep in a bed. We were staying in the resort town of Palanga that's nestled right off the Baltic Sea. We were dropped off, and as soon as I could, I was asleep in the bed, and it was a very comfortable bed as well.

The next day we got up early, and we had a busy day ahead of us, but first we had to eat breakfast. We ate at the hotel restaurant, which would become the norm for us while we were there. I can tell you ordering food in a foreign land is quite interesting. If you order bacon and eggs, that's exactly what you get: bacon and eggs as one. But besides the actual food topic, during this first day of breakfast, I heard a very familiar song. In the background, there was this song in a language I do not know, but I knew the song. It took me about fifteen seconds and then I realized that the song was in the game of "Project Gotham Racing2," so now any time I hear that song I am instantly taken back into that hotel restaurant in Lithuania in the wintertime.

Like I said before, we had a very busy day. It was the day before Christmas Eve, and we had many different places to see and do. One neat thing I did was walk over the Baltic Sea on this pier-like thing. While doing this, the waves were very choppy and the clouds coming ashore were quite ominous. A whale of a sleet storm backed up their ominous appearance. We quickly took shelter under the pier, but it quickly passed and we went back to the car. We visited with many different people on that day and saw much of the western part of the country.

That night we went to our guide's children's Christmas party/play. It was an odd sensation to see a play and all the interactions but to not understand a word from anybody. It was neat to see that the interaction between parent and child is the same there as it is here.

After all the walking, we were very tired that night, so we went to bed expecting to sleep until morning. We were both wrong on that assumption because around 3:00 a.m., that wonderful thing called jet-lag hit both of us. Somehow my dad knew I was up, and he asked me if I was and I replied that I was wide-awake. Instead of fighting it, we decided to stay up and read the books we had brought. To a tourist this experience may have been a bad one, but those two and a half hours were some of the most memorable of the entire trip. Maybe it was the sense of safety in that hotel, or maybe it was the fact that I finally realized I was halfway across the world, but whatever it may be, I will always remember those hours reading and being with my dad.

We finally got back to sleep, and we got up and it was Christmas Eve. We ate breakfast again and the same lady waited on us. My dad asked her how long she worked because it seemed like, regardless the hour, she was there. The answer she gave was shocking. She stated that she worked from 8:00 a.m. to 10:00 p.m. six days a week! In all the places I've been, it is the people stories like her that I wonder where they are as I write this. Is she still working sixty-hour weeks? How can someone do that and appear to be as content as she did? I could go on and on with those type of questions, but there's more of this trip to talk about.

Once again, it was Christmas Eve, and after eating breakfast, we went with our guide to this house where a birthday was being celebrated. But this wasn't just any birthday. This was a birthday for a woman who was turning one hundred. That is just mindboggling for me, because she would have been alive for the pre-Soviet era, the Soviet era, and the current state it is now. Those eyes would have seen so much. And I better not forget they also saw WWII. At this party the people were quite friendly toward us American strangers. They asked us what it was like in America, and this one older woman was very intent on wanting to know why American movies were generally violent. All in all, it was a very memorable experience. Also, of personal note, that party was the first time I drank anything with alcohol in it. I had a glass of champagne. I didn't willingly drink it, but when handed something and the person seems quite intent on giving it to you and you don't speak their language, I thought it would have been quite rude not to accept. Only later did I know what it was.

That night we went to our guide's church service (by the way, our guide's name was Darius) and I felt almost ashamed that I wasn't paying attention in church, but I had to keep telling myself that even if I paid my fullest attention, I would be unable to understand a word anyone spoke. So after that I went to the side room and continued to read.

After the service, I was in the back of the church just observing, and again I was shocked on how the interaction between people is almost identical to ours over here. Not that I was expecting a polar opposite or anything, but it was very weird to see a parent care for a child, but the words make no sense.

After the church was locked up, we went to one of the elder's houses and had Christmas dinner. The family was very nice to us and, for the most part, all spoke English. It was very intriguing to see Christmas customs of another country. The niceness of those people made me wonder why America isn't as warm. The sincerity of the people is something I have never witnessed before. That warmness from people would be experienced on the next day as well.

Christmas day was just like the day prior, except the hotel restaurant was closed, so that was a bummer. Thankfully, Pringles taste the same over there as they do here, so I munched on those, and the Cherry Coke's taste is also quite close (don't taste the Sprite though!). During the course of the day, which would be our penultimate day, we went to three different churches and saw the place where a very big church used to be, but it was destroyed in the war.

It was indeed Christmas, but for me it didn't feel like Christmas at all. Christmas for me is all about routine and being with the same people, so while the calendar said it was Christmas, it didn't feel like it. In fact, not even the temperature felt like it, as it was considerably warmer there than it was in my home in St. Louis.

The next day would be our last full day in the country. Sadness started to creep in, as I am very much sentimental and every little thing I saw I knew it would probably be the last time I saw it in that place. For instance, that morning would be the last time I would have those bacon and eggs; that night would be the last night that I would walk into my room.

That day would bring news of the terrible tsunami, but hearing the news reports in a different language kept us from knowing the full effect of the disaster.

The last day we did some more touring and videotaping, and we also went to the Amber Museum. That museum was one of the weirdest I have ever visited; not so much because of what it is, but because of its surroundings. Its location is in the middle of this large park, and on this cold, snowy day, there were no people about, but in the middle of this park, there was a massive museum. Behind the very large and heavy doors were actually people who work there. It was just very odd, because it was about a half-mile walk to the place, and not a soul outside was to be found, but inside there were people. It was just a bit strange.

That night we had our final dinner in Lithuania, and what a dinner it was. We ate at this pizza place that isn't more than a quarter mile from the beach, and let me tell you, it was the best pizza I have ever tasted. If I ever have a lot of money, I may have a spur-of-the-moment urge to buy myself a plane ticket and fly over there just to have that pizza. It was so good, it should be outlawed! During that great meal, it was fitting that the sun was setting, because the sun was also setting on our journey. In less than eight hours, we would be headed back to Vilnuis to board a plane for home, but as that meal lasted, it was such a fine end to such a wonderful stay in a wonderful country.

As I walked into my room for the final night, I silently got misty eyed, but my tiredness let me fall asleep fast enough before I broke out into full-blown sobs.

After a short five-hour sleep, Darius was there to pick us up, and I said goodbye to my bed, and room, and hotel, and then to Palanga as the lights fell behind the horizon outside the rear window of the car. I slept the rest of the way to Vilnuis, and as the sun rose it was time to enter the airport and start the long trip home. Our first stint would have us fly to Warsaw; then from there we were back to Frankfurt.

Our layover was to be just two hours long, and because we were going to be flying back on a 747, we barely had enough time to finish our McDonald's meal. We got to the gate right as it was starting to board, and we were set to make our final voyage back to home ... or so we thought.

We boarded the plane normally and then we started to pull away normally, but then I noticed that a lot of little lights were flashing above all the steward stations. Then I noticed that all of them were on the phone, and I knew that this wasn't a normal situation. I quickly thought worst-case scenario: Was it a bomb? Had we been hijacked? What was wrong? We started to creep back to the terminal, and I told my dad something was wrong, but he quickly dismissed my fears. They were found out to be somewhat grounded, as the captain came on the PA and said that there had been a small fire in the air-conditioning duct. The repair time was only an hour and a half, so after that we were back up in the air headed to Dulles.

When we got back to American soil, we quickly had to get to our gate because of the prior delay, but thankfully we made it. But then, because nothing for me can ever be normal, our plane we were on for the last leg of the trip wouldn't start. After another thirty-minute delay, we were finally taxiing toward the runway. That's when the captain came on the PA and said some very unnerving words, "Okay, folks, as you noticed, we wouldn't start and we were able to fire the right engine, but the left won't fire. I'm hoping as we go full throttle the air will kick-start the left and everything will be fine. This is a normal procedure, but you may feel some tugging as we go down the runway. Like I said, this is a normal procedure. I haven't done this before, but we should be in the air momentarily." I know people like to tell it like it is, but did he have to say that he had never done this before?

As you can tell, we made it because I'm writing this, and after a long trip we were home, but my luggage was not. Somewhere it got lost in between Dulles and Lambert, and it would be three days before I would get it back. In my luggage were the mementos I had been given from Darius, so I was very nervous that they would be lost, but thankfully, I received them with my luggage. The mementos are in a white box that was taped at the Vilnuis airport, and I have yet to open the box because I fear it would be too painful, because the memories of when I received them were of such joy that I don't know if I could handle the memories now.

Jetlag hit me bad, and the next three days are somewhat blurred. I bowled in my bowling league on the twenty-ninth, and then for some reason I drove to Indianapolis to see my mom, who was visiting my brother. I had slept from noon until eight the day prior, so I was awake enough to drive, so at 1:00 a.m., I decided to go.

It was a very foggy and nerve-racking trip. The fog was dense enough that from the right lane you would be unable to see the median, and all the while I was being passed by trucks and cars who were doing at least twenty miles per hour more than me and I was doing sixty, so I quickly picked my pace up because I would much rather do the hitting than be hit.

I made it safely to my brother's house at six in the morning, and my mom was up to meet me. Later that morning my mom and I ate at IHOP. We talked and I talked about my trip and all that had happened since the last time I had seen her. I really wanted to see the Brennons, but contact could not be reached so my hope that the prior Christmas could be relived was dashed (Okay, I made one reference to a prior piece.)

That evening, due to the jetlag, I went to sleep at 4:00 p.m., but because my brother's place is rather noisy, I was awakened at 10:30 at night. I knew that I would be up for some while, and I didn't want to sit and do nothing for the entire night, so just as spontaneous as my decision to drive to Indy, I made another one to drive back just twenty-one hours after I started my way there. My mom didn't like this, as she wanted to be with me for New Year's, but like I said, I didn't want to do nothing all night, so I left and headed back home.

Something happened on that drive home that was most unexpected. My former girlfriend, Emily, called me and we talked for a good forty minutes. As she started to go, she said she would call me back after she ate, but in true Emily form, she never did, and to this day I haven't gotten that phone call back.

That brings us to the end of the turbulent 2004. Will 2005 be any better?

As 2005 started, jetlag was dogging me much like a mosquito that keeps buzzing your ear. I just couldn't shake it or get my hours back on a somewhat decent track. On January 4, I slept an astounding seventeen hours, and then I finally regained some control of normality on my sleep schedule.

A week and a half later, my dad talked to the Linger Production Group. They are the ones who produce ABC's telecasts of the Indy Racing League races and the Indy 500. He talked to them about getting me an internship of some sort, and on first talking with them, it seemed like something could be worked out. Five days later it was said that I would be working the St. Petersburg race.

January 30 would mark the day that I would start to really take my writing seriously, and after that day I have been firing off pieces left and right.

February 4 marked my twenty-second birthday, and in true typical Aaron fashion it was a rather depressing day. For me nothing is more depressing than a birthday. It's one more year toward the end, the end of what I don't know, pick something and that's what's closer to the end.

Eight days later I would be watching Speed's coverage of the ARCA race from Daytona. It was a crash-filled race with several red flags and one extended red flag because a car destroyed the catch fence and it needed to be repaired. Later in the race, on the next to last lap, the screen flashed quickly to a car upside down sliding down the backstretch. As it slid, it got back into the grass and started to tumble, then it was hit hard by another car, and immediately after that happened, the shot changed and the angle was now looking straight down the backstretch. As the angle changed again, more cars could be seen flipping, and one car flew as high as the top of the catch fencing. It was, to put it mildly, a horrific scene.

Speed's coverage of the aftermath was horrible. Not a mention of the crash in the post-race interviews, and they went to their NASCAR pre-race show as if nothing happened. This scared me, as in the racing world no news is bad news. Had a driver been killed? Or more, did a car off the screen fly into the lake or into the stands? What happened? The Internet sites were mum about it, and for the next hour and a half there wasn't a single word about. I went absolutely crazy in fear that something horribly bad had happened. In the end, just one driver was moderately injured, but that time of anxiety was very, very great.

Four days later, it was confirmed that I would be going to Kenya later in the year. This was great news, because I was getting very depressed because I wasn't doing much of anything and there wasn't really any progression of any sorts on any topic, so this was much-needed news.

That weekend saw the running of the Daytona 500, and it was a very depressing time. It was the first time in over six years that I would be watching the race alone. Prior to 2005, I either saw it with my dad, or from 2001–2004 I watched it with Emily, but since she hated me, and my dad had a business obligation, I was relegated into watching it by myself.

Two days later, though, all that would be forgotten, as my dad and I were headed to Indy to have a meeting with the Linger Group. My dad said that the meeting went well (I couldn't tell if it was a good meeting or a bad one), but it was decided that my first work would be the Indy 500 and not the St. Pete race. This was decided because the Kenya trip would interfere with that race.

Two days after that, on February 25, it was time to get my shots for Africa. Prior to this day, I had a streak of 386 days without a hospital visit, but this day would see that streak end, but not of my own doing.

I don't remember much about that day, and the first thing I remember is grimacing in pain as the yellow fever vaccine was injected into me; then suddenly everything went black. I don't know how long I was out, but as I awoke temporarily, I thought I was getting out of my own bed to go get the shots, so it was quite the shock when I was dressed, sitting in a chair, and the lights were on. I simply asked, "Dad, where am I?" and before he could give an answer, I was out again. I have snippets of memories of that time and the time I came fully aware of my surroundings in the hospital. It wasn't a pleasant experience at all, as it felt like I had been awake for a week with no sleep and no food. What had happened was the needle had hit a nerve and it triggered a very long medical term but, for space's sake, it caused me to faint.

Not much of note happened between that incident, and it was time to go to Kenya on the twenty-first of March.

At this point in time, please refer back to "Kenya."

I probably saved myself three hours by doing that, but I'm sure if I had rewritten it, it probably would have been the same anyways … As hectic as December to March had been, the first three weeks of April were very dull in comparison. Bowling on Mondays and Wednesdays was about my only excitement, minus the weekends I flagged.

The twentieth saw me to see a coworker I knew six years prior. Her name was Carol. It was very nice to hear how she was doing, but it was also saddening because I instantly remembered all the memories I had. And when I mention memories, I just not only remember the time working with her at the bowling alley, but I remember the entire time era that I knew her. So Linda was remembered, and the days I would go over to my dad's apartment and play "Grand Prix Legends" and the afternoons where I would go to play golf at Forest Park. It's amazing what one person can do to unlock so many memories.

Two days after that meeting another incident would occur. I was flagging a practice session, and at the end of it the primary race director wanted to chat about where the next race's starts would be, so he got this flatbed (not a pickup, imagine a golf cart, but without a top, longer, and with just one seat), and we were going to drive out to the finish line. As what I mentioned in the parentheses, it only had one seat, so I was seated on the flat part. Bad idea! As he drove toward the track and made the turn onto the track, the vehicle was traveling too fast to hold me, and I was flung off much like a rodeo rider is bucked off a bronco. I landed on the ground, thankfully feet first, and I was able to take about five steps before falling, and those five steps let me land on grass and not asphalt. But in the end, I had a sprained ankle, and another trip to the hospital would be necessitated.

The prognosis was good, and it was only a mild sprain, but the hospital visit would prove to hold more boxes of my calendar than just April 23. The trooper that I am, I flagged the next day; granted, I was hobbling, but I did do it.

May 2 would be a day that would shape the rest of the year so far. Before this date, I was still looking forward to working for the Linger Group and being at the Indy 500 as an intern. But on this morning, I would wake up with a phone call saying that ABC had taken over the dealings concerning interns, leaving me cold and in the dark. It was a very bitter day for me. I had been told that it was going to happen, and as so many things have happened before they fall through.

Three days later, I went to a baseball game with my stepbrother, Mike, and normally a game itself isn't worth putting in something like this, but during this game, the other team had runners on first and second with no outs, and Mike said, "Boy, a triple play would be nice in this situation," and no sooner than he finished the word of situation, a triple play had happened. Not too many people can say they have seen one of those.

May 9 was the day I completed reading A Tale of Two Cities, and I'm not much of a reader, but that was a really good book. It was very depressing, as I saw myself in one or two of the characters (too bad for you, I won't mention who), and it was a rather bleak book. The next day I would start to get very sick, a sickness I will never forget.

May 10 I woke up with what I can only describe as a pimple on steroids on the back of my neck. On this day, I would think nothing of it except some mild discomfort, but the morning of the next day would prove to be very bad. I woke up with a fever that eclipsed the 104-degree mark, and I woke my dad and we went straight back to the hospital (this is why I mentioned prior that the hospital visit would be in more boxes).

I was admitted to the ER, and the ER doctor lanced the bulging abscess and then put me on IV antibiotics, and for the first time in my life, I was admitted to the hospital for an overnight stay. I wasn't feeling like myself at all, so I didn't care where I was so long as I was getting those nice blue pills that were killing all the pain, but what I don't understand is why they wake a person up, like myself, who has just fallen asleep to give them medicine to help them go to sleep. Also the constant bothering of checking my blood pressure and what not got to be very annoying, but I guess it's their job to make sure the patient isn't dying.

The next day my fever was still persistent, and my primary care physician was actually going to discharge me, but my dad called the nurse, and since I wasn't getting any better I was going to be kept another night.

The second night into the third day was one of the most depressing times of my life. My dad was headed to Ft. Wayne, Indiana, and I talked to him at 4:00 in the morning, but after that, I couldn't sleep. I thought of how many people I used to know and how they would never know if I died there on that bed. At the time I didn't know what was wrong with me, and even if I did, with all the pain and pain pills, I probably could not grasp whatever condition I had, but sadly I did realize how lonesome I was. I wondered if Kyle would ever know, or Emily, or Ashley, or anybody. When the mind has nothing to do but think upon itself, it isn't a productive experience.

On that morning I was scheduled to have my next dose of all-important painkillers at 6:30. The nurse shift change started at 6:15, and 6:30 came, then 7:00, then 7:30. Each quarter hour I buzzed and said that I really needed the medicine because the pain was so great that there were times that I wished that I were actually dead or in a coma. As bad as the pain was, either of the two would have been just fine. Eight o'clock became 8:15, and then finally, finally after hours of pain that no one should endure, I got the medicine. At the same time I was told that the reason I was so sick and had a big mass of something on the back of my neck was because of a staph infection. A doctor looked at me and then said she would do surgery in the next two hours, and sure enough, I had a surgery. While I remained awake for it, it was rather painless except for the pain-numbing shots that were injected. And some of those needles went in about an inch!

They needed to go that deep because that's how far she made the incision, and not only did she make an incision, but she took out the entire mass. The mass of infection was about the size of a U.S. quarter and the depth of approximately one inch.

After the short surgery, I was back in my hospital room, and Mary, my stepmom, was on her way to pick me up. I had not seen what my neck looked like, and at the time I was not aware of the fact that part of my neck was gone. But as she arrived and as the nurse was telling her how to pack the wound, I knew it was bad, because when the nurse took off my bandage, she looked like she saw a ghost. When I got home and saw in a mirror what my neck looked like, I could not believe my eyes.

The falling apart of the internship may have been a blessing in disguise because had I been up in Indy, I may not have said that I needed to got to the hospital for fear that I may not be able to work. So what does this mean? I probably would have just dealt with the pain, and that could have had fatal consequences.

Even though I still had a hole in my neck, we went up to Indy to attend the 500. It was a great race and a great time all around, as we went to two races the day prior to the race and also saw Star Wars Episode 3. So many good memories abound from the end of May.

The entire month of June was mainly wasted away playing "Forza." During this month, I was the number-one rated player in the world, so I had to maintain that status. I did apply for a job in this month, but I think I'm glad that they would just keep my application on file because the more I think about it, the more I believe that a normal job could kill me. Oh, the application was to the bank that I formally worked at.

The start of July was more like what I'm used to with that being stuff outside the norm. July 2, my best friend, Kyle, got married, but I wasn't invited to it, so I don't really know what that means, if anything. But after that, not even a week after, a hurricane was brewing in the gulf. It was less than nine months removed that Hurricane Ivan ravaged Pensacola, and this new storm with the name of Dennis was on the same path. So what do we do? Well, since I guess we hadn't had enough adventure in the previous nine months, we went down before the storm so we could be in the storm.

Dennis, when it was 150 miles out, was a category-4 storm bordering on becoming the worst category of a five. We were somewhere near Mobile, Alabama, when it hit, but we were on the west side of the eye, so we didn't get any severe weather, but we got winds that were still over fifty miles per hour and torrential downpours.

Somehow I made it through without getting injured, and thankfully for the citizens of that area, the storm weakened and it wasn't as bad, so on July 12 we got back to St. Louis.

After that, once again, there was a lull in any noteworthy activity, until August 1.

On August 1, I went to the baseball game and I was expecting a good game, but I wasn't around to see the first pitch. Of course, something bizarre had to happen to me. I was walking back to my seat after getting a bottle of water and this vendor passed me and said, "Excuse me," then as soon as he passed me, he cut in front of me stopped suddenly. I tried to avoid him by walking left, but I made contact with him, and as my luck would have it, I slipped on previously spilled Coke and ice and I went backwards into a wall with my head; in the end I suffered a concussion and whiplash. I can't even go to a simple ballgame without an episode from bizzaro-world hitting me.

I spent about six hours in the ER and was released around 2:00 in the morning, but I don't remember too much about that. Since that time, my short-term memory has been a bit shaky, and the dizziness and headaches were brutal. They are slowly diminishing, and I hope that they will go away in full shortly.

So what does the future hold? Today on box 285, I wrote that I heard from a friend I had not heard from in ages (Josh), and also that I have a meeting with a man who owns a sprint car. Will the boxes in the future hold good things? People live their lives looking so far ahead (I know I do), but sometimes one has to look within four lines to see a box and realize that there are days, and within each box a life-changing experience can happen.

THE PIT AND A.EQ

Yet another interesting and intriguing title. I'll get to both in this piece because they go hand in hand.

The pit is what my mind can do if it starts thinking on one thing for too long. For this piece, I will use money because of a recent incident.

Earlier this month I suffered a concussion. I don't remember much of the first five to ten days after, and about two weeks after I started to be able to drive again. At the same time everyone in my house was gone, so that left me with a lot of time to do nothing but think. Even though I was playing Xbox, my mind is overly qualified to multitask. In this instance it was just going on and on about money and what expenses are to come.

To start, I'll say that at the start of the month I had around seven hundred dollars. For someone like me who has no real expenses, that should be a comfortable sum, but I'm not like anyone else, and when someone sees seven hundred dollars and no current expenses, I see seven hundred dollars and this formula:

Bowling is to start later in August. I will be in three leagues for thirty-six weeks with the combined lineage totaling forty-eight dollars a week. So 48 x 36 = $1,928. I have a car payment every month that's around $130. So over the next six months that equals $780. Also to add to the melting pot is the Xbox 360 that is released this year. I have fifty dollars down on it, but it will retail for $399. So that leaves $349, but that includes no games, no S-video cable, nor an extra controller. So that will be an estimated $510 in the end. So just by that alone, the money going out, not including taxes or weekly food, is a scary $3,218.

This is the pit. For one thing, in that formula I am calculating expenses that will take place nearly nine months in advance. I cannot help this. I also can't include in all that money that I don't currently have. Add on top of this thinking, a concussion and pain medicine and fear beyond imagination ensued. The only logical option I could find in my time of weak thought was to risk it. And as they say, "The house always wins."

This brings me to my A.EQ, or Age Equivalent. People always talk about IQ, but for a person with Asperger's, I believe an A.EQ is more important. Why so? Well, in some areas I am decades ahead of my peer group, but in others I am maybe eight or age ten at best. This is where the problems occur in these weaker points. These areas, I believe, aren't as pronounced in times of stability, but rock the boat (or the head in my case) and irrational conclusions and solutions will be thought up. Even if they are partially wrong, and even if I know they are, the partially wrong is better than doing nothing. This can be applied to more things than just money. Relationships are deeply affected by this as well.

I don't know if an A.EQ exists, but it should if it doesn't. The clashing between the inner minds that are older and the younger side is one of the most disabling things about Asperger's. Does this mean I need a babysitter? No. What's the solution? That answer I do not know.

The A.EQ really rears its ugly head it times of stress. Maybe this is why, in all my pieces, relational problems come in times of other stress. The handling of hardships is not of a twenty-two-year-old, but maybe of an eight-year-old. This is the true pit, and the two go hand in hand.

EMOTIONS

Just a note from Dad... One aspect of autism and Asperger's that many professionals use to define the malady is an inability to demonstrate social or emotional reciprocity. The following has touched the hearts of professionals who are astounded, to say the least, at Aaron's unique ability to express life at an emotional level.

A FRIEND GONE

Recently, I lost a close friend. This is important for one, because I don't have many friends, and like me, she was quite shy. We shared many traits like that, but she's gone now.

We were friends for over thirteen years. She was always there for me when I needed her and sometimes when I didn't need her. She somewhat shadowed me. I didn't mind this, though, as like I said, I don't have many friends. But the friends I have are close and very important to me.

I don't have many friends because I keep to myself. So did she. Her name was Amsterdam. That is a very odd name unless you are a cat, and then any name goes. Yes, this close friend was a cat, and what a wonderful cat she was.

Much like twenty-six months ago with Missy the Maltese, I had to make the decision to have her put to sleep. I can't think of a more difficult choice to inflict upon someone. I knew her from when she was less than three weeks old. I bottle-fed her when she was just larger than softball, but now instead of nourishing life, I had to make the choice to end it.

Amsterdam was always there for me. At first, she was excessively shy around everyone, including me. Then one night, she was walking around with a piece of dog food in her mouth. She wasn't eating it but just carrying it. So she dropped it by me, and I threw it toward the front door and, like a dog, she went after it and grasped it with her mouth and brought it back. We repeated this throw-and-retrieve game at least a dozen times, and after that we were best friends until the end.

She was there for me when it was Missy's time. In a way, she took Missy's spot on my bed, and she became very doglike in her loyalty toward me. I guess it's sort of ironic that she took Missy's spot, but the same ailment that took Missy away would claim Amsterdam.

Shortly after Missy was gone, Amsterdam was losing weight, so we took her to the vet. The vet did a blood test, and it came back with all the signs of kidney failure. The vet gave her at the most six months to live. That was twenty-six months ago.

I don't know what drove her, but she didn't go quietly and did not succumb to the all-but-terminal news. It was like she didn't get the memo that she had six months, because shortly thereafter she put on the weight she had lost, her gums regained their color, and she got her youthful step once again.

I think she could feel the deep loss I had over Missy, and she wasn't going to put me through that again so soon. Time went on and I forgot about the grim diagnosis that the vet had mentioned.

Every morning when I got up, she would either be on my stomach, at the foot of the bed, or in my dresser that lies about two feet from my bed. I have had a lot of health stumbles myself this year, and the past month I didn't realize that she was no longer by me when I got up. Instead of being near me, she was either under the television in the entertainment center or in the front room's main window. I also did not realize the weight she was once again losing.

Then, just a week and a half ago, while I was about to go to sleep, I was eating some string cheese. This is my other cat's favorite food in the world, and Amsterdam didn't mind it either. On this night I gave a piece to Amsterdam, and she started to eat it and she spat it out. I was about to give it to Siam when I saw what appeared to be blood on it. I assumed that it was probably a tooth or something else that would just go away.

The next week she didn't move about the house much, and I was still oblivious to her declining health (I had a concussion this same month, so I was a bit slow). Then one morning while eating after going somewhere, Siam started to be extra talkative for no apparent reason.

He is a very talkative cat, but his tone and sense of urgency were different. After I thought for a brief second, I called for Amsterdam and got no response.

She was very loyal and would always come to the calling of her name. This panicked me, and I went flying through the house trying to find her. I went down into the basement and called for her again and there was nothing. As I got back upstairs, I heard what sounded like the mail slot opening, so I went to check the mail, but there was no mail. As I turned from the front door I heard this faint meow, or an attempted meow. The past two weeks she didn't make much noise but just made the motion with her mouth of what would be a meow.

As I looked at her, she had this shiny substance under her mouth. I walked toward the kitchen and kept calling for her, and she followed quite willingly. As we made it to the kitchen, I picked her up and then it was made clear. It wasn't a hairball, or thrown-up food, but instead it was the crimson color of blood. She was dying.

I knew immediately what choice I would have to make on that day. The choice was clear, but the timing was so sudden. I had not had the mental capacity that month to realize she was on her way out. So for me this turn of events was quite sudden.

I called my dad, and he came home and then I spent my last moments with what was one of my last remaining friends. I sat her on a chair adjacent to mine and I just petted her and talked to her, and she just sat there as if she knew what was going to happen and she showed no fear. While her body was going through its last stanza, she purred while I held her.

With what would be the last time I would hold this dear cat, I held her over my head and I just looked at her. All her life, she would just keep eye contact for a brief moment, but during this she just stared at me to the point that it appeared like she was looking straight into my soul. The way she was looking at me was with a sense of contentment and fulfillment. It was almost as if she was speaking straight to me through her eyes, saying, "Aaron, it's time. Thank you for taking good care of me. This isn't the end, as I will see you again."

Whether she really was saying that or just going senile as her body was going away, I will never fully know. I can say that in thirteen years she had never looked at me like that, and I know it wasn't a look of pain.

After she pierced my soul, it was time to hand her off to the car ride that would be much like a condemned prisoner taking his last walk. As I handed her to my dad, I kissed her head and I told her, "Thank you for being such a wonderful cat," and then she did something she had not been able to do for two weeks. She meowed. And then she was gone.

Mary, my stepmother, told me that while she walked into the humane society holding the box that Amsterdam was in, she talked to the cat, telling her that she was just about to arrive in kitty cat heaven. Then for what I think would be the first time ever, she meowed to Mary. Amsterdam kept to herself and never really liked Mary. In fact, she pretty much just liked me and barely tolerated everyone else. I guess from her viewpoint, everyone else was just a distraction and a barrier that could get in between her and me, so it was a precedent that she would talk to Mary. I never had thought about it, but after the soul-piercing look and her response to Mary's comment, I am sure that pets are much smarter than they show and that each of them has a soul.

Mary had to take her because I know that I would not have the inner strength. From the time they left with her to the time I got back, I worried so much that she might have panicked. I hated myself for this. But then I remembered that look of contentment she gave me, and it was almost a preemptive look of forgiveness.

She never looked at me like that before and she did, and I am fairly confident that what I thought she was telling me is true, so, Amsterdam, I once again thank you, and I know it isn't the end, and someday I hope I get to see you again so I can apologize for not being able to take you myself.

I ...

This piece is very open-ended and is probably intended for someone with ADD, because I will probably be changing subjects faster than a politician who doesn't want to answer questions...

I wonder about a lot of things, but most of all I wonder what exactly I am. The first logical answer that comes to mind is a bunch of water, but beyond that, what exactly makes me tick? The dumber version of that question is "Who am I?" I know exactly what I am, but knowing that makes me ask the question because it is so paradoxical. Since no one can fully know who they are, one who does doesn't really know. The illusion is what they think they are. This is what Asperger's is! With all the firsts and rules, it is very clear what I am and who I am, but in real society that simply doesn't work.

As confusing as that first paragraph was, I assure you that it is all the more confusing for me. The summary of that paragraph can be compared to the phrase, "One who thinks they know it all knows nothing." I believe this is the self-awareness aspect of Asperger's. If someone is so keen on knowing everything about them, it creates a slew of issues. One thing is a closed line of communications because they may think, I know who I am, and you're wrong, end of story! Another example may be that they don't want to communicate any emotion, because since they know it all too well, it is just overwhelming. And lastly, they may come full circle and get to the part of knowing nothing and be so scared that anything and everything is just mind-jarring. I know each of these, because at one point or another, they have happened to me. Which is worse? Pick one, and whichever one is happening at any given time is the worst one, because all of them are undesirable.

I want to know why I am so open about this thing I have. All my experiences and my limited outer knowledge of Asperger's has told me that people with it are tight-lipped about the issue. I certainly am not so, but why? My only thought on that is the fact that the pain is there all the time, so if I write or talk about it, it remains the same as if I were to just keep quiet.

Another thing I ponder about is the trade-off. What trade-off? In life, for every positive there seems to be a negative. My mom recently read some of my writings and said that she was so proud of me and that I have done more things than most people will do in an entire lifetime. That may be so, but at the same time there are some things I will never be able to experience even if money, time, or age were not issues. I have traveled the world, but a simple open conversation with my peer group is nearly impossible. Think about what that must be like for a second.

Imagine being able to do nearly everything you have ever wanted to do. I have been halfway around the world, driven multiple race-cars, flown an airplane and numerous other non-normal activities, but I often ask myself if the trade-off is worth it. What trade-off? Going back to the pendulum of positive and negative aspects of life, the trade-off is the benefits and shortcomings of Asperger's.

On one hand, I have an uncanny ability to recall information. The negative of that is the annoyance factor I have of those around me. I know I can annoy my dad by correcting him on a statement he may make about something that happened a decade ago. I know the exact details, so I have no choice but to interrupt and make the correction. And it doesn't take people long to learn this about me. A teammate I have on a bowling league asked me within four weeks, "Aaron, do you remember everything that has ever happened and then some?" Sadly, I do remember most everything that has happened to me, and I can recall it way too fast for my own good.

Another aspect is self-awareness. Some people have none, some have a little, and there are those few others who have too much. I believe I fall into the "too much" bracket. Again, there are two sides to this coin, and it is debatable if in the end it's better or worse. On the positive side, I am very hard to sway on issues (that is, if I tell you my stance on an issue), which means I am a firm believer in what I believe in.

With self-awareness comes self-knowledge. This can be bad, because I can be very hard to sway. It is truly a double-edged sword. Yet another paradox I live with. If I had a dollar for every paradox I live in, I'd at least be able to buy Boardwalk. While this self-awareness is good, it can cut communications with others. And it can also make what other people have to say null and void. It pains me at times to hear other people's opinions about issues when I already have my mind made up. This, I believe, was the true wedge in my relationship with Emily.

I wish more people could understand who I am. I know Emily didn't, and I know anytime I mention Asperger's, people think it's a new vegetable or new diet trend. In other words, they have no earthly idea what the heck I am talking about. This pains me straight to the heart because I know they will never fully grasp the pain and extreme heartache I feel every day. Maybe this is the reason why I write. Maybe I am hoping that someday someone will read this and for a brief moment they will understand. Understanding is the only thing I want.

Last night I accomplished something on my invisible life-accomplishment list and that was bowl a game in excess of 297. My score wasn't perfect, but it was just a stick off—299. Near perfection, but whether it would have been a 298, 299, or 300, it didn't matter. People wait their entire lives to get to that high echelon of bowling greatness, and I did it and I thought, okay, what does this mean? I did get excited for the ring I will be receiving, but that is no satisfaction of the fact that I did something that people will try forever to do and will never be able to. I will admit, I did feel pressure going for the perfect game, but afterwards there was no glee or self-satisfaction except for the fact that I get a ring.

Could this be related to the closed mindedness I mentioned earlier? I have observed from others that most people's best experiences come when shared with friends, but since I kept to myself during that game so much so that most others around didn't even know I was going for the 300. And when one is isolated, their happiness is only as much as their mind will allow.

As I shot for the 300 and got a nine count, I showed as much emotion as I would have had I gotten the 300. I had a smile, since I knew I got the ring, but besides the materialistic gain I would get, there was no self-satisfaction of the extremely hard achievement I had just accomplished. I wish I could tell you how much that hurts. Someone called me a word artist because I have been told that I can paint a vivid picture of what it's like to be me, but I know not how to describe the emptiness that should be filled with happiness. I have seen people throw 300s many times, and the jubilation on their faces is of such that if they were to die, they couldn't die happier. For me, besides the ring, there was nothing! Absolutely nothing!

I did call my dad just because I asked for permission that if I ever bowled a game higher than 280 that I could call him. And since he said yes, I had to call him. I do think I did sound happy, but all thoughts were on the ring—an insignificant, materialistic thing. Many times I told Emily that jewelry and rings were pointless. And now, there I was, and that's the only ray of light that made that game any different than a 199. What for most people is a lifetime achievement for me could be the most depressing thing of the month. Not because I did it, but because of the lack of feeling that I know should be there.

I know there is no worse feeling than knowing something should be there and you realize that it isn't. Take, for example, a room. If you walk into a living room in someone else's house, you expect to see similar items universally. A couch, a television, and perhaps a phone are all things common in probably 99.9% of U.S. households. Now let's say, you go to someone's house and there's a couch facing an entertainment center and a television is absent. Your eye would catch that, and you might find it odd. That's how my brain is. I know that the proverbial television should be there, but for me, all I have is the glamorous entertainment center made of fine oak, but the television is not there. In this instance, the entertainment center would be very eye appealing, but no one buys an entertainment center as a stand-alone product. It is always bought to house the true gem of the room, and that's the television. For me, the television symbolizes emotion that should be felt, and I know it should be felt, but there's just an empty space that is filled with nothing but air.

That's all the "I's" I have at the moment, but I know there has to be a sequel to this, because I's always come in twos, unless, of course, you're a Cyclops.

THE IMPORTANCE OF THE STORIES AND IMAGERY

As Hurricane Rita barrels towards Texas, my fear, along with many others,' is that America will stop caring. In the past fourteen months, Americans have become familiar with the likes of Charlie, Frances, Ivan, Katrina, and now Rita has entered the water cooler talk. How much room do people have to care?

I have witnessed firsthand the devastating results of Ivan and Katrina. In September of last year, I saw the wrath that Hurricane Ivan left in its wake. The sights, the smells, and stories of survival are of such I will never forget. Then along came Katrina. To take nothing away from Ivan, Katrina was far and away more destructive on every level.

This is where a "medium" comes into play. The common American will only see and hear the stories from CNN, The Weather Channel, or The Fox News Channel. Before a storm hits and up until it passes, the primary pictures are that of the traffic jams or the idiotic reporter being blown around in the wind. So far this summer, outside of the flooding of New Orleans, the primary media have said little to nothing about small towns like Biloxi or Gulfport. Sure, they made the news, but only to the fact that the casinos were destroyed and ravaged. No one mentioned the heroic rescues under the rubble in these towns.

Yes, the dramatic air rescues in New Orleans were a sight to behold, and a sight we hope we'll never see again, but lost in the flair of it all were the true stories. This is where the careful choice of medium needs to be considered. If you just show aerial footage of neighborhoods flattened, you've just lost your audience, because with this succession of hurricanes people have a "been there, done that" mentality.

This is why I think the pictures and video my dad and I have done have been very vital in informing people. Much like a crowded mall is noisy, so is the news and coverage of a major hurricane. The news covers the hurricane, but there is little to no emotional attachment to it, unless one has family or friends there. I was in Waveland, Mississippi, shortly after Katrina, and Rev. Matthew Harrison was interviewing this husband and wife who had survived the storm and were sleeping on the ground that once was the foundation of their home—I realized the human element of the storm. I hope the video conveyed that message as well, but in all the chaos the individual human element is lost in all the clatter the national media gives us.

Through just one interview with people who weren't rescued from a rooftop or a group of evacuees, it dawned on me the human tragedy of such a storm. Through one story and the imagery of the surroundings in this small, but leveled community, the entire scale of the storm and tragedy were finally learned. With all the clutter and hearing over and over that 500,000 homes damaged and 2 million people were without power, it is easy to forgot that in those 500,000 households, just one household has a story that will break your heart.

THE AGING OF FEAR

I rented the movie The Sum of All Fears today and watched half of it tonight. Something struck me as I watched it, and it was the evolution of my fear. Two or three years ago, when the movie was released, I had a tough time afterwards because of the threat of nuclear attacks and the fact that the bomb goes off in Baltimore. This immediately struck a chord with the name association with Linda and, all in all, it was a nerve-racking experience.

That was then. Fears of terrorism, death, and any mention of the town of Baltimore were commonplace. In fact, if any of those fears were triggered, it was absolutely disabling. Again, I will say, that was then.

As I write this, I am currently immune to the fears of terrorism, death, and I can hear the name Linda without a second thought. While that probably is a big accomplishment, I must mention that those fears have evolved into a much more hideous animal.

As my awareness of myself has grown, so have the internal fears. The fears mentioned above are mainly external threats. Death can't be avoided, terrorism is uncontrollable, and Linda is crazy. However, looking back, I wish those were my only fears, as now the agony of the current ones are of such that the only word I can think of to describe them is madness.

But what are these current fears? As I mentioned in the previous paragraph, my self-awareness has increased over the past two years. A lot of situations that could have turned out be fatal have occurred. Call it a distorted "realization of the real world," if you want, but my perception of the world has been greatly changed in the past three years.

The summer that the aforementioned movie came out, I was just two years removed from knowing Linda, one year from 9/11, and still in an overly safe relationship with a person with the gung-ho attitude of a three-toed sloth. During that time, there was no thought of myself, but it was all directed outward. The Taliban, Osama Bin Laden, taxes, nuclear war, anthrax, and chemical warfare raining down from the heavens were all the thoughts in my brain.

Enter the year 2003 and the loss of Missy and my house. Little did I realize that the cascading effect would not be realized until tonight. Gone are thoughts of random packages holding a bomb of some type that is here to kill all of us. This would seem to be progress, but, sadly, it is not.

The fears I have now are all internal. Knowing about my condition is almost like having a curse put upon me or being scarred across the face and having people always looking at the scar and knowing people will always look at that scar until the day I die. This is what it is like. The knowledge that there is nothing I can do to change is downright horrifying.

I mentioned the cascading effects. What are those? Accompanied with my newfound knowledge is the vast array of other attributes that come into play. I look now and wonder how I could have been so scared of foreign terrorists when the true terror lies within me. Instead of the fear of being vaporized, I now fear loneliness. Instead of fearing death, I now fear dying alone. Instead of fearing and mourning the loss of my friendship with Linda, I now fear the future friendships that will be unable to take place because of what I am.

Yes, this truly is a nasty beast. While a doctor of some sort would probably say great progress has been made with the "moving on" of the previous four years, I say it is much worse. All the little catastrophes that happened have merged and moved internally. The great fears I had of the outside world have imploded, and now the only fear lies within me.

Lessons learned from those experiences have helped this self-awareness thing, and what was learned is the problem. I always thought that the problem lay with Emily and Linda and their wacky ways, but the block that was there that prevented me from thinking about my short-comings is gone.

I have Asperger's. No one can understand this except me, and even my understanding is vague at best. The fear of the tomorrow is now with me. Formerly, it was the fear of the pain of yesterday, but today it is the fear of tomorrow. Gone are thoughts of regret, but now I deal with the realization that what I am now and the situation I am in now will never change, and that is the scariest thing I think anyone can think about life, and sadly for me, that's where I am now.

MUSIC

Just a note from Dad… There is a talk show that I listen to sometimes at night that warns listeners that the show might contain "psychological nudity." I never thought much about that statement until I read what you are about to read.

I used to ask Aaron why he listened to this song or that song. I didn't understand why he would never answer.

What I have learned, and I think other parents could learn, is that sometimes it is not rudeness or rebellion that causes silence. It just might be the fear of "psychological nudity."

By the title, so many options are at my disposal to write about. I could write about a concert I went to, or I could write about my theory on music theory. However, those would be rather boring, so this topic of music will be much more intense (at least for me) than anything about music theory or any other assorted musical topic I could throw out.

If there is one thing I know Emily couldn't stand about me, it was my evasiveness on the topic of music. Questions such as, "Well, Aaron, did you like this one?" or, "Aaron, what is your favorite genre?" were all answered with the generic answer of, "I don't know." Here lies the issue of music. Do I truly not know what I like, or is more at play here than meets the eyes?

In school, I loathed music talk because I knew the "What music do you listen to?" question would always come up, and every time I would skate around the issue. What was worse than answering the question was the part of thinking about the question. This pattern has steadily gotten worse as I have aged. So what on earth could it be?

Enter "Aaron's music theory." This theory isn't boring like talking about half notes and treble clefs all day, but rather the thought process and near-disabling effect music has.

The first thing when asked about a particular genre of music that comes to mind is an actual song. When one song is thought of, another pops up, and then another, and so on and so on. A lot goes into just a small question, well, at least it does for me. If I were typical, I would assume that music is just that, music. However, for me, music is much deeper than notes and instruments. It is almost a direct path straight into the memory core of my brain. What do I mean? Take, for instance, my drive through the Rockies west of Denver. I had the CD that I made playing at the time, and attached to the songs that were playing each and every quarter-mile is permanently etched into my memory. Or another example is that morning in Lithuania where I heard the song from PGR2. Hearing that song instantly made me remember not only the notes of the song, but all my surroundings in that hotel.

Music for me is a scary thing and unknown entity. But, of course, the question I haven't asked is why am I so private about my music choices (writer's note: There will be a future piece entitled "Privacy," but it won't be written until I open up a little bit more)? That would seem to be a hard question to answer, but I have an answer that requires no second thought. It's simply the matter of that I don't want to think about music. To think about it is to put me right back to a time or place that I heard a song, and then I instantly remember all the emotions of whatever era that song is associated with.

Could this be related to "firsts"? It very well could be, because if a song is playing that is not offensive, a "firsts" possibility in my opinion is quite possible.

But now, back on the issue of privacy of music: Let's say someone asked me if I liked Cher's "Do You Believe in Life After Love?" I instantly will become jammed, because I don't think about the actual song, but rather the time frame that I remember hearing it. Sure, a song can be heard many times innocently and not a second thought will pass, but when something special happens and a song is playing, the two get linked like a very special chemical bond. The song mentioned above was playing when I got my first non-league 300 while I was working at the bowling alley. So, if someone does ask me about the song, I instantly try my best not to recall the times I heard it, but it never works and I go back in time to the place where I heard it.

The association of that Cher song then takes me right back to that hot summer night in 2000 working a Wednesday that saw zero paid bowlers. It was practically empty, so Carol let me bowl until patrons showed up. The scores I threw are irrelevant because that's not what I remember. What I remember is those nights working and being content with my surroundings at that time. What I then remember is the short-term future of that memory and the nights coming home and playing my retro gaming systems and all the life discoveries I found in that summer. All of that is thought of from just the simple question of whether or not I like that song.

Why this happens, I know not, but what I do know is that somewhere there is a very tight bond in my brain that helps music cripple me. I'll just throw out some examples of songs and then list the triggers they trigger... "Ode to Joy"–Hearing someone I know, and wish I still knew, playing it to perfection on a piano.

Any track on the Titanic CD–My entire year of 1997; the car ride I had with my mom to Gordon, Nebraska, in 1999; seeing a tornado on that trip to Nebraska; my entire trip to Kenya; driving from the South County mall to the mall in Crestwood.

Songs from "MVP Baseball2005" and "Burnout3"–These are weird ones. I owned both games, but then sold both. Two days ago, though, I had this deep desire to own both games again, however, it wasn't for the games but rather for the songs that are included in the games. For "Burnout 3," I remember late summer 2004 and the start of the 2004 NFL season. Also, it was the beginning of the end of realizing I would never see Emily again. On "MVP," the tracks take me back to the second month of 2005. I picked the game up the day that I had my meeting at the Linger Group. Also, it was the day I received from my sister a picture that has Missy, Siam, and Amsterdam in it. Also the tracks from "MVP" were in my head right before the hostage incident in Kenya.

I'm out of examples at the moment for the sole purpose of not naming songs you may ask me if I like or not. I want it to be noted that just because I listed the songs above, I do not necessarily like them.

I am truly overloaded while I write this because I am reliving so many things by just mentioning this effect music has on me. One could say that with the memory I have, my life has been scored musically. A soundtrack of my life, one could say.

In a movie, music has a big effect on the moviegoer. It is debatable as to whether or not the movie Jaws would have had the same impact had it not been for those famous spine-tingling notes. The movie Titanic certainly would not have had the same emotional impact had it not been the resounding theme. So, with that being so, what if that same principal carried over out of the movie theater?

Maybe a theory has been done like this before, or perhaps it has already been proven. Whatever the case may be on that, the thing that is important is its effect on me.

Privacy is the part that confuses me. As I have written this so far, I have realized that there is more to that than I first thought. When answering with the same generic answer, not only am I keeping what I like private, I'm also keeping what those songs are tied to private. If I tell someone I like a song, for me it's like exposing to them memories and thoughts on the memories. To give that much away is to give them the keys to my car, house or, heck, why don't I just give them my Social Security number so they can steal my identity? For me, music is more than just notes; it is my life and the gateway to all my memories, and I don't want anyone to know fully the linkage from every song, so if I say, "I don't know," don't take it in offense, but realize that the answer I give is just like clothes: they hide what lies beneath, and if you know what songs I like, I am virtually emotionally naked in your eyes.

TRAVEL

For as many bad things that have happened to me, I have also had a lot of good experiences traveling, and for that I am grateful. I do realize that a very small percentage of people my age have traveled the miles that I have. This could be an important part of why I am still sane. I am very fortunate that I have had many a mile logged.

As I said, I feel fortunate that I have been able to see the sights that I have and that this may be a reason why I am still sane. But what did I mean by that? There is something really odd that happens to me when traveling to a destination that isn't home. It is a feeling of liberation and pure freedom. All prior stressors and mental clutter are gone and my mind is at ease.

If I am in a long car ride, it is like having the recycle bin in my brain emptied. For me, when at home under normal circumstances, my mind is constantly thinking. Even when there's nothing to think about, my mind will stress upon the fact that there is nothing to currently think upon. After a while, that gets really old! But for me, when traveling, there is so much stimuli. Driving for twelve hours in any direction will generate many miles of things to think about. Colors of cars, beautiful landscape, and the thrill of crossing a state line are all examples of some of the minor thrills that make traveling so liberating.

Through all the chaos of the noise of the road, the constant hum of the motor, and ever-changing scenery comes the most tranquil feeling

I know. I do find it odd that something that is so taxing on the senses is one of the most tranquil and peaceful feelings I know.

For what long car rides do for me, long flights and long layovers do even more. As they say, "Half the fun is getting there." For me, it's more like, "All the fun is traveling to and from wherever I am going." The two times I have traveled internationally are the two most peaceful times I can remember. It is very odd that something most people hate is one of, if not the most, peaceful times I know. The long layovers are so nice. Maybe it's the fact that you have to sit and wait and there's nothing you can do about it, so the only thing there is to do is to take in the atmosphere of the airport and watch humanity pass you by. This goes for a long drive as well. Unlike a day in my hometown, a long drive is quite structured, and the matter of the day is not done until the destination is reached.

It is very much like a sporting event. If you go to a baseball game, you know that a regulation game is nine innings; if you go to a soccer match, you know regulation time is ninety minutes. So too is traveling. For flights, you may know your exact estimated time of landing, even if that landing is over six thousand miles away. For a long drive, you will know that if you've gone fifty miles on a five hundred-mile trip, you are one-tenth of the way there.

For me, when on a long drive, all is known. While driving down the road in a car, it is like being on another planet cutoff from all other human interaction three hundred miles at a time. Thoughts regarding money, Emily, the future, and the like are gone, vanished from my mind.

Maybe the feeling I have while traveling is what it is like to be normal. To be able to have a clear mind and not overthink about the importance of an irrelevant fact or emotion is why travel is so liberating. Perhaps this is the true reason travel is the supreme bliss I know.

The thing that is so blissful is the constant change of the cast of characters. When I travel with my dad, the only constant is him, and the world and the other people are always changing. Because of this, my preceptors on my shortcomings and the way people may look at me or think I am different are gone.

On a long plane ride, I would compare the feeling with that of being just two hundred people left in the world. All communication is essentially cut off for the passenger. The outside world is just a tiny speck on the ground, and everything that was stressful is miles away.

Is this an example of running away from a problem? The answer is no. While it may look like it is, it is not, because during the process of getting to a destination, my mind can make sense of the world and not get overloaded.

I always look forward to a long trip. The short time I get to experience normality can't be simulated by any other activity. Because of this, in the back of my mind I always want to ask, "Please tell me that we're not there yet and that we're miles and miles away from our destination so I can enjoy this feeling called normality just a bit longer."

WHAT *HAS* BECOME ... ?

In all the choices I have made in my life, I have always been under the impression that I will be able to see what has become of everything. Time and time again, though, I am left in the dark. What has become of people I used to know? Where is the epilogue that I expect to see?

But why am I under such an impression? This question has rattled through my brain many times with no clear answer. That is, until I thought of my "firsts" theory and movies at the same time.

Nearly every movie or television show right now ties all the loose ends by the time the movie or show is over. Commonplace is sequences of what happened after the story, where the characters are now, if they were based on a real person, and ninety-nine percent of the time, there is complete closure of the story. This, too, takes place in most story-based video games.

It's almost an obsession on how movies tie loose ends. I don't think it used to be that way, though. In the few books I've read that weren't from this century or the last, I noticed the ends are always sudden and vague. Imagination is needed to complete the story, and the story is not handed to you on a silver platter. "What happened next?" is not answered. Flash forward to today and very few TV shows or movies make you ask that question in the end.

What am I getting at? Well, as I said above, the extreme choices I have made, I had no concept of a complete cutoff from other people. When I made my choice on what to do with Linda, I figured I would always know how she was and what was next for her. Same thing applies with Emily. I thought I never would ask the question, "What has become of her?"

"What has become of …?" is a question I have asked many times these past four years. I never realized, though, that in life there aren't answers readily available to that question. If "firsts" is true, then a child who watches movies or television may pick up on something. That something is the fact that one will nearly always know how the story ends.

This is a scary notion, if true. Life experiences shattered my belief of what life was in this regard. I still constantly wonder that question of "What has become …?" and it drives me into this huge mental jam. I think that I should not have to ask that, because I should know the answer. Why? Because that's the way life is supposed to be. Then the true-to-life experiences tell me that is not so. Then I wonder why it is portrayed that people always know. I lost dear friends because of this thought that a complete cutoff of communications isn't possible.

The media that bombard us everyday are very dangerous for children. That statement is a bit old, but in this instance I am not talking about violence or drugs, but rather in perception of life. I'll use myself in the example when I learned the concept of "the end isn't really the end." What does that mean? How many movies have you seen where a person who dies isn't really dead? Or another example is a relationship that was destroyed becomes stronger in the end.

So I learned that the end isn't really the end. That concept isn't a bad one to have when you're five. However, as time goes by and that concept isn't overridden by experiences, there will be a problem.

Right now, I believe I don't miss Emily at all, but the pain comes in the fact that I don't know a thing about her since the end of our relationship. Just that thought brings so much confusion. The truly painful thing that I am aware of is another reminder of what I have. It isn't the person I miss, but facts that I don't know. In other words, it's not them at all. It is another example of my incapability to feel emotions toward others. The same thing holds true for Linda.

I don't know if a person can even try and imagine what this feels like. On one hand, I have the immense pain of not knowing how they are. But, furthermore, I realize it isn't them I am feeling pain about, and that is the biggest, deepest hurt there is, because I realize that it will always be like that. To know that I am unable to grieve over a loss of a friend, except in the knowledge I have lost, is about the worst pain I can feel. It totally destroys my self-esteem because it makes me feel cold and heartless, because in those movies and television shows, it never played out like that.

This distorted logic is quite dangerous because the question of "What has become ... ?" can be applied to anything. I often wonder what became of that aluminum can I have written about on separate occasions, or the flight attendant on the flight from Lithuania to Poland that smiled way too much, or the bellhop from the hotel in Kenya, or a dollar bill I may have had in my wallet for a month. The possibilities are endless.

Life is hard to live, though, while constantly being drug into the past with those questions. It's much like a driving a car. If you are constantly looking in the rearview mirror, you cannot see where you're going, and then you won't recognize the objects in the mirror because you didn't notice them while you were headed forward, so then you are always a step, or many steps, behind. Me, I'm years behind. By the way, "Whatever became of the ... ?"

FEAR VS. FEAR

One of the best baseball games of all time took place about a month ago in the National League Divisional Playoffs. Atlanta and Houston were deadlocked after some heroics on Houston's part. What happened after the heroics was a marathon of scoreless baseball. What started as an afternoon affair turned into a game that saw the start of dusk. Chris Burke broke the tie in the bottom of the 18th with a walk-off home run and ended the longest playoff game of all time.

Let's say, though, that all the players were so tired that no one had the strength to hit a home run, much less swing the bat. The game would be in equilibrium and neither side would have the chance to win, making the game go on forever. Granted, a team would eventually run out of arms on the mound and someone would eventually hit a ball long enough, but in this instance, let's say that wouldn't happen. Both sides would be exhausted and nobody would be able to win, making the game last forever.

This is what it's like for me. Neither side of my fears can win. The interesting thing about the two fears is that if one would prevail, the other would be taken care of. Instead of being taken care of, though, they are currently in the 105th inning of play.

So what are the two fears? One of them is the much-repeated topic of money. The other one is the fear of the pain of working in society.

Let's talk about the money fear first (fear A). So far in the second half of this year, I have made some money to get to my goal of what I would be comfortable with, or so I thought. After nearly a year and a half chasing that goal, I achieved it, but the fear didn't go away. In fact, the anxiety increased by an alarming amount. Instead of fearing having zero dollars and not having the goal, I now have double the fear of zero dollars and triple the fear of falling below the safe level.

As I have mentioned before, it is always something. There is always something that my mind will obsess on and worry about. What is truly interesting, I believe, is the fact that I was more comfortable having little money. With having it, I now worry about losing it. I tend to look at the big picture (referring to time and future), so the only thing I can see is expenditures and not possible income.

On the flip side is the fear of the work place (fear B). (I think it should be noted that when I use the word "fear," I don't mean it as, say, a fear of spiders or rabid rhinos from the zoo that may escape, but rather the deepest fear that one can have and that is internal fear.) If I were able to work, the fear of money would be negated because there would always be income. On paper this seems really easy, as logic would dictate that if this fear was broken, all would be fine and dandy.

It's not that easy, though. The multitude of stressors at a job is too much to bear. Some of them are socializing, the irrelevance of being perfect, and the time of it all. Every day I wish I could be in the normal crowd and just live with it, so both fears would dissolve away.

So those are the two fears that are battling it out now in the 106th inning. Neither side is willing to throw in the towel and the cruel game continues. To be stuck in this is aggravating beyond belief. To realize that it would be so easy to conquer fear B and that would dissolve fear A. But at this point the two are engaged in this eternal tie game. The deep sadness that fear A gives me is equal to what fear B causes me. In other words, just like the ballgame, they are equal.

That is the most aggravating thing of all. Much like a strong river that has a piece of driftwood caught in two currents, I am stuck in the middle with no free will, bound by the two currents. I can think all I want on the matter and neither side gains or loses anything. It is a very sick and twisted game.

I've had this equality of fears for as long as I can remember. Even in school I thought of this. It was a bit different, as fear B would represent school instead of the workplace, but I still feared money. I was always told that one must go to school so they can make more money, but the pain of school made for the first game of fear versus fear.

Time progressed, and I got a job at a bowling alley. I wasn't affected too much at the time; because since I was sixteen and I was ahead of the game and I wasn't forced to be there, it really wasn't a job, but rather getting ahead. However, as many other things in my life, time progressed and I did not. From getting ahead to falling behind, it was quite painful. People I knew were going to college and, as I was told, college means money. But yet again, the evenness of fears made me go through life much like that piece of driftwood. I could do nothing except stay on the path I was on.

So here I am now, stuck in the middle with the game, about to go to the 107th inning. By this time in the game, all the fans have left, and even the television network has cut away. The players are all alone. With the pain that being stuck in this game has brought, so am I.

SENTENCE

A sentence is a scary thing. Not the type of sentence that is written on a computer or with pen and paper, but rather the type convicts receive. Outside of the death penalty, the highest of sentences is the life sentence. When the felon hears the verdict of a life sentence, all is lost. Everything before is irrelevant, as for the rest of their lives they will not be free. I didn't commit a crime, but the day it was told that I have Asperger's it was very much like a gavel crashing down, finalizing my fate.

Before my sentence, I always knew I was a bit different. I always thought it was just because I was smarter and more mature than others my age. I always thought that my rigidity came from the fact that I firmly knew I was right and everyone else was wrong. Little did I know the truth that it wasn't them, but me.

After I knew my fate, I slid into a deep depression. Knowing what I had made me think that all my life was going to be like a train on tracks in that I would be unable to deviate from where the tracks take me. The tracks in this example are the limitations of Asperger's.

Not only was it hard for me, but it was surprisingly hard for Emily. At first she wanted to hear none of it. I don't know if it was denial or not wanting to hear a label put on me (she hated labels). That deafness turned into an intense and resounding hatred of it. "You'll never be able to like me!" and, "You can never change nor accept me," were some of the quotes I heard. Not only had I been sentenced, but with it came solitary confinement.

She was partially right, though, in the fact that I cannot change. However, the part about being able to like is completely false, but I don't show it like a normal person. In the end, this sealed the deal and resulted in the end of our relationship. When I needed someone the most, I was abandoned. This was a "first" in that I knew no one could like me because of what I have. My mind knew solitary would last forever.

With the sentence came the knowledge that normality would always elude me. Love? Forget about it. Not having weird little obsessions? Ha! Friends? Get used to spending evenings with reruns on television. The sentence is about the most depressing thing I can think of because it within itself shows no hope. And to know what I am missing is the worst feeling I can think anyone can feel. I've heard people say phrases such as, "All you need is love," and, "Friends are what make the day worthwhile," but neither one of those phrases can apply to me.

Time has progressed, and I have often wondered how things would be if I didn't know. They say, "What you don't know can't hurt you," but this raises the logical and relevant question of just who "they" really are. Finding out why I am what I am was very important. If I had never known, I believe there would be more self-hatred, because instead of blaming a syndrome, I would blame myself.

Finding out about it has changed my life forever. The sentence was read to me by a doctor, but even if I had never found out, I would still have a soul and be an Asperger's sufferer walking.

CRIPPLED IN ADDICTION

Addictions are generally bad. There are many hotlines for people who have addictions. Whether it be gambling or drinking, there are organizations that exist to help people with their addiction. But what if a person can be addicted to anything? What then?

Everything I do is done based on an addiction. I don't do anything unless I'm addicted to it. Perhaps the word "obsession" is better suited rather than addiction, but "addiction" is a stronger and more powerful word, and furthermore, obsessions aren't always viewed as a negative. For me, addictions cripple me.

If a person does everything that they are addicted to, then one could not do new things. For me, one of the addictions is the routine of things. If I do something the first time, I must do it the second. I remember that the first time my dad and I went to the Supercross event in St. Louis, we stopped at a diner. The year after, I insisted, and we did so for the next five years. Then I met Emily and went to the annual event with her, and, you guessed it, we stopped at that diner to eat every year after until 2004. The past two years, my dad and I have not done so, and I felt a great deal of remorse and anxiety. It's almost as if that diner takes on a human existence, and to not stop there is to hurt its feelings. This is just one example of dozens of these routines I live by.

The example above mentions an annual event. If something on an annual scale is strong, think about daily and weekly routines that are there. Emily and I always went to a pizza place before Monday night bowling. She is no longer with me, but the routine of going there has not died. It isn't that I want to go there (well, maybe it is), but rather that I have to go there. To not go there is unthinkable.

The scope of addictions, though, goes farther than just routine. The repetitive thoughts I have don't disappear. Money, global politics, the idiocy of why there is no Interstate 50 are just some of the thoughts that keep going around and around. But, for this example, I will use money.

Of all thoughts, money takes up the most. There is nothing feared more than money. Of all addictions, this is the one that creates the most fear. I am unable to fathom "money coming in," meaning money that is coming to be but not here yet. There isn't a bigger anxiety causer than this. As I have stated before, I generally don't trust people, so then I always think that I will never get the money. Then, as the thoughts go on, I calculate the future expenditures and in the end of the thoughts, I am penniless and asking for dimes on a snowy street corner in Duluth, Minnesota.

The part that hurts about this is that I am unable to do anything about it. I often think about working at a bank again, but many other addictions clash. There should be a movie entitled When Addictions Clash, because there isn't anything scarier. And for me this causes a crippling blanket that keeps me in stasis.

For example, let's say I got a job at a different bank. First thing is, it wouldn't be the old bank. Secondly, I'd have to meet new people. Thirdly, I would start thinking about the possibility of being robbed and shot. Don't tell me that this is a self-fulfilling prophecy, because I am already starting to think about that and I haven't even filled out an application. This feeling of being stuck in the middle of two addictions is downright crippling. And not only crippling, but it constantly gives blows to my self-esteem that a heavyweight fighter would be proud of.

An addiction can be anything and everything. And, as good or bad as one may be, it is extremely painful to be interrupted. Back when I lived with my mom and worked at a bowling alley, I would always play the same games when I got home. And about fifty percent of the time, my mom would want to talk or have me do some irrelevant chore that could easily be taken care of in the morning. This created extreme friction, because she was hindering me on what I was doing. At the time, I did not realize why I got so mad, but now I do. It was that I was addicted to what I was doing. This trend of being interrupted is still around. Ask my dad how reliable I am at taking out the trash or a pizza box if he asks me to do it while I'm doing something.

I just had an interesting thought. Perhaps my money addiction is based upon the fact if I had enough, I wouldn't be interrupted by the thought of it. Then, if that's so, the addiction of money is clashing with the addiction of routine, proving further that the psychological thriller When Addictions Clash could be the scariest thing to hit movie theaters since the time that one movie did that one thing.

I'll mention this again, I don't know if the use of the word "addiction" is right. Routines, obsessions, or compulsive behavior may all fit. Whatever the word is, it is irrelevant because it doesn't change the fact that I am still what I am.

Back on topic now, what is it about being interrupted that is so aggravating that I could literally get so angry that I could break something? Just the small thing of someone closing a door can break my mode of thought to the degree that I want to scream. I constantly tell myself that it isn't a big deal, but then I'm just lying to myself because to everyone else it isn't a big deal, but to me it is strong enough to raise my pulse to the point I can feel the blood flowing through my fingertips.

Perhaps a good analogy would be a train. They do call it a train of thought (has anyone seen the real "they," because they say lots of things?) and when a door shuts or I am asked to do something, it is like taking out ten feet of track, and when the train gets there, it makes for a spectacular derailment. This derailment process is a big problem I had at the video game store. When there were constant sales I had no problem, but in the middle part when the manager would ask me to do something that I deemed stupid, it immediately derailed me.

This is saddening to realize because I know how stuck up or snobbish I sound. What gives me the power to deem a task stupid? Why should I have gotten upset when my mom wanted to talk? Why do I get so upset when someone closes the door to the room where I write this? The answer is, I have no power to say so, but that doesn't change the matter that I feel so much anxiety when any of those things happen. If you were to step on a cat's paw, they would possibly strike at your foot. What gives them the power to say no to the fact that you're on their foot? Not only are you bigger, but you're considered their master. But the reason why they'll strike is for two reasons. One of them is the simple fact that it hurts, but the other is the attempt at self-preservation.

When derailed from an addiction, I get so angry that all life is deemed nearly irrelevant. Depression, anxiety, anger, animosity, and self-hatred are all experienced. Most of the time, my brain is like one of those bullet trains in Japan. In other words, it is going really fast and my brain likes it that way. But when something out of the routine comes in, it knocks that speeding train right off the tracks, then my thoughts aren't in that controlled environment that most addictions provide (this doesn't include money).

I know I have to look and sound weird when a wrench is thrown into my routine. The sad part is that I realize this. However, attempting some self-preservation trumps the looking foolish part. So important is the need to be speeding down the tracks that I will do anything I can to prevent a derailment. This within itself is an addiction.

Emily learned quite quickly that I get a tad bit on the testy side when things don't go according to the plan. And I get especially angry when it involves tardiness. One time when I went to pick her up, she was ten minutes late getting out of the house, and those ten minutes were ten minutes of pure loathing. To compare this to my time being held by murderous homeless boys in Africa was not as great of mental trauma as sitting in my car waiting. Think about that. A life-threatening ordeal was not as bad to my overall psychological well-being as sitting in a car in a comfortable climate with nothing remotely life-threatening happening.

My least favorite day in school was always the topsy-turvy day. This was when the regular order of the day was thrown out and each subject up next was determined by a draw. Not knowing what was next threw me outside the routine and the addiction was lost. For those days, it was like stopping an addiction cold turkey. These days only occurred in second and seventh grade, but I made sure to do everything in my power to avoid going to school on those days.

Now I have to mention the racing aspect. A racecar driver is always traveling. Drivers may have a race in Phoenix during the day, and by midnight that night they are back home in North Carolina. I can't think of a better living than that. Through the madness of constant change comes sameness. I know this is true because this is what the international trips I have been on are like. There isn't enough time for a "constant" addiction to occur; therefore, I am free. I'm sure my dad would say I am somewhat different on trips, and this is the reason why.

There is addiction in my writing style as well. I always use the same font type for the title and then for the actual piece. I have tried to change it just for change's sake but am unable to.

I don't know of a solution to this problem. My brain is wired to the point that to take these away would be almost like removing Windows from a computer. Yes, you'd still have the computer, but with no operating system, it would be useless. I wish it were as simple as just switching to Linux, but that would be just too easy, wouldn't it? And then there's the fear of learning a new OS, then what happens if it malfunctions and their customer support team isn't good, and what if…

MUST ...

In everyday life, there are many things that must be done. Eating and sleeping are examples of this. Our minds are programmed to tell us when these are needed. For me, there are other things that reach obsessive levels that don't go away and the only way out is to just do them.

"I must think of a way to make money" is a common "must." I must think about it. Beyond the fact of thinking about how to make the money, I think about the process of must thinking about money. It's like spyware on a computer. Your computer may be running properly, but hiding deep within a program it is silently running and, at moment's notice, produces a popup ad on your screen.

These near obsessive thoughts are vigorous in their pursuit to make whatever their objective is to be done. Maybe it's a spur of OCD, but whatever the case, there is no known way in my mind to break the cycle when it starts.

This can easily be tied into "firsts." Once a thought comes into the mind, it is there for good, and the only way to end it is to achieve whatever the must is. One of the two examples I'll use in this paper is my mission to become the number one racer on "Project Gotham Racing 3," more commonly known as PGR3.

PGR3 was a launch title for the Xbox 360. Previously, I had been number one on three other racing games and my mind was set on making this the fourth game I was top of the world in. You could say that it is motivation that is pushing me to get there, or pure desire, but neither is the case. The only reason is that I must get number one. There is no alternative to this. Number one is the only option and nothing else will do.

When I got the game, I adapted quickly to the new console and new game. I got the system four days late, so that meant many people had a leg up on me, so I needed to learn quickly, and I did so. I quickly moved into the top one hundred, top fifty, and after a week, I cracked the top ten.

In online games there is a "lag" factor. With so many servers and Xboxes communicating with each other, there is always the risk that a person may "lag out," meaning they are dropped from the race. The person who is so unfortunate will see on his screen that everyone quit the race, but in all reality, they are the only one that dropped out. The main race will finish and the driver who lagged out will take a last place and lose a lot of points to everyone else, because the system will think that the driver quit.

As I cracked the top ten, I hadn't suffered a lag out, but my luck was up. One lag out and I dropped from tenth to sixteenth. Shortly thereafter, another lag out dropped me from fourteenth to twenty-third. This was devastating! I was good enough to be number one, and circumstances outside my control were preventing me from getting there. Oddly, I felt the most anger toward myself. The thoughts were that I must be number one, but with this lagging out, I'd be unable to, but even so, I must be on top for no other reason than to just be there. It's not to prove that I am the best, or good, but simply because I must do it.

Because of that driving force that is "must," that is the equivalent of a mile-long coal train traveling downhill at fifty-five miles per hour. I kept at it. Twenty-third became twentieth, became fifteenth, then back to where I was before the lag outs began. With me recovering, I went on a winning tear and cracked the top five within a day and a half. I got up to fourth and the top three was in sight.

One thing you must know is that the rating system is called Trueskill. It was developed by two professors at Cambridge University and is loosely based on the chess ELO system. Because of this, the interval between third and fourth is much greater than it is from eighty-ninth to ninetieth. When I say much greater, it is much like the Richter scale in that a 7.0 earthquake is nowhere near as strong as an 8.0. That being said, when I got to third, it was a milestone. Now there were just two spots left, and I must overtake those two spots.

The next day I worked at it and I got second. I was now within one spot of the position I must be in. Then fate dealt a cruel blow, a lag out. Then, if that wasn't bad enough, fifteen minutes later it happened again. I fell from second to ninth. How could this happen? I was so close! The feelings I felt were of deep, deep rage. I constantly hit the arm of the chair with enough force to sprain my left hand. With the "must" I had in my mind, there was no option than to be first, and now it seemed like it would be impossible.

I regrouped and again went on a winning streak like no other. Ninth turned to seventh, seventh turned to fourth, and I was back at the pen-ultimate position. I knew the gap between second and first prior to me taking second was like the gap between New York and London. I worked and worked and finally I got what I set out to do and I was number one. But now what?

Was there joy? There was a little, but nothing overjoyous. The obsessive must thoughts were put to ease, but what was left was a void. Literally, my mind thought, Now what? I worked and I worked and I worked at it and I got it, but unlike the runners in the New York City marathon that have a fanfare at the finish, I had nothing except a number one by my name.

Perhaps in the obsessive nature of having to get first, the rareness and greatness of that spot's meaning is lost. Anyone who is in the medium skill level would probably give an arm or a leg, or maybe in the least one hundred dollars just to be number one for a day. There are over fifty thousand people and I was number one. Skill might have gotten me there, but there was no other option because I "must" be in that spot.

"I must" isn't isolated to global domination of a video game. It can be as minor wanting a candy bar just because I might need to eat it five days later. A quick example could be the sunflower seeds I eat. I have a tub that has several bags worth in it. If I were to eat an hour a day, there would be at least a week's worth in it. I keep a couple bags in reserve just in case I run out. At 2:00 a.m. last Friday, I used my last reserve bag and I literally panicked. While I had a week's worth in my tub, there was no reserve. So I got my shoes on and in the middle of the night I went to the store to buy more just in case I were to run out.

Somewhere in my life I was taught that I always need a reserve. This is where "firsts" and "musts" meet. The "first" is needing the reserve; therefore, I must have the three extra bags. The two may seem the same, but they are separate entities, albeit intertwined with each other.

The final example I'll use is of this game I bought today. For the Xbox, I bought (please don't laugh) "Karaoke Revolution Party." As the name implies, it is a karaoke game, and you play by using a microphone and it uses voice recognition to know if you are on pitch or not. The game has fifty songs, but I looked on the game's downloadable content and saw that for a certain price you could download one hundred more. If you read about the sunflower seeds, you already know about the conflict to come.

I haven't played the game yet, but I knew there were more songs. Immediately, I must have those extras, but what about the price? "It will drop me close to my limit I don't want to drop below, but I need, no, must have it, but the cost, but I must!" is a clip of the constant barrage of bantering that went on.

In the end, I could not withhold the urge and I purchased the additional song packs even though I could've in the future when I'll play the game and have more money.

Both primary examples, while completely different, are of the same nature. Once the mind is set, there is no alternative. I feel that the musts are a stem of firsts. Firsts are the rules that the mind lives by, and the musts carry out the rules. Yes, this makes perfect sense in the PGR case. The first I learned is that I need to be in first (I believe I picked that up in school because in most everything I always was so); therefore, I must be in first. When such expectations exist, there can be no joy in getting there because it is expected, and when something is expected it is of little relevance, because that's "just the way it is supposed to be."

Impulsive buying remains somewhat of a mystery to me. Once I learn of a product I want, my mind will not stop until the product is in hand. I'm sure retailers love that mentality, but I know I do not. Perhaps the collectible market racket's clients all have Asperger's, because they all must purchase the next product.

Musts stem further than those two examples. When in a new conversation I must get the upper hand and have most of the control so perhaps racing can be talked about. Musts are the results of firsts and could be the survival mechanism that keeps the mind on track. As unbreakable as a first is, a must is even more so. Firsts taught me so.

THE HAZARDS
OF FIRSTS

(Possible chapter two to my thesis)

After writing "Must ... ," many thoughts came into my head, so many thoughts, in fact, that I am unable to sleep. The thoughts just keep coming. As I write this, it is 5:00 a.m., but I feel as if I am in the middle of the afternoon.

As I wrote in the must paper, the "must be" attitude stems from firsts. You could almost call the must the judge, jury, and executioner of the law created by the firsts. This can be very good, but it also can be very, very bad.

All aspects of my life are dictated by firsts. The firsts are the groundwork for who I am and the musts are the things that keep everything in line. This can be very bad, as a must is very hard to ignore. Single-track thinking is very common once a single must is the sole thought.

I've written before that it can be very scary and bring a lot of anxiety when there is nothing to think about. That's because there must be something to think about at all times. This is where it gets tricky. If life makes it to where a must is impossible to get to, all chaos breaks loose. Extreme rage and hatred of everything will pulse through my entire body. This can be caused by the smallest of things like a lag out in a video game.

Using what I would think to be a normal person's logic, a position in a video game would be of little consequence in the grand scheme of life, but for me, because it was what my mind was focused on, it became everything. Think about that. My mind was so focused on what the must said I needed that it was everything. When the lag outs happened, to say I was devastated would be an understatement. I was nearly paralyzed by having my circuits blown. It was much like an EMP burst that changed the magnetic field that in turn knocked my internal compass off so I had no idea which way was which.

That example is the hazard of firsts. In the grand scheme of life, it was not even a minor setback. A number that represents rank in a game that awards no prizes was lowered by a tiny fraction. I can't imagine the devastation that someone with Asperger's would feel if something bigger was lost, much like I lost a little bit of rank.

This concept of firsts keeps getting scarier for me because, now if musts are true, an Asperger's mind is much like a game of "Jenga." If you play the game right, the tower of blocks will be steady, but all it takes is just one block for the tower to come crashing down.

I've read and heard that many people with Asperger's have just one interest. This is the biggest security blanket and further proves my point. If a person has just one field of interest, change will be little. I've also heard that those fields are normally in a safe and constant environment; therefore, the firsts and musts can be played out with little to no interference.

Interference for me is a very discomforting event. I'd call the mentioned lag out more than interference, so I won't use that as an example. However, minor events that change the way the formula works can create a minor meltdown. Formula, you ask? It works like this: The firsts are the way it was; therefore, it must be like the first.

One of the major interferences that comes about is in rules. Rules were not meant to be broken. Let's take "Monopoly" for an example. I will fight tooth and nail to keep in force the ten-percent interest fee to get back-mortgaged from the bank. "Oh, that's a stupid rule," is a comment often heard with that rule, but it's in the rules and it's been that way since 1935. I do have some "house rules," as they are called.

Minor tweaks that are added to the game, but the ones I have are perfect, and at another person's house I will not bend on my rules. To do so is to create a rift in the order of things. If a game of "Monopoly" can be canceled just because of these firsts and musts, I can't imagine the bigger things that can come about.

I guess I can imagine the bigger things that could happen, and none of them are good. Marriages destroyed, violent outbursts, and loss of life come to mind. I believe these could be avoided; however, a near perfect environment has to be preserved for life, and, as we all know, life isn't perfect.

With that being so, it's becoming clearer and clearer why one with Asperger's may have an obsessive fascination with a certain brand of car. A 1955 Chevy will always be a 1955 Chevy. Whoever designed it then will always have the credit of designing it, the number produced will never change, and it's a constant, and every other aspect of that brand will always be constant. Same thing goes for any other oddity like cars, trains, planes, presidents, the 1911 baseball season, and any other thing like that you can think of.

So as I have mentioned, when the internal compass gets derailed, bad things happen. What can be done? Parenting is the first and foremost important field of defense. Parents themselves can't change what the firsts and musts become, but they can prevent certain ones from forming. Also, trying to change ones that are planted could lead to rebellion or fits of outrage.

I can remember back when I was seven, I had a dentist appointment at eight at night on a Saturday. Yes, I know it was an odd time for an appointment, but it was made worse because it was the Saturday that NASCAR has their night race at Bristol. To make matters worse, I would be able to watch the start of the race, then I would be forced, against my will, to go to the dentist. I can remember telling the dentist that he should hurry so I could get home. When he came back with the snippy comment of, "That isn't a way a good patient would act. Don't you want to be a good little patient?" I snapped. I remember crying aloud. Why didn't he understand? Bristol was on and I was missing it! I told him a race was on and he was completely clueless that they even raced on Saturday night. This confused me. Why didn't he know, and furthermore, why wasn't he hurrying?

As you can tell by the emphasis, this was a very heated moment for me when I was seven. This is the type of interference that I was talking about. Racing was implanted in my mind as a first; therefore, I must watch the race as it happens, and this dentist didn't have the foggiest of idea of the need I had to get home. I'm sure my parents were confused of this strong desire to miss that appointment and to the severity of stress it caused.

That type of scene is probably repeated day in and day out with little to no thought as to why a seven-year-old can want something that seems irrelevant so badly. Therefore, as I said, parents are the first line of defense. If they were to know that this existed, scenes like this could be minimized. Had I not had good parents, that outburst could have been repeated, but with worse consequences later in life.

Each day is like a tightrope walk. Interference can't be avoided. I'm thankful I realize that fact. Without that, I would easily fall off the tightrope and plummet to whatever lies below. However, when musts are interfered with constantly, there can be no balance good enough to keep me on the wire.

I believe the good thing is that I have discovered this hazard, and as long as a hazard is known, it can be dealt with. The worst of times is when there's a problem, but no reason is known as to why there's a problem. Parents who are unaware could literally drive their kid/teen/young adult to death trying to help when they are actually doing everything that is just the complete opposite of what needs to be for stability.

I know it would be next to impossible to change the firsts I have. If firsts are true, as I believe them to be, other people with Asperger's will have the same traits; therefore, the only defense for families is knowledge. The family will not be able to change the individual, but they may be able to change the individual's future so it is much brighter and happier.

MEDIA AND "FIRSTS"

The purpose of this piece is to do my best and explain the severe hazards of today's various media. I believe I have written about this in segments but never in one big piece that all relates to firsts ... This is a stupid comment, but we live in a world in which we are constantly bombarded by media. Print, radio, and television are just a few. In fact, some people wake up to the media via their alarm clocks. In a perfect world, this isn't a bad thing. Add Asperger's to the equation and things get a bit tricky, as well as possibly dangerous. Why do I believe it is dangerous? To start, we must go back one hundred-plus years.

I heard somebody say that autism spectrum people are on the rise statistically speaking. Is it that the numbers are really on the rise, or is the means to notice it getting better? You see, one hundred years ago a person couldn't really live comfortably, as survival was above living. Perhaps maybe this was true 150 years ago rather than one hundred, but the number is irrelevant, because it's the fact of the matter that is important.

Since I can't agree on 100 or 150, I'll use 125 as an example. Survival was paramount. People didn't worry about missing a television show, people weren't aware of the fact that a Top 40 countdown of music could exist. There was only one thing that mattered: survival! Sure, the aristocrats were able to enjoy a life of luxury, but the numbers then are much less than they are now. The point of all this is that a person with Asperger's would not have been as noticeable as they are now. Two reasons I assume this: 1) survival was the ultimate first, and 2) their lives could not be influenced by today's media.

Let's flash forward to today. Knowledgeable five-year-olds in a middle-class home may have multiple forms of open-ended media at their disposal. Not that many years ago, print media was it and nothing else. Now, the five-year-old can have video games, television, and the open-ended universes of the Internet at their disposal. The amount of information at anyone's fingertips is mind-boggling, and for someone who may take many "first" snapshots, it is too many.

Twenty-five years ago video games were limited to arcades that were primarily teenage hang-outs. Today with the Xbox, Gamecube, and the portable systems, a video game can be played nearly anywhere. If a first is developed, there may be no other world for a child with Asperger's except within the game. Since the child probably doesn't have to worry about starving to death, the game becomes life. With this being so, why would the child need social interaction? They wouldn't need it because they don't know it. This is sort of like a drag race, and, in this instance, the game won with socialization finishing a distant second and, therefore, it is never given a second thought.

With the example above, the child learned to play the game, and since it became a first, it won't leave. What's the point of everything else if only the game matters? Using that logic, what would the point of anything be if it doesn't include the video games? This is a small example, and I can think that this one-track mind can be expanded to include anything and everything. Much like a computer program being programmed for one and only one function, so too is this proverbial child who takes a devout interest in video games.

Television, too, is a scary medium. There are so many genres of shows, and as of now, I can't think of one that is beneficial. I'm not trying to sound like the chairman of the FCC, but for a child with Asperger's, the television medium is a barrel full of firsts that can destroy a child's way of thought.

If a family watches the news, the child with Asperger's will quickly learn of the evil in the world and quickly hate everyone because of the death factor. It used to be that a child learned about death through the loss of a grandparent, but now, turn on the news and you will hear of a suicide bomber in the Middle East, a murder-suicide in New York, a workplace shooting downtown, a small plane crash in the mountains, and the list goes on and on.

A century ago, the world for most people ended on the street corner. This would be ideal for an Asperger's person because the evil would be unknown. Now, though, we live in a global community where all the evil of the world is known. For a child with Asperger's, this is very, very bad! I can remember at the outset of the Desert Storm asking repeatedly, "But why will they fight, and why will people die, and will it happen here?" I think I was fortunate in the fact that I was able to express this concern, but had I not those fears would have sat there and gotten worse and worse over time.

The TV also affects interpersonal relationships. If firsts are able to form at any age, very bad habits can be picked up at an early age with no one knowing the long-term ramifications. The television wants us to believe that a murder and a co-worker romance conflict can be cured in one hour or less minus those all-important commercials. They cannot under most circumstances, but if the first has been laid down, it becomes confusing as to why not. I can take my relationship with Emily and apply this mode of thought. I broke up with her many times, but I always expected things to be the same after we got back together, and since I already said it in this sentence, I always expected to get back together.

One thing television doesn't do fast is change. Yes, I know the camera angles change much faster than they used to, but shows and characters move as fast as an eighteen-wheeler going up a steep incline in the snow. This is good that it doesn't change, but when the inevitable happens, damage can be done. I am curious for the current young people who have Asperger's who watch "Jeopardy" as to how they were affected when Ken Jennings, the seventy-four-day-straight champion, left the show. Because he was on for so long, a routine had to have been developed, so I wonder if there were any issues with his departure.

With all the forms of media, I believe the symptoms of Asperger's are more prevalent than in the nineteenth century. To make an analogy, in the nineteenth century, every person had the same Operating System—survival! But today, it is like having normal people using Windows and a person with Asperger's using a Macintosh. While both get the job done, the two don't intermingle all that well.

The bad thing with the current forms of media is that they are almost impossible to avoid. For a normal person, these can be enjoyable half-hour escapes from the stress of daily life. For a person with Asperger's, it can be the Bible of which life should be lived, and then when the real world hits, there is no reset button, no power button, and the channel can't be changed, and the sad thing is, there may be no understanding that everything won't be wrapped up before the eleven-o'clock news.

FUTURE

If there is one thing more frightening than any other object, fact or fiction, in the entire universe for me, it is the future. They say that if you don't know history, you're bound to make the same mistakes. Well, that's fine and all, but that does nothing for what might or might not happen in five, fifteen, or twenty-five minutes. Could there be a phone call? What if it says that the number is unlisted? Will the doorbell ring? Will someone shut the door I loathe?

All the above questions get asked every second of every day. They are relentless. The questions range in variety, though, and they stem from something as simple as the time of dinner to what I will be doing in a year's time.

With all the time and effort my mind puts in trying to calculate the future, it takes a major toll on my overall psyche. In most cases, I am only comfortable when I am able to predict the outcome. To make a simple analogy, it would be like a small child's toy that when you press a button, it makes a noise. Before the button is pressed, there would be great anxiety because I wouldn't know what exactly would happen, but after one time, it becomes like second nature.

That analogy works great on simple things, but one must remember that I try and figure out what everything will be. Let's do some math … There're sixty seconds in a minute and sixty minutes in an hour and twenty-four hours in a day, making the week 168 hours long. Now to make the true pain of my mind be known, let's multiply sixty seconds by sixty minutes, then we see that there are 3600 seconds in an hour, and now that total times twenty-four hours gets us 86,400 seconds in just one day. Every second I am up, I am constantly telling myself what's going to happen next. When the current next comes and goes there's another one, and another one, and it just keeps going on like that.

If I had no previous worldly experiences, this wouldn't be bad. If I did not know of the outside world, this wouldn't be that bad of an existence, but because I know of the world, it makes it all the more difficult. I have to throw in variables of death, money, change, and a whole host of other things that can change everything. I do know this holds true for everyone, but I try and prepare for everything, and regardless of the situation, it is practically impossible to prepare for all circumstances.

This is why games are so alleviating. In the instruction booklet, the game makers have done the work for me by giving direction on all possible situations that come up within the game. I wish life were more like chess. Chess is bound by the rules of movement. A bishop can only move diagonally on whichever color it started on, a king can only move one space in direction, and so on and so forth. Life, however, is like the queen in that she can move in any direction at any distance on any given turn so long as there's a straight line. If every piece within the game of chess were allowed this movement, it would be all-out chaos; so too is life.

With all my thoughts on the future, I am able to withstand not knowing so much; however, when too many variables become present, I slow down and get irritable, much like a computer with too many Web browsers open while using a 56k modem. I can handle the unknown of a few things, but open it up by just one too many and an interior meltdown is imminent.

I know what I'm saying is impossible in this life. I can't imagine the pain people have that don't realize this. At least I can recognize that the various variables are the cause of the pain, but if I did not know, I believe the pain would be worse and I might go looking for answers in all the wrong places. I believe this was one of the fatal blows with Emily; at the time I did not know what was going on and why I am who I am. With the knowledge, there is still pain and severe anguish; however, it can be directed inward instead of outward, and that will minimize the amount of other variables I'll have to contend after the initial ones that are the current stressors.

MY PERCEPTION
OF LIFE

There is no greater influence on a person on how they are in the world than how they perceive the world. Perception is vital to survival. A normal person is lucky in the sense that their perception can easily be changed. However, for me, it can't be.

The most terrifying perception I have, and the hardest to get over, is the one that people in general are evil and untrustworthy. That sounds harsh, and it might be, but for you, the reader, try and imagine if every person you met was as evil as Satan until proven innocent. I am lucky in the fact I hide my suspicions about people, but could you imagine what it's like to think of people I don't know as being pure evil? I've heard the cliché that "the first impression is the lasting impression," but for me, since they are deemed evil, that impression is one that is hard to overcome.

But where on earth did this disdain for others come from? In my mind, I have no concept of the kind stranger who would help me if I had a flat tire, even though it has happened to me twice. In my mind, I have no concept of someone willing to help me in hard times. Even when I was with Emily, I could not fully trust her (she was ninety-eight percent cleared from being evil, until the aftermath where she was deemed guilty of being what most of society is ... mean and evil).

This makes a two-way conversation hard. Let's say, for instance, someone tries to talk to me. On their end, I'm assuming they see me and think I might be intelligent and they try and start a conversation. On my end, the first thing I think of is, "Okay, what do they want from me? How are they going to use me?" So, like I said, it makes a two-way conversation hard because you have the other person playing an offensive tactic to move the proverbial ball down the conversational field, and you have me playing a goal line defense doing an all-out blitz to prevent any sort of movement, because in my mind only bad things can come out of it.

With this sort of mentality, it is no wonder I fear the future. If the few people I trust are gone, what will become of me? This is the root of my money fear, my always needing a little bit more than what I need at that moment, and the absolute primary reason I know nobody. It's not that I'm unlikable; it's that I don't let anyone within my exterior defensive shell. If someone on my bowling team asks anything personal, they will get an answer that will be vague and also end the conversation because my personal likes are completely off-limits to all. I don't even think my stepbrother, sister, brother, or mother could say what my favorite movie, color, song, animal, planet, or anything else in this universe is.

This is where my perception kicks in. If they know nothing about me, it can't come back and haunt me. Also, it minimizes the chance that a common bond is formed, and if a common bond is formed, a conversation about whatever that thread could be would be inevitable.

In my perception, money is a big mystery. Furthermore, I have no idea why some metal is considered to be worth anything (Warning! Rant coming!). A dollar bill is worth something because it is government issued; however, a gold bar will always be a gold bar. It will sit there shining, doing nothing. Same thing applies with platinum, silver, and any other valuable metal. It's just metal, folks! People are starving in the world, and these metals have more value than the combined income of ten thousand people in the impoverished country of Somalia. I know I'm not helping considering I quite frankly don't care about such countries (at this time, a first hasn't been developed yet), but yet, why on earth are rocks worth anything more than a pebble found in a playground at an elementary school in the middle of Nowhere, North Dakota?

As you can see, I have very rigid perceptions on things like this. Emily would get so mad that I thought rings, necklaces, and the like were irrelevant, but they are. Why do people hide behind glittering things? To not be sexist, I say the same thing about sports jerseys. Have you seen how much sports attire goes for? Why on earth is it so much? Does wearing a Michael Vick jersey give you his powers? Anyone who wears a player jersey I instantly frown upon and associate them with the evil in the world. I know I have no logical reason other than it's just stupid that people pay an insane amount of money for irrelevant objects (no fair using the "it's illogical for you, but not to them" logic!).

One's perception is completely dictated by how they were raised. This being said, "firsts" are more important than either you or I can believe. I do not know where I got my dislike of others, but that is beside the point. On this front, I am a lost cause. However, what happens if there are more people like me who are really young. If they get the same firsts I got, the world would be a dangerous and hostile place around the said individuals.

Perhaps I was raised too well. Having such high ethical standards doesn't mingle with the rest of the world. This could be the root of my hatred of most of the world, because I have no concept on why they aren't the way I am.

I believe I am right most of the time; that being so, if someone else differs, they are wrong, and I was taught being wrong equals being bad, and in my mind, bad equals evil and it's a vicious cycle. I realize that no project has ever been a one-person show. The Empire State Building had a multitude of workers to build it. But, with my perception, I almost cannot allow a team. As I calculate the future of that, it ends up being rather lonely, which, oddly enough, is how I perceive the world. Maybe I'm right after all.

THE TRAIN

Of all vehicles in the world, the one that comes to mind as being unable to stop on a dime is a mile-long coal train doing fifty-five miles per hour. The sheer inertia of the vehicle is mind-boggling, at least for me, but it is a great example of my mind.

I may have written about this in some form or another, but never as a one-off piece, but I feel this is important because this can, or rather could, explain some choices that are made rashly.

So what is a train in the way I describe it? It is a topic, person, event, or anything else in the world that my mind will start to dwell on. You could call this obsessive thinking, but that is a clinical term and puts no face or spirit in the devil that this train has. Much like that coal train's inability to stop, so too is my mind's train of thought when one topic is locked in. Furthermore, in my case, this train heads down a hill, so now we have inertia plus gravity speeding the train.

So that was the definition of a train, but what is it like? Since society would not deem me of a "normal" mind, I can't make an example that I'm one hundred percent sure would be understandable, but I'll try. Have you ever had a song stuck in your head, and I don't mean just for a minute, but for days on end? I'm sure by the fourth, fifth, or sixth day, your nerves are on edge. For me this happens much faster and the train creates something I like to call hyper-focus.

Let's say you have a song stuck in your head for a week. During that week, you would probably have heard other songs, but none of them replace whatever tune it is echoing through your brain at all hours of the day. In other words, no matter what you hear, it won't replace the original song that your mind won't let go of. If you know that or can imagine that, you may just be able to understand what the train is to me.

When a train starts, there is no stopping it until whatever the train's motion is achieved or ended. It can be something as simple as walking to my car, or something as complex as planning out the next thirty-one days. In either case, I almost go on autopilot because my mind uses most of its ability to focus on nothing but this train.

I'll use money as an example, because this train is always chuggin' along with its engines at full blast. My mind will do nothing but think about it and the expenses to come. Then I may think that blackjack is the answer, and my mind will use this formula over and over, "Okay, if I put one hundred dollars down and win, one hundred dollars becomes two hundred dollars becomes four hundred dollars becomes eight hundred dollars and eight hundred dollars is enough. The house has a 50.8% advantage, so nearly one in two, so winning eight hundred dollars starting at one hundred dollars is a one in sixteen chance. Those aren't good odds." Then as soon as it ends it begins again, "One hundred dollars to two hundred dollars to four hundred dollars to eight hundred dollars... One hundred dollars, two hundred dollars, four hundred dollars, eight hundred dollars..."

(Pardon the interruption: Just a note from Dad... Mary and I were in Washington, D.C., to videotape an event at the Russian Embassy for the National Council for Adoption. We no sooner walked into our room and Aaron's mother called me from South Dakota and said Aaron was in trouble. What had he done? I called him and he said he went to a casino on the Mississippi and lost his fanny. He was crying and said he was driving eighty miles per hour down I-55 and looking for a bridge. It was a tough afternoon but we got through it.)

It is mentally draining to have thoughts like this and to try and fend them off each day. Thankfully, as of late, I have been able to control the urge to go for the one in sixteen shot. However, regardless of the odds, the damage is done in taking up the proverbial RAM in my brain.

What the pain is with money is only the tip of the iceberg. This sort of training effect runs across the board and may be why I get caught up in so many incidents while walking.

During nearly anytime or anyplace my mind is thinking on what I'm going to do next, and just as I think of the mathematical odds on blackjack, I will think along the lines of, "Okay, walk to the car, put the key in, try and look normal (repeat until mission accomplished)." So very much like a train, my mind can't be easily stopped until the objective is met.

Like I said, clinically, it could be considered obsessive thinking, but it is beyond that because my mind runs like that across the spectrum of life.

As of the day I write this, Osama Bin Laden released an audiotape yesterday. I read the transcripts and at the time I thought nothing of it, but as it got time to go to sleep, the train rolled out of the station and I started thinking about all it had said. From that, I drew conclusions on the possibilities of what attacks may come, and from that, what the markets may do, what lives will be effected, and, above all else, how much life could be lost.

After I reached every conclusion, I restarted each sequence of events over and over again. There was no stopping the train, because at the end of the day I will not know the outcome of events that are yet to happen.

Those are the major trains that can get started, but let's go to a lower scale and talk about conversations. I am great at a one-on-one conversation that is flowing well and has one central topic. However, if there's more than one person and the topics are changing, I am rather silent. This is so because my mind starts the train up and is trying to think of a way to get it on one topic. As soon as a solution is made, a variable is thrown in and the train changes tracks and has to start all over again, making it a very awkward scene.

Once my mind as a train is going, there is little to no stopping it suddenly. Whether it is something as simple as wanting a certain piece of candy or wanting to talk in a conversation. Simply put, once the mind wants something, it will continually think about whatever is wanted until the mind figures it is one hundred percent impossible or until it gets whatever it may be.

Close-ended conversations are the best for me because it is much like a train route from one side of town to another that only has one line and is only one way. Having a train route like that minimizes the need for a complex system to know how the traffic is flowing. However, add four more routes and intersect them and things become a bit more confusing, and in my mind, you could say, each person in the world I meet adds one more track to an already screwed up layout of the tracks.

With any train, the worst-case situation is a derailment, and this holds true in my trains as well. Whatever I'm thinking about, if something comes along and derails me, I get very angry and filled with pure rage. Unlike a real train, I don't have the power to destroy anything that stands on the track; but instead, I'm as flimsy as a 1978 Ford Pinto.

With that being true, repetition is very important because it lessens the trains that happen and, on top of that it, makes the trains more bearable because those variables don't have to be considered.

I often get a train when I start a new game on the Xbox that I know I could be number one at. I won't stop until I get what I sought out to do. In other words, the train leaves when the game is in my hands and the destination is arrived at when I get to number one. When I get to number one, there is normally no jubilation. I often wonder why, and then just now, I realize it's much like a trans-Atlantic flight. When a person flies for so long, as happy as they are to get to the destination, they are normally too tired to enjoy it. So too am I, but I am so mentally tired from the constant reminder that the train tells me that I need that number one spot.

Whatever the case may be, there are always trains in motion. They can be big or small, but sadly in my case when the train rolls by in my mind, a memento of flattening a penny, like people can do on a real railway, can't be made; instead, I am left with anger, pain, and pure mental exhaustion, but, nonetheless, the train rolls on, even if the destination is unknown.

UNWRITTEN PAGES

Everyone's life should be a book. Each person, alive or dead, has lived an interesting life unique only to himself or herself with his or her birth being chapter one continuing on to present, or death.

My book that is life is still being written with each day. However, I am learning that it isn't pages past that give me such agony, but rather the days to come, or rather the unwritten pages.

How I came to that conclusion is, as I write this, I may move to Las Vegas away from my current home of St. Louis. The move within itself is a logical one since I'd be moving to what appears to be a very promising job in a field that I'd do anything to get in (racing). So with that being said, why is there this incredible chill in my brain that has frozen all my thoughts?

In recent days, my mind's calculators of the future have been on overdrive. With a typical novel, one can usually deduct which way the author is going to go with the book, so I try and figure what will come next. However, I not only try to figure next day or week, but I take it up a couple notches and try and figure what the baseline will be for the next year of unwritten pages.

So with a move, not only will everything I thought of before go by the wayside, but I have to try and get a new sense of direction and recalculate pages and pages that I had already spent way too much brain power on.

There's more detail, though, than just using a blank page as an example. A good novelist will always provide vivid detail of the surroundings. While I don't think of what adjectives will apply to the future directly, I do use current ones and have grown accustomed to them. This is an example of the routine of life, and it's very small things that get filed into this.

In my pages that have been written, I have a vivid account of noises and smells. So if I were to move, all these noises that I have grown accustomed to would be gone. These small things are part of the routine that keeps some sanity to life. Such things include the noise of each person's footsteps in the house, the sound of my cat pawing at a door, and the acoustics of the room that I watch television in. All of these things are very minor, but a great novelist would surely write about these things if my life were a novel, and with that, if the author left them out, there would be some sense of something lacking.

I know there would be new things waiting, but I hate change, and if I hate change on the level of someone's footsteps, how can I bear a change of house, zip code, and even state? And it's true; the change in zip code alone is one that causes me to cringe a little.

With suspense novels, the author has the luxury of turning the story around without hesitation. A plot twist is expected, but in a way that is only known to the author. This is a good example of life; however, when trying to predict these, it can cause much pain to the brain. If I accept the change in scenery, what will happen where I used to live? Will the cat still paw? Will the footsteps still have that same pitch to them for each person? If the worst should happen and someone were to die, or disappear, how can I adapt when the change isn't instant?

Change is more bearable when it is instant. This is backed up by my ice-cold reaction and action to having my two pets put to sleep. But when I think about what my reaction would have been had I been gone causes me to fear the outcome. So I constantly ask the question in my head of how would I react should something bigger than a loss of a pet happen?

With the future, everything is unknown. If you watch the news, often the future has somewhat of a depressing theme to it. Nukes, bombs, and elections all are constantly on the radar (C'mon, do you really want to watch three months' worth of campaign commercials? I thought so!), and they don't paint a pretty picture. I take into account with the pages that aren't written yet. So with so many variables, it's a wonder my mind hasn't cooked itself yet for exceeding its processing capabilities.

As much as I fear the unwritten pages, the knowledge of the fear is even more depressing. To know the fear and to be powerless to do anything about it is worse than fear itself. Then the two feed off each other and the two become stronger. The third element to the painful equation is trying to calculate just how I will react to each disaster I conjure up. With that trio going full steam, I can barely breathe.

In the end, though, I would have to compare this with a horror novel. As scary as the pages a reader is reading through, if they want to know how the story ends, they have got to keep reading. So must I. However, in the suspense novel, the story is already written and its end already chosen, but for me, the end is still blank pages. Never before have empty pages seemed more terrifying than anything Stephen King has written.

ONE THOUSAND OUTCOMES

Everyday life can go in one thousand directions. The car could break, the lottery could be won, donkeys could invade any given series, and a helicopter landing in your front yard are just some of the nearly infinite possibilities each day brings. These events are of major proportion, but for me thinking of big things isn't as big as thinking of each possibility of small things.

In most social circumstances I would consider myself to be a bit slow. It isn't, though, that I'm dumb and uncommunicative, as it's just the opposite. What's going on in my brain is trying to figure out any of the one thousand outcomes that may come from the next sentence I'm going to use. Okay, so it may not be a thousand, but regardless of the number, it's way too many.

This would explain why I'm nearly normal when it's a one-on-one conversation, but if one extra person gets added, I become silent. It's simple math. Let's say I'm talking to one person, so, therefore, in my thinking, the thoughts are a multiple of one. If we throw in one more person, not only does the multiple go to two, but it goes to three, because not only do I have to try and calculate how the second person is going to react, but now I have to think about how the first person is going to react to the second person. Did I say this was simple math?

My mistake. If we throw in a third person, the math becomes of such that someone could go for his or her doctorate in mathematics trying to solve that equation.

That was the conversation example, but this type of thinking applies to everything. It goes down to the simplest level of seeing someone walk by my car. As I see them approaching, I begin to wonder if as they pass by will they smash my window. Will they pull a gun? Will another car hit them? As my mind goes through these motions, it's as if time freezes for the outside world while it creates all these scenarios and then possible reactions on my part. With all the thoughts that come, rarely does the predictor of the person just walking by normally come into play, but that's what's always happened.

Having a mind like this is quite tiring, as nothing is ever a quick decision, but it's almost a requirement to know what's going to happen before it happens. With that, it lowers the amount of thought when something actually does happen. This can be quite bad, though, because when something that is completely from left field happens, I go into mental shock and I have no idea how to react.

This thought process of one thousand outcomes wouldn't be bad if a person was in the weather business or park ranger business because these fields, while unpredictable to a certain degree, have limitations. People on the other hand could have 1 billion outcomes. So, as much as I try and prepare, I'm only going to get it right a very small percent of the time.

There is no practice in preparing for the unpredicted, and, in life, what separates the great from the not so great is how one reacts to the unpredicted. (When I say "great" I'm not referring to great leaders or great inventors, but rather to the people that live life with happiness, as that is true greatness.) I react very poorly as I at first don't react at all. Then, when enough has happened, I'll do everything in my power to rid myself of whatever has given me too much unpredictability.

This affects all aspects of life, as everything will eventually throw a curveball at some point in time. Using my math formula, it's no wonder why school was so detested. If there are one thousand outcomes for one person, and one thousand x one thousand x one thousand for three people, I do not even want to imagine the mathematical nightmare that is a full classroom. And if that formula is scary on paper, try and think of what it is like living it!

There is no slowing down the outcome process, as it is needed to keep sanity. As tiring as trying to think of everything, it is not as bad as that random element. To let you know how broad this system is, I'll tell you that I'm constantly thinking right now, Do I want to save this? Is it worth saving? What could come from this? Possible reactions? Will this cause an uproar in an Arab state like that cartoon? Geeze, it never ends.

THE CONSCIOUS COMA

Despite the truly bizarre title, I'm not crazy. I did mean one hundred percent to put consciousbefore the word "coma."

All my life there have been many time spans that stick out because of something that, before today, made them almost as if they never happened, or, in the least, they felt like a dream. These spans could last for a day, a week, or the longest one that I recognize lasted well over six months.

So what is this "consciouscoma"? My definition of it is a state that a person (like myself) goes in that is for the most part self-absorbed, so much so that the outside world sort of just goes away. During this time, the person's contact with the outside world will be minimal and utilitarian at best. To others, it may seem that the person has become dumb, uninterested, or just plain rude. However, while these may seem true, the amount of inner thought has made it nearly impossible to comprehend any stimuli from outside sources.

If one of these comas lasted forever, the person would never really have to deal with actual reality because the perceived reality of the coma would dominate. For me, though, there are awakenings, and every time these happen, all the stress and bad things that have happened since the previous awakening flood in at light speed. To make an analogy, it is sort of like a family that goes on vacation and they don't get anybody to pick up their mail. A day goes by, then a week, and then finally a month (long vacation). When the family gets back, the amount of mail to go through will be quite substantial. In this example, the mail represents all the stressors and things of the like that, under normal circumstances, are dealt with and then discarded. But if everything arrives at once, the smallest of small things can be overwhelming.

In my writings, I have hinted at something like this but have never come to this full-blown conclusion. At this time, I don't know what starts or ends one of these because each time it is something different.

The best example of this coma happened back in June of 2004. Six months prior, I had broken up with Holly for the last time. On this June day, I was working a practice session at the racetrack I work at. One of the drivers asked me if I'd take his kart out to give him some setup advice. I happily agreed to, and within fifteen minutes I was suited up and on the track. After about six laps, I had an incident that would awaken me.

Going into the third turn, the left rear tire decided it would be better if it operated alone rather than in unison with the three other tires. Turn three is a fast right-hander, and the left rear is a very important tire for that turn. As the tire came off, I was sent into an immediate snap spin that nearly rolled the kart. While spinning, I was also nearly hit by three other karts on track. During the spin, I awoke. The chain of thought was like this, Boy, I can't wait to tell Holly this. Wait a sec, Holly, Holly, I don't think I talk to her anymore. Why don't I? What happened? I think I broke up with her. Oh my goodness; it's June! Where did the last six months go!

I do remember those months, but while spinning, it was as if all the bad stuff was just then being registered. As much as the forces were of the severe spin, they were nothing to the vacuum that sucked my breath away due to the pain of suffering from all the things from the past six months.

That's the story side of it, but there's more to describe as to what it is like while in this consciouscoma.

Another way I can think of describing it is to be on a pendulum that has an irregular track from back and forth. While the pendulum is on side A, life is as normal as it could be for me, but when it shifts into side B, things change completely. This wouldn't be so bad if the side chose one or the other, but it doesn't seem to work that way.

While in this state, as I've said, emotions are on delay. It is a horrible feeling for me because I know I should feel something about any given situation, but nothing is there. This isn't to say that I'm completely numb, as if there happens to be something with shock value, I will have a response right away, but it won't be a with full intensity. This is sort of like a paper cut. When you first cut yourself, there is that immediate pain response and then there is lingering pain. During this coma, I just feel the immediate pain, then all emotions fade back into darkness.

I now fear this back and forth cycle because depending on how they fall, a lot of bad emotions could be waiting and they could overload me. In another piece, I theorized that a person with Asperger's would be more likely to "go postal" than someone without it. This consciouscoma helps to further solidify this because there normally is a time delay before someone decides to take action. This time delay could very well be this consciouscoma. And when the individual awakens, they finally have to deal with the change of life and routine and it becomes unbearable and then blood is spilt.

There is a difference between just not wanting to express emotion and this coma. One is by choice, and the other is a state where no matter how much I want to, I simply can't feel in the general sense. This isn't to say that all emotions are dead, but rather feelings are still there, but they just sort of get on a system like TiVo where they will be felt at a later time.

While in this consciouscoma, the only thing that matters is what my mind is thinking about. This does sound odd, I know, because it states that there are two different states of being with the exterior never changing. What this does point out, though, is why on one day a certain activity will be completely bearable and on another it will be completely unbearable. I would think from my experiences that while in this coma, the ability to stand variables and lots of people drops. This is because the mind is on such hyper focus that it is like a person on a very thin balance beam on a gusty day and all it will take to knock the guy off is just one big gust. And, of course, nobody wants to fall off a balance beam, and I don't want to be knocked off my thinking. This could explain how I broke up with Holly a dozen times only to call back the next day expecting things to be normal. If she knocked me off track in my thinking, the automated response, regardless of whom or what it is, is to cut it off so I can be whole again in my thinking.

This has been one of the hardest things I've written because it is so deep and mysterious. I'm only starting to understand this, and I never would have discovered it had I not been thinking deeply about why there are times where life is one way and others where it's different. I hope, with more experience, to write in better detail what it is truly like to be like this. I can tell you I fear this now knowing it. Could this be the tip of the iceberg on fully understanding Asperger's?

FOREVER
CHANGES DAILY

Is there anything worse than having your favorite television show canceled? Okay, so there is, but bear with me. Now, after your show has been canceled, let's say you have the mindset that no other show will ever be worth watching except for the show that was canceled. If this were so, the future of your television viewing would be rather dim. This is half the picture of this side of Asperger's. What side? Calm down, I'm getting there.

The other side, using that television analogy again, is, let's say, you've watched a certain show for many years and a new show debuts opposite of the show you've watched for years. And, for the analogy's sake, let's say you are very cheap and will not purchase a VCR or TiVo, so that means you've got to choose one or the other. After careful consideration, you abandon your show of many years and cross over. You thought for years nothing would ever take you away from the show you've viewed for nearly a decade, but a show greater than life itself debuted and you made the switch.

Those examples are what life is like for me every day. The second example is rare, but it can happen if something is over the top and so much better than whatever it replaced. However, the key point to take from that second example is that there is no middle ground. It's one or the other. The first example, though, is the more important one, as it is the object that causes many stresses and hardships.

To complete my analogy, let's say the said television show can be anything—an image, a person, an idea, a weather forecast, or just about anything else. Those are the shows, and in this example the television is the brain.

Since life is with constant change, many things get canceled. When this happens there is extreme anxiety and anger. A cancellation may be of a relationship, a minor change in plans, or the loss of a chance that nobody else ever knew you wanted. It gets down to such a small level that it is on the point of being absurd.

Whatever show is playing is intended to be forever. There is safety in the concept of forever, as this means change is nullified. Unfortunately, for people like me, nothing is forever, thus, for me, forever changes daily.

These changes are for the most part small, but no matter how small it creates pain and anger. It can be as stupid as a change in a stoplight pattern or as big as losing a job. Regardless of what is lost, the thing that creates the pain is the thought that nothing can ever take its place (okay, maybe the stoplight thing doesn't go down that road of thought). In other words, it's like having a television show canceled, but no show takes its place. Forever and ever it will be dead air, so to speak.

With this fear of forever changing, I can now understand why some people get so obsessive on such small and, what appear to be, trivial things. I have to push myself to leave the house every time I do. If I'm at home and isolated, I have complete control. There can be no shows that are just in my imagination canceled and I am in complete peace. Sadly, I understand that life can't operate that way. I wish so much it did, though, because every situation that results in a cancellation throws my whole perception of life out the window.

I believe this can be a very confusing thing for those around me. All can seem well, and then instantly I'm in a depressed mode for what to them are unknown reasons. And because whatever may have triggered this is all in my head, I am not about to share whatever has created the disturbance. This further drives home the message to me that perhaps it's better just to stay at home.

It almost sounds like I'm completely narcissistic in that my mind believes whatever it thinks should come to be. This isn't the case, though, as having that mindset keeps the only bit of sanity there is intact. Without it, the world becomes too big.

The other side to this is the second example I used. This is an example of when one thing has been obsessed on and, at the time, it appears nothing can ever get in the way. This is an example of a favorite food, an obsession on the fascinating topic of the top one hundred cleaning services in America, or a week fling as a birdwatcher. During the times when those become important, they are the only things that are important. Then, as my analogy states, a new show runs rival to it. It becomes one or the other, as having two interests is unthinkable. The end result is a change on what appeared to be a hobby or interest that was going to last forever. This example differs as the changing of forever is self-induced, thus making it okay.

That's the difference. Example A is world-induced, and example B is changed by one's self. In any case, I'm sure it is confusing to family and friends because it is all so baffling. Why does a change in daily routine cause a breakdown, but yet in the same person jumping from a hobby of birds to planes creates no issues? It all comes down to control. The way I operate is to mainly take the path of least resistance. If it is easier to be interested in the sport of golf rather than becoming a grandmaster at chess, then golf will be my thing (the only thing for me that has been forever has been racing). This isn't to say something won't be done if it's hard. Far from it! The path of least resistance isn't external resistance, but rather internal. The thing I think my brain thinks about is: What will have the least amount of variables and pain and change?

Yes, forever changes daily. Neither you nor I can help it. When it does happen, there is grief and, most of the time, nobody understands. At least I have the realm of writing where only I can make changes and what I type is forever. Uh oh, I'm at the end of this; that means it's spell check time. No! Forever is busted again. No place is safe from the changes in forever.

SORRY, WE'RE OPEN/HAPPILY, I'M CLOSED

This is a two-part subject, but the two go together in a way.

If the world were to have a sign like a storefront has, I would give it "sorry we're open." The open is the open-ended-minded society we live in. This is killer because I can barely operate in this environment.

I may have written about this before; If so, sorry for the rehash, but this is a critical topic.

As I have said many times, my mind is always trying to think of what's going to happen next. In a linear world, this is easy, as there's a start and an end. However, that would be like a drag strip, and the real world is like the interstate system going every which way.

Let's take a recent trip I had that involved stopping at a fast food place. Here in St. Louis, they have this special deal I always get, but on this trip to this restaurant, they did not have the deal. I was paralyzed in self-thought. What do I get? What do I get? What do I get? What do I get? is what my mind was hung on. The routine had been broken, and I was as helpless as a man stuck in the middle of a cornfield on a cloudy night. I knew no way out. Something as simple as changing my order created the most uncomfortable feeling I have had in a while.

It's almost embarrassing for me to admit that this simple problem was so major, but it was. On the outside, I looked like I was trying to make up my mind, but this was just a silent scream, as on the inside, I wanted anything but to be there.

The normal world is open and can accept change like that. The normal world also likes asking open-ended questions. Every time I encounter a situation like this, I get like I was trying to change my order. It's so bad that if I hear someone else ask an open-ended question, I get uncomfortable because I fear that the question asked will be asked of me. There are no scarier words than when "what" is followed by "is your…"

If you want to have sadistic fun, ask any person with Asperger's a question such as, "What is you favorite movie and why?" A simple question such as one directed toward a preference of color isn't too bad, but give a broad topic like movies, games, years, presidents, and so on and so forth, and you can create a silent scream and totally ruin that person's day. My food choice debacle was three days ago and it still hurts.

Why is this, though? Normality asks empty open-ended questions every day, in fact, probably, every half-hour, and I can't change my order at a restaurant! Normal people routinely say what their favorite movie is, but if you were to ask me, it will send me into a sputtering spell that Porky Pig would be proud of. Not only is there sputtering, though, but immense pain. On paper, I'm sure this looks ridiculous, as something such as a favorite movie is commonplace to be asked, but for me, it is enough to make me hate all of life.

But again the question is why is this so? As this title stated, it's a difference between the open world and my closed world. A drag strip is quite simple in that there's a quarter mile of track with runoff within the confines of concrete walls. The normal world is the vast interstate system with many cloverleaf exits, turnpikes, tollbooths, sharp turns, elevation changes, and the list goes on and on. If you watch drag racing, you'll know that at the top level the cars are specially designed to just go straight and the motors last about three seconds longer than needed. Now imagine driving one of those cars and needing to drive from Pensacola, Florida, to Richmond, Virginia. It would be fun to watch but most certainly not fun to try, as it would be impossible because the top fuel dragster may be able to do in excess of 330 miles per hour, but I'm sure those occasional stops for gas on whatever interstate would be taken would be fun to watch, as parallel parking is certainly quite the chore.

That metaphor probably lasted too long, but it proves the point. If something is designed for a specific task, it probably would function too well outside the confines of whatever it was designed for. I didn't have the luxury of deciding how I was designed, but outside the friendly confines of a situation like a closed drag strip, I am on edge and screaming on the inside.

I know I've said this before, but whenever I do something, I know what I'm going to do and I plan on how it'll go. Let's continue to use that restaurant as an example. Let's say that some stranger came up to me and asked me what my favorite song was. This would cause more stress and anxiety than you can possibly imagine, as not only do I not know this person, but they are also asking a question that I can't possibly answer. Furthermore, it was a situation I had not planned, furthering my downward spiral within. The situation would be different if they asked a factual question about something I like or am very knowledgeable in. This might sound confusing, but it's much like a safe; if you find the combination, the doors open up.

As long as I can remember, I have done everything to keep some sort of sanity. These things that were done were to keep me closed to a degree. If there were a reason for me to be doing something, then the openness would not be there. In school at recess, I would always be the referee for the kickball games. If I was the ref, then I had a reason to be standing there and I had the ability to talk, because I was not talking as myself, but rather as the ref. This, in essence, closed me off on the personal level, and I was merely operating on the level of directing the game.

I was at my sister's over the past weekend, and for her son there was a small plastic swimming pool in the backyard. For some reason, there were a lot of people over, including their kids, and one kid stood out because he had all the traits I've heard of that come with Asperger's. And, on top of that, he did what I would have done at that age. What did he do, though? While all the other kids were splashing in the pool, he established himself as the lifeguard. This closed him off on the personal level but gave him a reason to be there. On top of giving him a reason to be there in the eyes of others, it made the environment bearable to be in, because he wasn't there as himself but rather the lifeguard.

For me, it was a sad sight to see because I could fully associate with what was going on, and I can tell you it doesn't get any easier as time progresses. I thought the world was open when I was six, but it's nothing compared to how open it is now on so many levels. To continue the metaphor, when a person is six, the world is a small two-lane road in a small town in the middle of Nowhere, Wyoming, but as I see it now, it's a hectic city interstate system that just got upgraded from four lanes to ten lanes… each way!

I'm happy being closed. If I kill a conversation by being closed, I avoid the pain and anguish of openness. So, as my title states, the world in my mind should be sorry for being open, as I'm sure it has no idea the pain it causes just being itself. Is there a chance that openness can happen for me? Don't know, but it would be kind of interesting watching a dragster go down the interstate system and deploy those ultra-cool parachutes.

INVISIBLE
REMINDERS

As I've written many times before, my mind is constantly thinking about everything. While awake there is no escape from my mind's constant scanning and calculating. With that being said, it would seem sleep would be the refuge from the chaotic thinking, but it is not so.

Since I always go upon the assumption that if it happens to me, it's the way it is for all, I never gave this topic much thought. For me, dreams are nothing more than an extension of consciousness. Every night I will remember all my dreams and in the sequence they occurred. Up until about two months ago, I thought this was so for everybody, but that was until a person looked at me as if I had told them that I was a ghost.

As successful as my mind is at creating stress while I am awake, it's even better while I'm asleep. The reason it's so good at stirring up trouble is the fact that I am fully aware during my dreams, and even further to make it sound false, I am able to be aware of the fact that I am dreaming.

In my piece I wrote about Linda (I think this is so, I wrote that sixteen months ago), I mentioned that I had a recurring dream. After a couple nights of that, each time the dream would start, I would know the plot of it. It was sort of like watching a rerun on television, knowing what's going to happen. I was able in those dreams to interact differently with the cast of characters, but the end result was closely the same each time.

It's quite odd to be able to act like myself completely in my dreams, yet be aware that it is, in fact, a dream. Maybe this power, or rather awareness has prevented nightmares. I can't remember having a nightmare like other people describe. Yes, bad things happen to me (I, for some reason, am constantly being electrocuted in my dreams by AM radio towers. I know, I know, I'm odd), but it is never scary. I would take nightmares, though, for the pain that dreams cause.

If something is troubling me, I will probably dream about it. The dream would go along the plotlines of trying to figure out all the possibilities and possible solutions to the problem. I may be aware of the dream, but I turn the television off, so to speak. If I'm awake, I do have the chance of diverting my attention, but while asleep my mind is able to do what it pleases. That being so, the reminders of what are, what was, and what will never be can't be blocked.

To let you know how aware I am in my dreams, I'll tell you about a dream I had last night. The location was a level from the game "Halo," and for some reason there was a concert there. During the time before the concert, I was worrying about things in the real world and at the same time thinking about strategies to use next time I play at that level. Right before the concert was to commence I was, for no apparent reason, attacked by a tiger shark. My conscious mind immediately pointed out that this could not happen because there was no water. I got quite annoyed because it kept biting my hand, and I was trying to tell myself that this was completely false, but it just kept trying to eat my hand. Because of this fact, I started thinking about sharks and then made a mental note to check the Internet for facts about tiger sharks.

Every night is like that to some extent. To further the incredible nature of this, I'll point out that as the night progresses, I am aware of, to a certain degree, what time it is, or rather how much longer I can sleep. This is done by the fact that as awakening approaches, my dreams become even more vivid. They become so vivid that sometimes I can't tell the difference between reality and the dream. As becoming awake nears, my dreams shift into a pattern of planning the day's activities. The first thing I do every morning is to call my dad just to see if anything is new. I'll dream about this before I do it, and sometimes when I awake I will have thought that I had already called him several times.

A couple months ago I had a dream about losing money while playing blackjack. I thought this was true for many days until I checked my checkbook and what I dreamed about wasn't there.

Before you get envious about me being able to recall dreams, you should know it's a curse! As I said earlier, my dreams tell me what is, what was, and what will never be. A high percentage of the time, I will dream about money and I'm not worrying about it. During this time I am fully relaxed; then morning comes. It takes a short while for me to grasp that what was invisible really wasn't. I'll also dream about having everything being right with Emily, I'll relive the Linda incident, I'll be the world's best racecar driver, and whatever else my mind thinks about.

The topics vary, but everything is an invisible reminder of what my mind is thinking about. Imagine someone giving you one of those prank lottery tickets and you think you've won a million dollars and then you find out it's merely a joke. I live this every night! Every night I'm normal, only to reenter this realm where all is not well.

I don't fear going to sleep at all, but I always dread what the morning will be like. Depending on how the dreams went, I might think about calling Emily, only to remember what life is really like.

There is nothing I can do about my dreams. For all I know, though, writing this could be a dream. My dreams are vivid enough and so lifelike that this very well could be a dream. Whatever the case may be, I will go to sleep and I will awake, but I have no idea what I'll be reminded of, and I have no idea what it will be that I will have had in my dream, only to have it cruelly taken away by simply waking up.

FAKING KANSAS

I believe there is going to be a very serious pandemic of this issue in the next five to ten years. Before I get into that, let me restate what exactly Kansas is. Kansas is the term that I use to describe the place where a person can operate unabated. To put it simply, if a person were paralyzed in every state except Kansas, where do you think they'd live?

From a young age I started to play video games. I still do, but from when I started to what the games are now is staggering. Last week I was in a race over Xbox Live that had racers from four continents! Not only were we racing, but via the headset there is instant verbal communications. This is light years ahead of the 8-bit stuff I started with.

While the graphic and all other aspects of the games have improved, there is one thing that is open for debate and that is the Internet aspect. A two-player game fifteen years ago meant that there would be two people in the same room. Now it could mean two people anywhere in the world. Yes, that within itself is a good thing, but what happens if this alone becomes Kansas? What happens if a person gets to the point where the only place they socialize is via the Internet in video games?

When I worked in a video game store back in 2001, the primary online game was something called "Everquest." I heard from a handful of customers who knew a son, daughter, father, or mother who got addicted to the game. The game was called "Evercrack" in jest, but it is a good adjective from the stories I heard.

"Everquest" had all communications via text. Move ahead two years from that and Xbox released their online service with a headset. This allows, as stated, instant communications with anyone else who has the service. From my experiences, at first, the average age was at least twenty, but now it seems as if half or more of the online community is under sixteen.

With my first theory, should a kid start at an early age playing games over the Internet, that will become the status quo. Furthermore, should the individual have Asperger's and can't socialize except on the Xbox, where do you think they are going to spend their time?

There are so many ethical and moral questions that are raised by this issue. Should a person only be able to have a normal conversation via the Xbox, then what happens if it's taken away? At some point in time the real world will beckon, but when is the line drawn? If it never starts then it isn't an issue, but there are so many kids and probably adults who have found a manufactured Kansas.

With so many twelve- to eighteen-year-olds now spending all their free time talking with friends online, what's going to happen in ten years? For now they may be happy, but what happens down the road? What if they simply can't make it outside? Where will they retreat to?

I am scared of the future for these kids. There are now big money competitions for video games, and a select few made over thirty thousand dollars last year. This sounds good for them, but one of the big winners was just fifteen and was already addicted to games. What is he going to think now? What value does the outside world have since he can now make his money playing games? For those who didn't compete, they can easily think that that could be them if they played more.

I have asked a lot of questions, and normally when I ask them I have an answer, but not this time. Once a person gets hooked, there is little to nothing that anyone else can do. If you take it away and that's their only Kansas, how will the person react? But if you let them stay there, the risk is there that they will never leave.

As time goes on, the game companies will find better and more clever ways to engineer Kansas more efficiently so the battle will rage on. There is a game being played but it's not on the screen. It's the battle for people's Kansas, and people's futures are on the line.

QUEST

There's one topic that I have talked about several times but have never had a definitive answer on. I think this topic is a main theme, and for me it is very confusing. This topic is near and dear to everyone, and everyone probably has a different opinion on it, but for me I am clueless to what it even is, and that topic is love.

Unknowingly, I started a quest when I started writing to try and learn what love is. What does "I love you" mean? If I don't know the meaning, am I able to love? We are bombarded each day by thousands of sources (primarily media outlets) telling us what love is. In movies, I'm sure the concept works on people, but that assumes that they understand the concept. I don't think I do.

In anything that happens with me internally, it's to the extreme. I either feel very strongly for or very strongly against something. However, with emotions I'm either content or extremely upset. There is nothing I know past content on the positive side. Does this mean I am incapable of love, or do I have to be content with being content?

Of all the things I am short-handed on, the one I truly feel sad about is this lack of understanding of the concept of love. As I've said before, the only thing I know about love is that I'd miss a person if they were gone. I truly hate that sentence, but that's all I know. Of all the inner rage I have, the majority is directed toward this enigma, this unknown emotion shrouded in mystery.

Without knowledge of what it really is, I fear I may get caught up in a horrible relationship. You see, when talking to someone, I get caught up in a tsunami of sorts. I may not like what's being said, but because I can't change a situation, I just give the answer of least resistance, so the tsunami rolls on. If a person in reality is caught in the middle of the ocean by a tsunami, they are at the mercy of the sea; I, too, am like this if I'm talking to someone.

Now what if I have loved, but it's simply so overwhelming that I didn't even know it? Say, like a circuit breaking? What if it was so perfect that it was unbearable? This could be, but I'd be scared if this is true because then the first, according to theory, could not be duplicated.

The above paragraph is talking about a relationship, but what about family? There should be something there, right? Again, I hate this. I absolutely hate this. In any situation, I can only think how the outcome will affect me. Call it selfish if you want, but I am unable to feel any emotion about another person.

My mom is constantly bugging me to see her, as she lives about one thousand miles away. Last New Year's, I drove up to Indianapolis to see her. It had been over a year since I had seen her. I bring this up because the issue of time is in play. She was so excited to see me, but I was impartial. You see, to love is to be bound by time. If my mind thinks differently in regards to memories, then for her it's been a year, but for me it's been just another day. The same thing will probably happen this year as well, and I'm sure she'll get misty-eyed and I again will be impartial.

Can love and time coincide? To love someone is to look forward to the future, but what if all I can see is what was? Does this mean I do in fact love, but only in the past? Can I only love what was and not what is or what's to come?

The last sentence in the last paragraph could also refer to the inability to accept change. Therefore, with the logic that I constantly love everything so long as it doesn't change; however, when it does change, that's when I knew I loved it. This obviously is false, but it does raise a point. If I am capable of love, will I only know if there's a change? I wish I could say how tragic this is for me not even knowing this.

While I continue to ramble about not knowing about love among humans, there is one love I do understand. It's a perfect love—so simplistic, so understandable. It's the love of an animal. With the wonderful animals I have had, there's no doubt what love is. With a pet there are no hidden strings, and by mere observation, I can deduce what the mood of the animal is. This topic is so overwhelming that it's almost impossible to write about it. With an animal, there is never a feeling of aloneness. The fear of the open-ended situation is non-existent; therefore, my mind doesn't overthink and I can simply enjoy the company of the animal. This has yet to be accomplished with another person, minus once.

With the above paragraph being so, does this mean for me to love a person she will have to say nothing and be as predictable as the sunrise? This would be impossible, so is all doomed? Perhaps this type of thought has been discussed and talked about by hundreds of the world's greatest philosophers, but none of them have been in the same ship I have been in.

Or could it be there is no such thing as love and I'm the only one who realizes it? What if the term is just thrown around to make sense of an otherwise chaotic and strange world? Could it be that the world, in general, uses every other person and that love is just a myth? I surely hope not, because that would make the world all the scarier.

As you can tell from this, I have plenty of questions and few answers. The quest will certainly continue. Where the destination is I don't know. Is there more beyond "I'd miss you if I were gone"? I've done so much in my life, but I'd trade it all in a heartbeat to know what love is, even if it's just for a second, because with my memory, that second would last a lifetime.

THE REST OF THE BOXES

(The sequel to 245 Something Boxes)

"245" Boxes left off with me looking to the future in somewhat of a positive manner. Sadly, four days later, my cat Amsterdam had to be put to sleep. I've already written about that, so it will be left out of this.

The story continues now as Hurricane Katrina devastated the Gulf Coast. I had been down after Hurricane Ivan in 2004, but nothing could prepare me for the destruction that was on hand.

We traveled to the Gulf region just three days after landfall. On our way down, we stopped in Jackson, Mississippi, to eat and figure out what we were going to do next. When I say "we," I'm referring to my dad and myself. While we were eating at a steak place off the interstate, my dad got a phone call from somebody saying that all the crime that was happening in New Orleans had spread to Baton Rouge (which is where we were going to be staying). I pleaded with my dad that I wanted no part in that and that I had already had my fill of hostage situations for the year, so he found a fellow pastor in the area and we stayed with them.

While staying at the pastor's house, I had one of the more surreal moments of my life. While we all were talking, the pastor asked, "While you're here, want to go fishing?" He asked this because an inlet of the Pearl River flowed right behind his house. I had not been fishing in nearly a decade so I immediately said yes, but the weird part was I had already seen the flooding and the catastrophe on television, and en route to the chaos, I was now fishing. Certainly, it was the last place I'd expect to go fishing.

I won't stay on the Katrina topic too long, as it's all been said before. From my perspective a person can't imagine how bad. No matter how many adjectives I use, or paragraphs, in fine detail, there is no way you could understand what it looked like and smelled like so I will not try.

We got back to St. Louis on September 6, and I was still having some issues with the concussion I had suffered the month prior. Nevertheless, just eight days after we returned to St. Louis, I would achieve a life accomplishment at the bowling alley.

It was just week two of the league, and in game one I started with the front eleven strikes. For a 300 game, twelve in a row is needed. The pressure of my last shot is something that I wish I could experience every day. It's not exactly a rush, as I hate that term, but it's all about the pressure. It's about hitting this for bowling immortality or screwing up and being the laughing stock of the alley. I did take my shot and came up just one pin short, a 299 game. Since I started bowling, I had waited for the day that I got a 298, 299, or 300 game, as with one of those scores a ring is awarded. Even though I did it, I felt empty, just as I do with any achievement. In fact, I actually felt worse after doing that because of the lack of emotion.

As October rolled around, we went back to the Gulf. This was one month after the storm, and it looked exactly like it did the previous time we were down. This time, though, my luck followed me down there, as on day three I grew some sort of mass on my leg that was probably another staph infection. Because of the dangers associated with that sort of infection, we returned home. This depressed me for two reasons. The first, obviously, was that my luck was continuing (bad luck, that is) and, secondly, we were staying with this family that was as nice as they get. I honestly didn't think there were "nice" people in the world, but this somewhat older couple welcomed us into their home and tried to make us as comfortable as possible while we there. I just wonder if there's anyone else like that out there.

As the next to last weekend of October came, I flagged the last race of the year for the St. Louis Karting Association. The final race of the year always bothers me, as I never know who is or isn't returning for the next season. It's also a symbolic event showing that winter is on hand. My memory isn't too good of that race, but according to my calendar/journal, it bothered me badly.

Nothing much happened between that and the time I went to Washington, D.C., with my dad in November. This has been a yearly tradition since 2000, and as a bonus this year we were going to New York City for a day and a half. I had been to NYC only once, and only for four hours, so I was greatly looking forward for this event.

On November 20, we headed from D.C. to NYC. Of course, the route we took was I-95, so that meant I had to go through about thirty minutes of agony while going through Baltimore (see "Linda" for details), but because of the destination, it wasn't as bad as I thought it was going to be.

As we entered the island of Manhattan, my dad needed to stop at a camera store. This sounds so simple, unless you've been to New York City. You see, one cannot just stop at a camera store, as there is practically no place to park. This meant I would get to drive around and around until he got out. I have driven at Pocono, I have driven a Formula Car, and it's a good thing, because I needed the experience to survive that ordeal.

With the driving issues gone my dad dropped me off at the hotel while he went to wherever he had to go. I was planning on just staying at the hotel and watching the final race of the NASCAR season, but then I thought about the fact that Times Square and so many more places were just a little less than a mile away. So, after much thought, I set out to explore as much as I could before the race started.

My first sight of notice was Rockefeller Plaza. This was actually a depressing stop on my tour because watching everyone skate made me feel like an alien. All the skaters and onlookers were talking to others and smiling. Both of those I do infrequently. While there are thousands of people in all directions, I felt truly alone while watching those skaters. Not the type of alone as if a person is dropped off in middle of Nowhere, North Dakota, but as in the type of loneliness that can't be helped. I don't know if this was a bad experience or a good one. In a way, I felt completely safe among all the noise and chaos of the Big Apple.

From there, I walked toward Trump Tower. The building itself isn't anything to write about (trust me, if I wasn't going to say what I'm going to say next, I would not be writing about it), but because I'm a fan of the TV show "The Apprentice," I just had to see the building.

From the Trump Tower, I walked over toward Times Square. On that walk, I noticed again how, even though I was among so many people, I felt safe. I normally hate large crowds, but this was different. Among all the noise there was sameness about it. The city was always moving; therefore, there was no change in the environment. Also, the people of the city were either tourists or business people, so they were all in a rush, and I can't recall one person making eye contact with me. It's sort of weird how a place of such high population density made me feel like I was so alone.

Times Square didn't impress me that much, so from there I went back to the hotel, or at least tried to, as I forgot what street my hotel was on. After walking past Fox News, though, I knew the hotel was a block ahead because I remembered seeing the signs when driving toward the hotel.

As I watched the race, my mind focused on my journey through the city. I was so confused as to the reason why I felt so safe among so many people. I hate loud noises and large groups, but I loved New York City. I then began to ponder if it was, in fact, my love of the buildings and signs (okay, I love signs, don't know why) overruled the fear of people. But there was no fear of the people. As I write this in June 2006, I'm going to a video game store tomorrow to pick up a game. I fear going because of the awkwardness of it. The whole eye contact and asking for the game I want is horrible, yet in New York I had no problem.

Come to think of it, my time in New York is the same feeling I get in foreign countries. In a way, I was a foreigner in Manhattan, as I come from the Midwest, and I had nothing to do in the city while everyone else scurried about on whatever business they were on. This made me nothing more than an invisible spectator that nobody gives a first thought about. When in Africa, it's the same thing. They know I can't speak the language, and I know they can't speak mine, so nobody talks and it's pure bliss.

My time in the gigantic metropolis was all too short, and we left the next morning. Leaving the city and watching the Empire State Building fade behind the horizon, I remembered the last time I saw the same image back when I was with my aunt in 2003 riding on Amtrak. So much had happened in those two and one-half years, but it was still the same image disappearing in the blue sky, so I wondered how much time and how much change will have happened next time I see the same image. Those thoughts kept me occupied all the way back to my aunt's house. I didn't even realize we had passed Baltimore! This was a gigantic step but also a huge symbolic step that the era of Linda, and the hole that was still there, was now filled.

We had Thanksgiving at my aunt's house (I forgot to mention, that's the tradition since 2000) and the next day, we headed back to St. Louis. That turned out to be the longest car ride ever, as my brand new Xbox 360 would be waiting for me at home.

The ride seemed to last an eternity, but we finally made it, and I went to work on the game "Project Gotham Racing 3." Eight days later, I would stake claim to number one, a mark I would have all the way until March of 2006. Again, as with the 299, I was so empty with this number one thing. There were more than three hundred thousand people who had played the game, and I was the best but felt nothing about it directly. Indirectly, I felt depressed because I know there should be some joy, but there was none. I've written about this topic as well before, so I'll leave it alone.

During the month of December, I had severe complications with the concussion. No fewer than four times I was up more than twenty-four hours. This lack of sleep caught up with me as we went back down to the Gulf over Christmas. I don't really remember that trip whatsoever, except that the NBC show of "Deal or No Deal" premiered.

On December 29, I drove to Indianapolis to see my mom, who was in from South Dakota. The next day, we went from Indy to Ft. Wayne to watch an indoor race. It was eight hours of nonstop racing, and it was such a good time; however, driving back I realized that time had passed.

It's only about a ninety-minute drive, but on that night it seemed longer than a trans-Atlantic flight. I don't know what exactly happened, but I finally understood that what used to be in Indy never would be again. I used to always anticipate going up there to play endless games of "Monopoly" and "Scrabble" and every other game under the sun with the Brennons, but time moved on. On that car ride, it dawned on me that the era was over, at least for them. I'll never move on, as I believe I am incapable of doing so.

With this newfound awareness of change, my year was going to end on a downer. Rightfully so, I guess, as the year started with my coming off a mountain experience after getting back from Lithuania.

On New Year's Eve my sister, mom, nephew, and I ate at the Olive Garden. This, too, was a reminder of what was and isn't now. I used to eat there with my mom all the time (not that location but same chain). I also used to eat there with Emily, but that, too, was gone.

I always hate the New Year's time, and this year I hated it even more. There isn't a more depressing time of the year, as on that day memories of what was and now isn't are more prevalent. The end of 2005 was rough. As the clock made that last tick and the only second of the year where the year flips over came and went—2006 arrived. As much power as that time of the year has, it really in all reality is no more special than this or the next second, but it just happened to be picked at random to start the next year. We have a linear calendar with a nonlinear thing (time). But for those final days of the year, it is all the more easy to reflect upon everything and the ultimate finality that will eventually come.

I write this in the middle of 2006. The end of 2005, though, is still fresh in my memory. As with all time periods, I wish I could go back and be in that one instead of this one. The hopes of then are the desperations of now. As time moves on, I stay behind. As I said before, the eras of what was may be over, but I don't fully understand that.

TOMORROW IS AN
ETERNITY AWAY

During a routine conversation today, it struck me that time for me is different. The conversation was about school and how something could only take two years. This thought of two years made me really uncomfortable and almost angry. It wasn't the thought of going to school for two years, but just the thought of time itself.

My memory is such that it seems everything in my life happened within the past day. This makes my life seem like the present and past are just a split second. This, however, compromises the future, because I have no time perception (like seeing with depth perception), so if my entire life only took an hour, then how many events will take place within a year?

Quite an interesting concept here, I do believe. Is this the reason why the concept of years of schooling sends bolts of anger through my veins? It isn't the actual time of being at school that makes me mad, but rather the complete lack of concept of time. This isn't to say that an actual year goes by slowly for me. I am constantly thinking that actual time isn't as far ahead as it actually is (it's nearly July already?!). However, to say now that something will take four months will create panic and fear.

There are two things going about time here. First is the lack of perception, and secondly, if something is going to take place in the future, then I'll have all that time to think about it. I am in a constant state of thought, and prolonged thought on an individual idea isn't a good thing, so when there's this long-term goal or destination, it's a guaranteed X amount of time that I know I'll be thinking about whatever it is.

This lack of perception, though, may be where the true problem lies. Perception is everything. Without depth perception, many routine tasks are impossible. Having this time perception, it feels as if my entire past has been a couple minutes, but the future is an eternity away. I have consistent issues regarding this. And now, come to think of it, if the memories in my brain all seem to have happened just recently, it is no wonder the pain of an event never goes away. The saying is that time heals all wounds, but what if I am incapable of putting that time in between any given event and me? Could this be the true reason that I am stuck in the past? Well, rather the recently perceived past?

As I have mentioned here, the future always seems so far away. A day is an eternity, and to describe what a month into the future is would be to use words not yet made to describe time. This all makes sense now. Because everything is so fresh and vivid in my mind, there is no time passed from that event. This is how I can recall names, events, and minor details that no one else would remember. I must drive people crazy correcting them on what they said and the order they said it when talking about a conversation from five years ago. For me it's easy, because we just had the conversation. For them, however, it's been those five years, and who in their right mind remembers something that took place all those years ago?

So is this a good thing or a bad thing? It's certainly good, because I know my facts about an event, but it would seem to have more negatives, because I'm disabled in the realm of time. I have a feeling, though, that I'm not the only one who has this. Could this be another reason I have the difficulties I have? In less than a week, it will have been seven years since I met Linda. I can't believe I used the number seven to describe the past time, because it seems like just a week. It's been a year and a half since I wrote the piece about her, and I could still write to the same detail I first wrote because it's still just as fresh in my mind. I don't want to spend too much time on her, but I needed to make the point about time passing at the rate of pigs flying. The Linda incident, however, is a major event, but minor as insignificant events also have that same level of memory.

If the past never really became the past, what would happen in the mind? There could never be anything that could be "let go," so to speak. Friends lost would stay lost and the initial grief would remain. The time spent away from others would seem like a second when it could be a day, month, or year.

This is diving deep within the workings of the brain. Once again, as with "Quest," it is almost hurting my mind trying to verbalize it. I do know that this is a key topic, and I feel there is a high percentage of a chance that this is a cause of a lot of issues. Can these issues be resolved, though? I hate to say this, but only time will tell, and that time, whatever it may be, scares me.

IF I WERE DYING OF THIRST ... WOULD I ASK FOR A GLASS OF WATER?

If a person wanted something so badly it hurt, logic would say that they would ask for it. Ask and you shall receive, but what if asking was virtually impossible?

During the past weekend, I directed a race in Iowa. It was a very eye-opening trip for me, as I learned a lot about myself and raised a lot of questions about why I do the things I do.

The race weekend was not what I was used to. The track owners had a very "hands-on" approach, and they were the ones who really ran the show. On Sunday, I found out that they had a flagman and that if I were to say that I wanted to maintain that position, I would break the heart of their longtime flagman because there had not been a big race at that track for nearly half a decade. This tore me in two. About the only thing I look forward to in life right now is to be the flagger; now I was put in an unfair position. If I said no to the old man, that would be taking away what may or may not be the only thing he looks forward to. Furthermore, it would make me look like a jerk and then the rest of the day the track crew would be most unhelpful if I needed them. Because of this, I allowed the old man to flag.

The track owner also did what I normally do in the race director duties. I still was on track, and ultimately decisions on protests and such were handled by me, but instead of me being the most recognized figure on the track, I was behind the curtains, so to speak. I guess you'd compare it to a football coach being moved to the general manager. Perhaps it's a move up, but the instant choices of plays are now out of the hands of the former coach. I know if I do the job, it will be done right, but at the races I was like a general manager who only got to handle the aftermath and not the actual game.

Because of all this, it was most obvious by those who see me at my main track that I was a bit flustered. "Smile, Aaron," was a quote I heard a couple people say. I still had one bright spot, though, as I was scheduled to race in the TaG Senior final. (TaG stands for "Touch and Go" and refers to a kart with an on-board starter.) As the day's luck would have it, though, that opportunity went away as well. Greg, a kart shop owner, who is also the series president and the person who was going to provide the kart, said he'd try and find a replacement, but I declined that. Looking back, I don't know why I declined the offer completely. I know another kart would probably have come from somebody else besides him, so if I destroyed the equipment it wouldn't be like wrecking something of Greg's. Also, if it's something that may or may not occur, then that would cause some anxious hours. After no alternatives were found, he said that at the end of the day I could take out the kart that had become unavailable for as long as I wanted.

That glimmer of hope got me through the day, and I looked forward to getting behind the wheel again. The day came to a close, and I returned to the pits, and as the awards ceremonies were over, the karts were starting to be loaded into the trailer. I helped loading them, knowing that when they went in, there would be no chance of me getting the track time I so badly yearned for.

The karts were loaded, and eight hours later sitting at a bar with Greg, he finally remembered that he forgot to let me get on track. I just nodded my head and went back to watching the television, and then he asked me for the reason why I didn't remind him. My mind instantly locked on that question, and I responded with something along the lines of I simply couldn't ask for things. This was the answer of least resistance, but it turns out to be true. I live for the moments behind the wheel; they are what keep the next day of life worth living, and on that day I could have had that chance, but as powerful as the need to drive is, it doesn't surpass the inability to remind a person of something they had said earlier. This is why my title is the way it is. Racing is very much like water for me in that it is required. I had a big pitcher of water lined up, but I was unable to ask him to hand it to me after he already promised it.

If something were already promised, then why would reminding a person about it be impossible for me? I figured at the time that because it was the only thing I was thinking of, how could he forget it? I thought that my appearance in the pit would be enough of a reminder, but it wasn't. As the time progressed and there was no driving, I instantly thought of no less than one hundred possibilities as to why I would not be able to drive. Was he mad? If so, was it at me? Why would he be? Was it broken? Question after question filled my head, and because of this, nothing was accomplished. I was essentially locked and could not ask because it would have been impossible for me to know which question was the real reason. Of all the questions, though, the most obvious one of "Did he forget?" was never thought of.

If there isn't a fairly clear view of what a response will be after a question, then I won't ask the question. In everyday life, every question usually can be answered with a yes or no answer. Those are only two answers, but there'd be at least fifty reasons why a person would say yes or no, and with so many possibilities it becomes impossible to know what the answer is and why the answer is why it is, and therefore no question can be asked. I had a chance to be alive again, but I remained silent.

I realize that if a person doesn't vocalize that they're thirsty, nobody would know that the person thirsts. However, I live in a world where I can't vocalize it. Be it anything in the world, whether it's the go-kart incident, or if I want to stop for food, or any other question that involves me, I will be most likely unable to ask for it. There are certain situations that I am able to, but as a general rule, I am unable.

As I think about this topic, I realize that this, too, is a major cause of internal strife. As I wrote in something a while ago, I can always think of the perfect thing to say while I'm driving home thirty minutes later. Same principal applies to asking questions. After enough time passes, my mind comes up with the solution and then I can ask, but if a person is in the desert and severely dehydrated, thirty minutes may just be too long to wait. I wonder how many opportunities I've missed just because I was unable to open the proverbial knocking door because I was unable to ask, "Who's there?"

THE LIMIT OF
COULDS

What would a title be without making you think? This piece is a big piece of the puzzle that I just realized tonight. I came to this by thinking of my "Thirst" piece. In that, I came to the conclusion that it isn't the actual answering of the question that's the problem, but the possible answer. I hope that makes sense, if it doesn't, I know for sure you'll understand at the end of this.

As the journey of life ventures on, a person's life can take many different proverbial exits. Someone who is normal can view these and await them with a limited amount of anxiety. However (hmm, how many times in all my writings after a sentence that speaks of normality do I say either "but" or "however"?), with the hindrance that I have, the anxiety level is kicked up. For instance, right now a could is, "Will I ever race professionally?" If I have just that, could life be bearable? For me, right now, though, I have several more, and with that being so it is almost paralyzing.

Being above or below my tolerance can be compared to that one drop of water that overflows a glass. Using water is a bad example. Let's say that drop is gasoline and below the glass is an open flame. In this example, one drop can create quite the problem.

What exactly is the problem, though? Yes, I worry about money, and, yes, I worry about my racing future, but what of it? This is where it may get a bit foggy. I'll start by saying that if I have no money at all, I am at peace. This is because there is no could at that juncture because the "Could I run out of money?" has been answered. It isn't the "is" that creates the problems, but the coulds that could kill.

Of all things it was my old fear of thunderstorms that truly made this clear. When I was younger, storms were crippling for me. However, when the storm came, there was no issue. It wasn't the storm itself that created the fear, but rather the "Could this be the worst storm ever?" that made my heart beat faster.

Also, with storms, there was "Could the storm hit here? Could the storm hit at this time?" and so on. A storm only occupies a sliver of a day. Imagine the stress of something that has many more coulds and lasts for weeks or months.

Diving deeper into this issue, I believe this is a problem for a lot of people on the spectrum. I realize in myself when that one drop of gasoline lights the fire. I'm sure there is a correlation between intelligence and how far a person is on the spectrum that dictates how many drops, or rather coulds, they could take.

When my glass overflows and the fire is lit, everything becomes hopeless. The everyday tolerance of minuscule events becomes nonexistent. To create a stable environment, the amount of coulds needs to be dwindled down. How is this done? Sadly, I don't think it'll be easy. It would be like having a job walking dogs in the desert but having a condition that makes you overly sensitive to the sun. In other words, it's a no-win situation. You can't get rid of the condition, but with sunscreen you could minimize the exposure. This is a big need regarding this situation.

Open-ended situations are ripe with coulds. It's important to note, though, that in any situation, at least for me, the end result is fine, but it's getting there that's the problem. Getting there may be half the fun according to the old adage, but for me in these situations, getting there can kill. I can literally become mentally lost when there are too many coulds. My mind becomes so wrapped up in trying to calculate all the coulds that it leaves no room for anything else.

If this is true, as I think it is for others, the simple fact of knowing this could reduce some of the anxiety. With the anxiety that comes from these coulds comes further anxiety of "Could this anxiety keep up? Could there be more?" So what happens is a vicious volley that keeps getting stronger within itself. If that continues, all would seem hopeless and the end results could be detrimental.

I think people have realized that it's the gray area of things that people like me have trouble with. I think I have given this gray area a name, "The Coulds," and I hope this helps others realize the true scope of the matter. I wonder if this could be true.

ASPERGER'S GEOMETRY

It's funny how things happen. Of all places to have a revelation about things was my stint at jury duty today. I wasn't expecting anything to happen on a personal level, but, alas, it did.

As I was doing some crossword puzzles waiting for the courtroom to open, I overheard the people standing right in front of me talk about bowling. Seeing how the topic of bowling is Kansas material, I started listening. There were three ladies talking and two were adamant bowlers. The third bowled, but she knew somebody that was a diehard bowler. She stated that this person, a co-worker at the St. Louis Bread Company, had been bowling since the age of five and bowled on two leagues presently. My heart immediately sank.

I probably should've gone right back to my crossword puzzle, but I had to eliminate the possible coulds, so I asked, "I take it you work at the Sunset Hills and you are talking about Emily." The lady looked very perplexed, as if I somehow were psychic before she nodded that I was right. I then mentioned that I was her boyfriend for nearly four years. She responded with the worst comment I could probably have heard, "Oh, yes, I've heard about you."

Heard about me? The amount of things this could mean is infinite.

Beyond that, everything that was is again. With the lack of time perception, it makes it as if everything is now.

This concept got me thinking, and it's very much like geometry. Let's say someone meets the person they marry on day X. Day X becomes the start of a ray. A ray is a line that starts at a given point and extends in one direction forever. Now let's say they get a divorce. Then, what began as a ray ends, creating a line segment.

Those two examples are what apply to normal people. As usual, the norm doesn't fit me. For me, when anything major happens, it instantly becomes a line. A line in geometry is a line that stretches infinitely in two directions. With that being so, I would ask you to try to find the start and end of the mentioned line. It'd be like trying to find the start of the equator. As confusing as it is for you to attempt to do the mentioned task, it is even harder for me. Why? As with all of my examples, the lines represent life. Now, when the proverbial person got married, their ray stretched out toward the future with a defined start. For me, though, with the time perception deficiency issues, I can't tell when something began and ended. I can tell you the dates of them, but the statistical numbers of the clock and calendar are comprehended the same way when recalled.

It's been twenty-two months since I last heard Emily's voice. A friend, if I had any, would probably say it's time to move on. That would be great advice, but seeing how my mind in regards to time has no defined start or end, it can't "move on" because it always is in an infinite state of being.

Questions such as: "Who has Emily become?" "What has she seen?" and "Is she happy?" will probably always haunt me. The tragic thing that happened at jury duty was that I was going to be able to perhaps get some answers, but just after she confirmed that the person she was talking about was Emily, and after she said she heard about me, the bailiff came out and it was time to enter the courtroom. Further, adding to the sheer tragedy of it all, she was picked for the jury and I wasn't, thus ending any hope of knowing anything more about Emily.

I never realized in grade school that geometry would come in handy. What I also didn't realize was the complexity of it. On paper, it seems so benign. Lines going this way, rays going that way, an intersection here, but when you start to think about it and those lines become life, well, perhaps I should have paid more attention in geometry so I know how it all ends.

THE INFINITY FACTOR

A follow-up to "Geometry"

I believe I explained a lot in my geometry piece; however, I believe I can expound on it even further.

In the piece mentioned above, I laid out the idea that for an Asperger's person, events become lines. This alone isn't enough to explain this, as on a two-dimensional piece of paper there is a defined start and end, as since we read in English, we are trained to start at the left and read toward the right. With that being so, a better analogy would be a three-dimensional sphere as if the line connected with itself, the beginning and end would not exist.

This is how most everything is for me. Once something begins, it feels as if there were never a time it wasn't. And if something was there always, there is no way to even try and predict what life would be if it weren't there.

You could consider this the linking evidence that "firsts" and my idea of the lack of time perception are there. If someone has no sense of time, all time would be at once, and because most firsts are forever, there must be a connection there.

Currently, after the jury duty incident, I am struggling with the concept that Emily simply isn't there. I know she's alive somewhere out there in the great wild known as St. Louis, but the story of her is lost, much like reading a book and having the pages become blank after the thirteenth chapter. I don't understand this concept because once someone or something enters my interior world, all thoughts are on the basis that what is will remain unchanged. Because of this, I can now see why I would break up and then immediately retract. And I know now that I could not conceive of the idea that perhaps one time would be the last time.

What is the last time? I don't understand this. Ends are a hard concept for me to grasp, if not impossible. Having a video-graphic memory, everything always was how it was as I remembered it. It is like living in a TiVo world. Sadly, though, when one is constantly watching last week's episode, the future can seem overwhelming.

Okay, I got a bit sidetracked, but endings are unbearable for me. I hate when traveling internationally if my dad starts talking to someone. If I hear the conversation and it's a lengthy one, I know it will end and that person will be lost forever. While the physical presence will be gone and what for others would have been small talk will, for me, become a memory of infinite proportions.

It doesn't take a long time for a line to be formed. If this is true for others, then this is a very dangerous thing, as it would be very easy to get caught up in something much like a helpless swimmer being caught by a strong undertow.

If infinity can start in a heartbeat, then a lifelong relationship of misery can easily be obtained; bad habits can form; and worst of all these lines, or firsts, or infinites are almost if not impossible to break.

It will be interesting if I ever have another girlfriend to see how long, if ever, it will take for Emily to disappear. These are grand questions that could prove to have valuable answers.

I can theorize that the pain will be shoved under a rug, so to speak. After the loss of Missy and Amsterdam, there wasn't too much grief, because I still had Siam. Four weeks ago, though, Siam was lost in the urban jungle, and I felt that he was gone for good. In my shock at that point in time, I was not only grieving Siam, but also the reality of Missy and Amsterdam hit hard. Therefore, perhaps once I have someone else the same rule will apply for Emily.

If the paragraph above is true, then it would seem to me that as long as there is a current line of something, life is bearable. But much like an orbit, if the lines disappear, they will burn up in the atmosphere. And if one's perception is that everything should be forever, how can one prepare for the flaming mass of destruction if something is lost?

WRONGS

The other week while I was driving home from working a race, I noticed that a car in front of me had one of those televisions for kids to watch a DVD or something on any given drive. This immediately sickened me on several levels. First off, are parents getting so weak that they can't talk to their kids? Secondly, and this ties into the first topic, if the kid is watching the television while the car is traveling down the interstate, it is creating a tunnel vision of sorts.

If the kid doesn't have Asperger's, then perhaps it's not a major issue, but if they do, it is creating a first that may be impossible to overturn. Let's talk about that tunnel vision. Let's say a family is traveling five hundred miles away from home across three states. During the drive, there will be new trees, cars, people, animals, and many more new things that the child may not have experienced. Should they be looking two feet away instead of a quarter mile ahead, then this is making their world very small.

I don't know the official stats on this, if any, but I'm certain that parents that resort to a TV for a car ride will be even more prone to use it at home. I have written before on my beliefs as to how hazardous the television medium can be, but now with thinking about shrinking the kid's world, it becomes a whole lot scarier.

This debate on whether television can harm a child has been raging since the dawn of the media. I'm not going to debate that on a large scale, but should a child have Asperger's, then it can be quite dangerous! With creating a tunnel-like life, the first will be that the world is only as big as the picture tube. The outside world will simply not be. By putting a television in the car, this is furthering that truth that may be picked up. This is a major wrong that if committed will create a lifetime of problems.

While a person with Asperger's is growing up, they will only know what they have been exposed to. Common sense doesn't really apply, because if it isn't exposed, then it won't be. This is why making TV the reality can be so deadly. If television is watched everywhere, and is the first that kids are being exposed to, what's the purpose of everything else? Reality is only as important as the individual's perception of it. This is why parents absolutely need to know and be taught what to do and what not to do if their child has Asperger's. Creating a reality that is comprised solely on media will destroy the child.

One hundred and forty years ago, the primary reality for all world-wide was to merely survive. For the aristocrats, there were operas and the like, but for all others, it was work hard or die. This, of course, is not quite the case anymore. And, with this, there is now a void of what the world is. This is again why the media is so dangerous. And the parents are the ones who are giving in to this.

It's not just TV that is creating the blur between real reality and the perception that is being created in young minds. Devices like the iPod that allow the person to listen to whatever they want whenever they want also create a smaller world.

I got lucky. I was very fortunate that I was born ten years before the big media turned into the behemoth media. Also, I was lucky to have parents who exposed me to a lot of things. I did watch television a lot, and I do not want to think about who I may have become had there been a TV in the car. The more I type about this, the more I want to call this the "cardinal wrong." Had my parents let me have my TV choice, I would not have watched the news at a young age and learned that there is a much larger world out there. It's through experiences that firsts are created and development can come from there.

Okay, I think I have beaten that topic to a pulp, so here are some other wrongs that, if done right, would alleviate much friction.

Parents should never tell their child such open-ended phrases such as, "Soon," "Maybe," or, "We'll see." From what I have seen, these are answers that are quickly said to try and shut the child up, and also to prevent the parent from having to think about the issue at that time. By using these phrases, you are essentially starting a trial, and from what I have done and seen, it creates the mindset of having to convince the parent to make a decision to say yes at all costs. The important thing I did was to try and get an answer as quickly as possible, because the question that was hanging in the balance was much worse than whatever the answer may be. I've thought about this, and it would be much better if the parent would say something like, "This isn't the time to ask that." By stating this, it's much like a trial judge setting the trial back one week; therefore, opening statements aren't needed. Whatever a parent says, it needs to keep the trial closed.

Another topic that I have seen is the anguish caused by parents trying to alter something the kid is interested in. If a kid gets set on a topic, their mind will only think about that topic and nothing else. Should the parents try and fight it, it will only turn out to be one of those Chinese finger traps. Ever if the child's interest is something as obscure as eighteenth century real estate agents, the parents have to let the child find their own way. In other words, the parents have to let the child figure out that their interest is stupid. If they never do, then that means it's not stupid to them; therefore, let them have it.

This sort of goes along with the previous paragraph, but parents should not force an interest upon their child. Why not? Let's take firsts for example. Let's say that the child has learned that they must do whatever the parent says but also knows that they hate being on a team. Let's now say that this child is in first grade and the parent loves baseball and forces the child to sign up for the team. With this example, the firsts are in conflict, and what will ensue is months of anguish as the child's mind tries to comprehend this gear system that isn't turning. The obvious resolution of this problem would have been before it happened and they would have asked the child if they wanted to be on the team. Even if after the force the parent thought that perhaps it wasn't the wisest choice, the damage is still done, as it will take some time for the child to work out the clash of firsts.

All of these examples, including the television one, can be fixed with one easy solution: Unselfishness. Gasp! What does that word mean? We live in the most selfish culture, and we live in a world where if you want it now, you can have it now.

Being selfish is to give your child a TV everywhere because that'll keep him quiet. Being selfish is to give him open-ended answers because you don't want to deal with it now. Being selfish is to thrust upon him or her your concept of what they should do.

It is imperative to be unselfish and to realize that the child is different. Normal practices may not work quite the same. In some instances, it may be that the child is hindered so much that it is truly a handicap. With just some simple measures, though, life can be easier, and that'll let you be a little selfish and boastful later in life when you can brag that you have a great relationship with your child.

THE FOURTH WALL

Just a note from Dad… One night when I was sixteen years old my father came home from a bar with a Bolex 16mm camera. In 1964 film was the medium by which images, both moving and still, were recorded. My father gave me the camera and told me to go make some money with it. He bought it from a man who had stolen it from a doctor's house.

I went to a local TV station in Oklahoma City and talked with John Harrison, the news director. I told him my father had given me the camera, told me to go make some money with, but I didn't know how the camera worked or how I would make any money with it.
He showed me how it worked, gave me two rolls of film, and said if something big happened on my side of town he would pay me fifty cents per foot of film they used in the newscast.

Wow, I thought, fifty cents per foot. But how many feet were in a news story?
On my way home I stopped at an intersection and saw a house on fire. I parked my car in front of the house, adjusted the camera like Mr. Harrison had said, and began shooting. I was there before the fire trucks. Now think about it. Where did I park my car? Right where the fire truck had to park.
Anyway, the firemen pulled two old women out of the house and the

house was totally destroyed. I headed for the station and ended up getting paid forty dollars for the film.

If you were alive in 1964, forty bucks was a lot of money. I was sixteen and had just become the youngest television reporter in American television.

Throughout my high school years I covered fires, accidents, murders, just about every bad thing you could think of. I remember the first time I went to an auto accident on I-35 where someone was killed. I had never seen a dead body, much less one in the condition of this one.

It was strange. As long as I looked through the viewfinder, whatever I saw was not real, at least not in an emotional sense. I was protected by the glass of the lens, the looking glass, if you will.

I was a reporter for most of my life. I saw things that 99.9% of people never see. But it was always very sterile. The looking glass kept it that way. That was until...

In 1981 I was a student at Concordia Theological Seminary in Ft. Wayne, Indiana. I was also a reporter for WPTA-TV. One afternoon my cameraman and I were south of Ft. Wayne when we got a call on the two-way radio that a train had hit a telephone company van. The van was on fire, and we were only about three miles from the scene.

Like my first story that made it in a newscast, we arrived before the fire truck. The gas tank of the white van had been ruptured. The driver, I think it was woman, was hanging out the passenger side window. Her body fat was burning. I had a very big problem. I wasn't the one shooting the video-tape, and I was not protected by the looking glass.

I looked at the body and wondered how her children would respond when she didn't return home? Would her husband want to see her charred body? Would her mother and father wonder why this had happened to them? Why couldn't I watch this through the looking glass and be immune from feelings and emotions?

When I returned to the station, I told the news director that I would never cover a fatality accident again. When he asked me why, I didn't have an answer. I didn't understand the importance of the looking glass, the glass wall that protected me from the horrors of life. As a reporter and not a cameraman, my protection was gone.

I grieve deeply that Aaron does not have a choice like I did. I told the

news director where my boundary was. He respected it. He never sent me on
another fatality accident.

I can't protect Aaron from those who break through the fourth wall. I
wish I could. If I did, though, would he ever grow up?

When one attends a live play, they are watching a pre-set production and script in progress. Normally, during a play, the audience has no say in what occurs on stage, as it is all pre-determined. I don't think any Shakespeare play has any characters asking audience members how they should respond to any given dilemma. Imagine how you would respond if you were sitting in the front row and the title character breaks the norm and asks you directly how they should proceed. If they were to do this, that would be an example of a breach of the fourth wall, that is, the imaginary wall in front of the stage that audience members view through.

The question is, though, how would you respond? Let's say you've been to one hundred plays and know every line, but then for some odd reason you are suddenly part of the play. Even if you knew what they should do in accordance to the script, I'm sure you would be frozen. This is how every day is for me. As I see life move about around me, I take the role of an audience member. I hope to be nothing more than a dark figure in a dimly lit room, simply viewing the proceedings that the world presents. As William Shakespeare said, "All the world's a stage," he probably had Asperger's, because it is true.

There are a lot of postmodern plays that purposely break the fourth wall, but it's merely the character talking to audience without the response altering the course of the production. For those who frequent plays, you would grow accustomed to this. I, however, am not able to make that transition in life to get used to myself becoming part of the production. In this instance, the production is life itself.

Perhaps this is why smaller groups are preferable because the fewer people there are, the better the chances that some random act won't propel me into the production. There is an exception to this, though, as I just realized; as long as I am the sole performer of any given act in life, there is no issue. Successful one-person plays are far and few between.

One would have to think that a person could grow accustomed to becoming part of the production, but literally there's a wall preventing it, no, not the fourth wall, but let's say the fifth wall that would be called a mental wall.

The more I think about this, the more it really sells the point. In all my memories of events, I always remember myself as an invisible observer of events unfolding around me, and I like it that way. As long as I'm not seen, there will be safety because I won't have to become part of the act.

Life doesn't have a script, but there are guidelines to how the play will go. Guidelines aren't rules. Therefore, they are the gray areas of life. If that is so, then how can I know how to act? My actions will affect the play going on around me, but how can I minimize the damage, as I am merely a simple observer? There's an issue with the answer, though. The easy answer is to stay home, or find a hole to crawl into, but yet, at the same time, while the play of life goes on around me, I have my own production of life going on.

It's a fine line, but one that has to be balanced. As much as I want to, staying home forever is not an option. The fourth wall will be breached, shattered, and stomped on every day that I live, and the fifth wall will prevent me from fully responding, but as they say, the act must go on, therefore I will.

HOW DO I WIN?

Early in one's life, the foundation is set on values, ethics, and over-all perception of life. This is quite dangerous for someone who has Asperger's. How so? With everything I've written, I have constantly said that the firsts are important, and in recent thinking, I have learned that it is even more so.

Parents with children affected with Asperger's have a fine line to tread. With my game theory, I stated that I operate best in a game because the rules outline actions taken. Life can become a game, though, and while the rules are unwritten, there's one underlying question that I still haven't answered, "How do I win?"

From the point one can realize their surroundings, they are sub-jected to ways to win. Television bombards us with winning situations. These situations come in all sizes, whether it is the Road Runner out-witting the Coyote, or a contestant winning a huge wad of cash on a game show. Sitcoms even have winners, as someone always wins some social situation.

If you aren't watching television, video games are chock full of win-ning situations, as I am not sure if there's any game that has an ending that is merely a tie. In movies, too, the good guy always wins.

So with everyone being surrounded by winners, how does one win the game of life? How does one know if they are succeeding? Beyond that, what are the criteria for even playing the game?

This is why parents have a thin sheet of ice to skate on and why they have to be completely unselfish. Should, in the early years of a child's life, the parent teach that anyone unlike them is bad, part of the game will be to hate others. Should the parent only care about them and no one else, the game of life becomes a solitary game. Should the parent physically beat those around them to maintain their dominance, the child will learn that the game of life is to have complete power.

So if the parent teaches what the criteria is, then when the child grows up, how will they know if they've won? The problem is they won't. Physical abuse will become worse because there will be no bells, whistles, or confetti that says, "Congratulations, you have complete control and everyone hates you!"

We are constantly shown graphics of how any event is going. Tune into CNBC and they'll show you a thousand different charts of how any given financial thing is going. Tune into ESPN and they'll show you a graph of how any given football team has done the past five years. With either of those two things, though, what is there beyond the graph? What happens after a team wins the Super Bowl? What is there left to do? And with the financial markets, how does one know when something has gone up enough? In other words, once you've won, why play on? What is there left to do?

Is enjoyment of life the way to win? If so, when does one fully win? We are taught that everything has a beginning and an end, as games have rules with ends, and your favorite TV show probably ends at the top of the hour, but how does one win this game? Is death the final way to win? Is life like a timed game of "Monopoly," and when the clock reaches zero, one is judged on the accumulated wealth?

All of these questions are truly relevant, but imagine what my questions would be had my parents been full of hate and rage. The hate and rage would have been passed on, and perhaps the questions asked wouldn't be so innocent. Life's goals may truly be unclear, and a winner may never be announced, but in the end, perhaps, it's not who wins the game, but how you play the game—even if you don't know what game you're playing or how to play.

I VERSUS IT

No, I haven't lost my mind. The title is as it reads. First thing you probably thought of was the question of, "Who or what is 'it'?" The answer
is not simple but could prove to be very valuable.

I started playing video games at an early age. After I could grasp
the concept that all the images on the screen were being controlled by
the same entity, the game became myself versus the computer. When
playing a game and the computer won, quotes such as, "That was a
cheap shot it did," were numerous. Right there in that sentence I have
given the computer an almost conscious mind.

I did and do know that computers are not sentient or conscious
beings. However, the detrimental effects of this are being felt to this
day. How could playing games as a child affect me now? Because it
paved the way for the thought that it is one versus one, no matter how
many individuals there are.

When playing a larger game like "Final Fantasy," there are many
characters on screen. Each character has its own traits and personality,
but they are all being run by one program. So, even though in one fight
you're facing villain A and the next time it's villain B, the fact is that
the same entity is being faced each time, It.

Let's assume that my first theory is correct (I don't assume it is, I
know it is). Because I played games from an early age, this concept of
I versus It got in the thought process. This means that the concept
carried over from the digital world and into the real world. How do I

know this? I bowl in a league tonight, and while there, I would not feel or comprehend the presence of 120 other bowlers, but rather I will see the mass as one. Yes, each person is different, but for me, it's like they are all just one program.

When I got to a big race like the Indy 500 and am one among three hundred thousand, I do not feel like I am in a sea of humanity. Again, it's like one presence.

This concept is quite deep, and I hope I can spell it all out in one piece. I do know videogames have this side affect, but is there anything else that can cause this? I haven't given it much thought, but I would have to lean toward the idea that television or movies may do the same thing, but I am not sure.

Back to the video game issue ... I don't know how this would prove accurate or if others have this "it" issue. I know two days ago, when, for the first time in my life, I had a thought that each person I'm talking to was a true individual was a truly scary idea. I understood the principle, but I could not grasp the true scope of it. If each person is his or her own person, the world becomes a much scarier place.

I feel video games gave me this concept, but perhaps it was already there. Either way, this explains how I am emotionally detached from so many things. I didn't flinch once at the sights we saw after Hurricane Katrina. I can theorize now that I felt like it was just part of the program playing itself out.

The idea of me being able to talk to a person one-on-one is still valid, as is the fact that I freeze if another person is added. Individuality is still in games, but it's one entity controlling it all.

I was thinking last night about this concept, and I realized that I never saw my parents as two, but rather one. This is very strange for me, because I know that they are each a different person, but they remain as one. This all probably sounds strange; I know it does for me. It's horrible to know the idea of different individuals but to not be able to understand it or grasp it.

Finally, this could simply be a defense mechanism. If each person in the world has his or her own thoughts, then the amount of thought I have to put in thinking of the random element becomes almost impossible. Whatever the case, the world is still viewed in the impersonal I versus It. There may be individuals within the It, but if I fully understood that, perhaps I would not be able to function, because the world truly would be a free place and the size and scope of 6 billion people would cripple me.

ALIASES

Personally, I have been baffled in my ability to do certain things, now knowing what I have. Some people are unable to talk in front of a large audience, but I can. Others are unable to, when working in retail, sell stuff to people who may or may not want whatever it is they are trying to sell, but I was phenomenal at it.

I have wondered deeply as to how or why I am able to do this, because a few people have said that I should be unable to do so. I have hinted before that the reason I am able to is due to the "Game Theory" I wrote about. While that theory is still true in my mind, I believe it goes much deeper than I thought. To work to its fullest extent, the game must have me doing something that isn't me completely; enter the alias element.

When I am race directing, I am not myself completely, as if I ask someone to do something, it isn't me asking but rather the race director. Yes, I may be the race director, but it isn't me who's asking. Confused? Let me explain more.

When I worked at the video game store and I was up-selling unsuspecting customers, it wasn't me doing the selling but the easy to like, "I'm on your side" salesperson I portrayed. If I were to have talked to that customer outside the store at the end of my shift, I could not ask a single question because then it would be me asking and then there is no protection. That's the important thing when in alias mode; there is safety in the fact that I am only whom I portray. When the protection isn't there, though, getting knocked out of Kansas is alarmingly close.

Let's take an example that happened at a race I was in recently. Earlier in the weekend, the team owner asked me if I could get some gas for one of his karts. To let you know, I am currently working at this owner's kart shop, so that made the alias factor easy because I could go to his customers not as myself, but as the data entry salesperson that I am. Two days after that, though, it was my turn to need fuel, and this eliminated any and all aliases from the equation. I could not be the salesperson because it was I who needed it. The fact that the other customers would not know the difference is irrelevant because my feelings are the only relevant ones, and this was just a horrible situation. The crisis at hand could not have been worse because on one side there's racing, which trumps all, and on the flip side was me having to leave Kansas. To make matters worse, I don't really know any of his customers personally. Yes, I do talk to them at the track, but I doubt any of them know the true me and only know the aliases. What did I do? I decided not to race on account of many reasons. I didn't want to be in the way, as I was six seconds off the pace (it was my second time in a shifter kart at a track where learning how to drive is difficult because the track is just plain hard), but when I told Greg, the shop owner, he started berating me with the same response I'd give someone in my position, that it's the overtaking kart's responsibility to overtake cleanly. I knew I had no logical counterpoints to this, and when Greg said that I can't let fear dictate what I do, I then mentioned, "Well, I don't have fuel, though." I don't know if he understood at that point in time if the whole debacle was just because I couldn't ask someone else for help. Whether he knew then or knows now makes no difference; the fact of the matter is, for the first time in my life, racing lost.

The important fact on this paper is not that racing lost (it is a very relevant topic, though), but the fact that this let me see the relevancy of the alias factor. When acting as someone else, the state lines of all other states from Kansas are very far away. I guess you could say I am in the geographical center of Kansas. So long as I am not myself, life is fine. The hazard for me is that the number of possibilities is endless. To a degree, one could make the argument that an alias negates the full effects of my autism. It may still be there, but because nothing is going to be personal, it makes the mind freer. If there is an insult given, it isn't toward me, but whomever I am portraying.

What I find fascinating is the fact that this doesn't work in reverse. I could ask that almighty question of, "Sir, can I help you find anything today?" but if I am asked that, I lock up.

This whole concept is taking game theory to the next level. The rules of the game create the persona that I am, and that is what keeps Kansas intact in those instances. Maybe Kansas is the wrong word here, and maybe this is a consciouscoma thing; either way, the two are close relatives, and if one is having issues, so is the other one.

Certainly this is a hard concept to grasp, as it truly is a difference of staggering proportions. I think people that see me in both areas will clearly understand this, but if a person has only seen me at the track, then they probably think of me as a very confident person with no fear in talking to people. If only they knew the truth. The few people I have let know the truth of what I have thought I was joking at first. This means my covert op works great. People who see me outside the tracks, though, when told that I speak in front of two hundred people, think that I am just making stuff up.

I will give myself credit somewhat in that, even if it is an alias, it is still me. If I weren't internally strong enough, there is no way this would be possible. This is a conduit I use to, perhaps, let the real me show through momentarily. If I have to portray something else to show my true self, then so be it. I just hope there are enough games and roles in the future so I can, from time to time, be as close to normal as I can possibly be.

IN THE END

With writing over a year now on my experiences and thoughts regarding Asperger's, I feel it is proper to write a final chapter. I write this in the same room I wrote "Scream" and "School" some nineteen months ago. This room is room number 312 in the Imperial Hotel in Kissumu, Kenya. This is a fitting place to write my final chapter, because it was in this very room, on this very bed that I first thought that my writings may actually be used for something. From that point on, I took my insights very seriously.

So with all that I have written, what have I learned? I have come to understand for one that I am, indeed, different. It's not that radically different, though, but just a different understanding of the world.

I have learned that I am very lucky to have such great parents who allowed me to be me. I have realized that I have had many experiences that "normal" people will never have. I believe that both of those things have allowed me to write these reflections.

Nearing the end, I think I should explain how all this began. At the end of 2003, I was officially diagnosed with Asperger's. In the middle of 2004, I lost Emily for the final time, and when I attempted to resume communications, she stated something along the lines of, "You have Asperger's. Why would I want to know you?"

I wrote her a letter that was essentially a mirror of my chapter "Emily," but not as long and not as harsh. I thought afterwards that perhaps it was marginally good and that I wanted to write it again, but this time, to share with others. I considered it a way to get back at her, but after I wrote it, I kept going. I wrote about Linda and then I started thinking about other things to write about and it snowballed from there. It was very much like the scene in the movie Forrest Gump, when Forrest starts running and he gets to the county line and he just keeps going for the sake of going. What started out as a means of sharing my story as an act of childish revenge snowballed into allowing me the opportunity to hopefully change many lives. Because of this, I can do nothing but thank Emily dearly for inadvertently unlocking these ideas I never would have had; because of this, though, I believe that my "Quest" has come to an end. I do believe that only the shock of a deep love lost could produce such wonderful ideas that I have had.

Finally, I have learned that Asperger's isn't the end of the world. I've heard stories from parents who freaked when they learned that their child had it. I was a bit spooked when I learned I had it, but now, yes, now, I am thankful I have it. Because of it, I lead a life I can be proud of. I don't drink, smoke, party, have fun (wait a sec, I have fun), or do other lewd stuff that may show up on a police report fifteen years from now. It allows me to act older than my age, and this has allowed me to do so many things at such a young age. I know that not all those affected will be as fortunate as I, but there can be a prosperous life. There is still much to be learned about it, and I will continue to think and write because I realize that I have only scratched the tip of the iceberg.

Just a closing comment from Dad... After Aaron's first kart race, I told him he had what it took to win the Indy 500. I think he still does. Several years ago, when Sam Hornish won the 500, I remember seeing how proud his dad was on TV.

If Aaron ever wins the 500, I, too, will be proud, but not nearly as proud as I am for this book. Why? If he won the 500, he might win a couple of millions dollars that he would spend on who knows what. This book, though, as he has told me many times, will make a difference that will last a lot longer than a couple million bucks.

Aaron has told me many times that having Asperger's is like bobsled racing. In a bobsled there is nothing you can do to go faster. Faster is totally dependent upon the friction coefficient between the blades and ice, and the fact that you can't change thirty-two feet per second squared (gravity). The only thing the driver can do is to not make mistakes that slow the sled down.

There is a lot to consider in this book about how parents, teachers, clinicians, and therapists deal with children and adults with Asperger's and autism. I hope they consider some new possibilities and modalities of care and therapy. I hope they find new ways to not slow down the development and possibilities for those with Asperger's. Maybe I'm nuts, but I really believe that Aaron has gone outside the box and found many answers previously unknown. I believe he has begun the process of decoding the enigma of Asperger's Syndrome.

May God richly bless him, care for him, give him a productive life, and may God bless you.

James Likens

"There is still much to be learned about it [Asperger's], and I will continue to think and write because I realize that I have only scratched the tip of the iceberg."

Aaron Likens, 2007

ABOUT THE AUTHOR AND HIS FATHER

Aaron Likens was born in Scottsbluff, Nebraska. He lived in Morrill, Nebraska, until November of 1983, when the family moved to Indianapolis, Indiana.

While growing up in Indianapolis, Aaron and his father would spend most May afternoons at the Indianapolis Motor Speedway watching practice for the Indy 500. Somewhere around five years old, he decided he was to be a racecar driver. The desire has never left.

His father's job brought about a move to St. Louis, Missouri, in late 1993. At the age of twelve Aaron began racing go-karts. Within a year he became the starter/flagman for the St. Louis Karting Association. Today he is the regional race director for a major Midwest/National racing series.

Diagnosed with Asperger's Syndrome in 2003, he began writing essays so he wouldn't have to talk with those at the Judevine Center, St. Louis, Missouri, who diagnosed him.

While he still looks forward to racing, he sees his current mission in life to speak to families, educators, clinicians, and others about his experience with Asperger's.

You are invited to visit his web site at www.FindingKansas.com.

Rev. James Likens was raised in Oklahoma City, Oklahoma, and became a television photographer/reporter when he was sixteen years old for KOCO-TV.

In 1978 he began his studies at Concordia Theological Seminary, Ft. Wayne, Indiana, and served congregations in Morrill, Nebraska, and Indianapolis, Indiana. In 1993 he assumed the duties as Sr. Video Producer for the Lutheran Church-Missouri Synod.

In 1998 he formed his own company, JDL Video Productions, and his adventures throughout the years have taken him around the world producing videos. He began taking Aaron on these trips in 2004, beginning with a trip to Lithuania. Aaron has been to Kenya twice and also Madagascar. In 2008 he traveled by himself to Latvia. Aaron also accompanied his father as a still photographer to the Gulf Coast to cover Hurricanes Ivan, Dennis, and Katrina.

Jim has been Aaron's advocate, encourager, and source of unconditional love.

You can visit Jim's Web site at *www.JimLikens.com.*